The Lively Ball

James A. Cox

A
REDEFINITION
BOOK

The Lively Ball

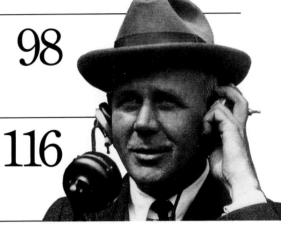

In the decade between the end of the Great War and the start of the Great Depression—from 1919 to 1929—the fellow who wore a major league uniform was worshipped by kids, envied by men, and adored by women. The uniforms are faded now, the gloves wrinkled and dry, but once they were sweat-soaked and full of muscle.

During the 1920s, the men who played the game mirrored the nation—brainy and strong, reckless and carefree, fearlessly honest and shamelessly crooked. The dead ball was gone, home runs were everywhere, baseball dynasties were on the move. It was the Jazz Age, the Roaring Twenties . . . and baseball was never better.

Say It Ain't So, Joe

Cincinnati's Dutch Ruether threw the first pitch of the 1919 World Series and for a while, Game 1 was close. But Chicago pitcher Eddie Cicotte, who was in on the fix, botched a grounder in the fourth, leading to five runs and a 9–1 Reds' win. A year later, the Chicago Daily Tribune *called it the "first crooked play of the world series."*

Baseball was Buck Weaver's passion—as well as his profession. The White Sox third baseman took none of the money earned by seven of his teammates in their plot to fix the 1919 World Series and played splendidly, but was banned for life from the game he loved for "guilty knowledge."

An underpaid star with a wife, kids and a heavy mortgage, White Sox pitcher Eddie Cicotte joined the scheme to fix the 1919 World Series, then, unable to cope with his guilt, broke the scandal open with his confession to a grand jury. "I'd give a million dollars to undo what I've done," he said.

n the spring of 1920, a restlessness, a vitality was in the air. The Great War was over, boys were back from the trenches of Europe, business was booming, and old rules were changing. Women were shortening their skirts and their hair. Dance bands played hot new music. The Volstead Act had closed saloons, but all over America people found ways to have fun. They never had it so good. It was the Jazz Age. The Roaring Twenties had begun.

As it often does, baseball mirrored the times. Fans said the ball was livelier than ever, and although baseball moguls claimed it was the same as the prewar version, home runs were flying out of ballparks as never before, especially in the American League, where a young slugger named Babe Ruth led the way. Even little guys were rattling the fences, games were more exciting than ever, and attendance soared.

As the summer rolled on, the Brooklyn Robins—nicknamed for their popular manager Wilbert Robinson—withstood a surge by the New York Giants and were well on their way to their second National League pennant in five years. The Cincinnati Reds, 1919 world champions, fell to an out-of-the-running third.

But the real excitement was in the American League. In late September, Chicago was battling Cleveland and New York to the wire. The White Sox played as a team in name only—a team torn by internal strife, a team whose players wouldn't even talk to each other, a team that since the 1919 World Series had been carrying on its shoulders an unthinkable burden.

On Wednesday, September 23, 1920, the Sox moved to within a half-game of the first-place Indians with a 10–3 win in the first of a three-game series at Cleveland's League Park. The next day Cleveland's Duster

Utility infielder Fred McMullin didn't have to do much to earn his $5,000 share of the Series bribe money, but he played his small part well. He slapped a meaningless pinch single in the eighth inning of Chicago's 9–1 loss in Game 1. He came to the plate as the tying run with two out in the ninth in Game 2, and grounded out.

Mails shut out Chicago, which hit .295 as a team that year, 2–0 on three hits. The Sox could be excused: their attention was focused on Cook County Courthouse, 200 miles away, where New York Giants pitcher Rube Benton was in his second day of testimony before a grand jury investigating the alleged fix of the 1919 World Series. Benton suggested that White Sox pitcher Eddie Cicotte could tell the jury what it wanted to know.

On September 28 Cicotte—except for Walter Johnson, the best right-hander in the game—unraveled to a grand jury in Chicago a tale about the heavily favored Sox losing to the National League champion Reds, five games to three (this was one of the best-of-nine years), in the 1919 Series. With little prompting, Cicotte told a lurid story involving seven teammates, a pack of gamblers, big bills that appeared under his pillow, and funny business on the playing field.

Fingering first baseman Arnold "Chick" Gandil and shortstop Charles "Swede" Risberg as the chief plotters, Cicotte confessed to the fix, implicating pitcher Claude "Lefty" Williams, left fielder "Shoeless Joe" Jackson, center fielder Oscar "Happy" Felsch, third baseman George "Buck" Weaver, and utility infielder Fred McMullin. Cicotte went on about his farm, a $4,000 mortgage, and the fact that he did what he did only "for the wife and kiddies." Cicotte added, "I never did anything I regretted so much in my life."

It was organized baseball's darkest hour. Legions of baseball fans, who had learned at their fathers' knees the sanctity and incorruptibility of the game, felt like jilted lovers. In the fall of 1920, America came perilously close to breaking off its affair with the national game. In truth, baseball had been deflowered long before, but the baseball moguls had done an excellent job of

Lefty Williams' pitching pattern in the 1919 World Series suggested something rotten. He held the Reds scoreless in 13 of the 17 innings in which he pitched, but wound up with three losses because, with runners in scoring position, the Reds went 8 for 14 against him.

White Sox left fielder Joe Jackson reportedly pocketed only $5,000 of the $20,000 he was promised for helping fix the 1919 World Series, but considering his performance, he didn't deserve even that much. His 12 hits matched a Series record, and he threw the tying run out at the plate in Game 6.

keeping the dirty linen from public view. As far back as 1877, the second year of the National League, four Louisville Grays—team captain Bill Craver, Jimmy Devlin, George Hall and Al Nichols—were bought off by gamblers. They dropped eight games in a row to lose the pennant and enrich their tempters. Rumors followed, President Charles E. Chase of the Louisville club called in the Pinkertons, and when irrefutable evidence was developed, NL president William A. Hulbert quietly, but promptly, barred the bad apples from baseball for life.

Object lessons are good, but they don't last forever. By the turn of the century, rumors of fixed games cropped up frequently. And why should that have surprised anyone? Gamblers have always followed the action, from racetracks to boxing rings to ballparks—and to the hotels and saloons where athletes congregate. In 1903 crooks tried to fix the very first World Series, as Cy Young led the Boston Pilgrims to victory over the Pittsburgh Pirates. In 1912 smart money had the New York Giants taking the Series, but if there was a fix, nobody told the Boston Red Sox, who took it four games to three. In 1917 White Sox players were accused of taking up a collection to pay two Detroit Tigers' pitchers to lose a doubleheader, ensuring that the Sox would win the pennant; Chicago won, but there was no proof of foul play.

Without hard evidence, proving a thrown ballgame is difficult. Pitchers don't have perfect control or their best stuff in every game. Outfielders misjudge fly balls. Infielders boot easy ground-ers. Everybody throws to the wrong base sometime. And even the best hitters have been known to swing at bad pitches. But sometimes too many things happen together . . . And in that 1919 Series, the questions began to

Shortstop Swede Risberg (above, left) and first baseman Chick Gandil (above) were ringleaders of the Series-fixing scheme, and were united in their hatred for tightwad owner Charles Comiskey. Gandil earned $4,000 a year and Risberg less than $3,000.

Center fielder Happy Felsch told the grand jury: "We've sold ourselves and our jobs— the only jobs we know anything about . . . for a few dollars—while a lot of gamblers have gotten rich. Looks like the joke's on us."

Buck Weaver (left), like the rest of the honest White Sox, never had a chance. Weaver, who led Chicago with 89 runs scored during the regular season, was tagged out by Cincinnati catcher Bill Rariden in Game 2, and didn't score his first Series run until Game 6. The White Sox, who averaged 4.8 runs per game during the regular season, averaged 2.5 during the Series.

arise as soon as the games started. The White Sox, widely considered to be one of the greatest teams ever, were heavily favored. Pitching for the Sox in the opener was "Shineball Eddie" Cicotte, the talcum-powder-ball specialist who had tallied 29 wins during the season. Cicotte's first pitch of the day, contrary to legend, was a strike. It was his second pitch that hit leadoff batter Maurice Rath in the back, supposedly signaling to those in the know that the fix was on. The Reds went on to belt 14 hits and won the game, 9–1, as the Sox sluggers flailed futilely at Dutch Ruether's offerings.

An off day for Cicotte? White Sox catcher Ray Schalk complained bitterly to team manager Kid Gleason that Cicotte had repeatedly crossed him up, disregarding his signs.

In the second game, Lefty Williams—a control pitcher who had walked only 58 batters in 297 innings during the season—walked three Reds in one inning and then gave up a triple to Larry Kopf, Cincinnati's weakest hitter. Otherwise, Lefty mowed the batters down, allowing only three other hits. But that one inning was enough; Cincy won the second game, 4–2.

The tale is told that during the game an airplane flew low over Cincinnati's Redland Field and brought gasps from the crowd as a figure fell out, landing behind third base. It turned out to be a dummy in a White Sox uniform "taking the dive." The boys from the Windy City were very upset.

Something else of greater import happened on the train to Chicago after that second game. Around midnight, White Sox owner Charlie Comiskey showed up at the door of John Heydler's sleeping compartment. Heydler was president of the National League and—along with August "Garry" Herrmann, president of the Cincinnati Reds, and Ban Johnson, president of the American League—he was also part of the three-man National Baseball

Nearly 70 years after it occurred, the Black Sox scandal was featured in director John Sayles' film of Eliot Asinof's book Eight Men Out. *In a still photograph from the film, Chicago second baseman Eddie Collins, played by Bill Irwin, is shown turning a double play.*

Commission that ruled the sport at the time. "I obviously can't go to Herrmann with this," Comiskey said, "and you know Johnson and I haven't spoken to each other in years, so I've got to tell you. Kid Gleason says he can't put his finger on it, but he's sure there's been some funny business going on with some of his players."

They discussed the matter. Heydler then got dressed and rapped at the door of Ban Johnson's compartment, in the same car. It was now past one a.m. and Johnson, a heavy drinker, was annoyed at being awakened. When Heydler finished telling his story, Johnson showed the depths of his antipathy for his former pal Comiskey by snapping, "That's the yelp of a beaten cur," and went back to bed. Since the Sox were in Johnson's league, Heydler felt that his hands were tied and did nothing.

Other rumors rumbled below the surface as this strange 1919 Series went on. The odds for Game 3 swung dramatically in favor of the Reds, but little Dickie Kerr won for the Sox, 3–0. Several gamblers, apparently unaware of Kerr's purity, reportedly lost a bundle.

Cicotte took the mound again for Game 4. In the fifth inning he bobbled an easy grounder and threw the ball into the stands, then kicked around a perfect throw from Shoeless Joe in left field, letting two runners score. The Reds won, 2–0. "In all his life," screamed Kid Gleason, "he never made plays like that!"

In Game 5, Lefty Williams pitching, the Reds scored four times in the sixth inning and won, 5-0. Sox center fielder Happy Felsch misplayed two drives and committed a throwing error in that fateful inning. Hod Eller, pitching for the Reds, set a World Series record by striking out six Sox in order

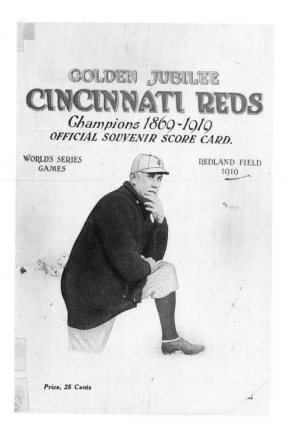

Tickets to the 1919 World Series were hard to come by, unless you were a member of the Base Ball Writers of America (BBWA). Then you got a pin good for admission to the entire Series.

over the second and third innings, a record, but one that begs questioning: were the White Sox swinging for hits or for outs? Game 6 produced Dickie Kerr's second Series victory, 5–4, assuring him richly deserved hero status, considering what his teammates were up to.

The next day the real Eddie Cicotte showed up, the White Sox played baseball the way everybody knew they could, and they prevailed easily, 4–1. What happened to the fix? The story went around that the fixers had short-changed the fixees; the deal was off and the Sox were now playing to win. After seven games, it was Cincinnati four to three, but still anybody's Series. Then came the rumor that a rival syndicate had reached the Reds. Edd Roush, Cincinnati's great center fielder, reported that starting pitcher Hod Eller had been promised $500 to lose Game 8.

Even if Eller had accepted the bribe—which he didn't—he would have had a hard time losing that game. Lefty Williams gave up four runs in the first inning before Gleason could rush in reliever Bill James. But the damage was done; the Sox lost, 10–5. What no one but a select few knew was that Lefty Williams was pitching under a death sentence from the Chicago mob: you win—you lose.

The Reds took the Series, five games to three, and the odor of fish was everywhere. The talk got so bad that Comiskey offered $10,000 to anyone who could prove that his "boys" had gone into the tank. There were no takers. But the offer had a hollow ring to it. Most of his players were recognized stars, yet he penny-pinched them unmercifully. Cicotte earned only $5,500 a year; Jackson and Weaver got $6,000; Gandil and Felsch, $4,000; and Williams, less than $3,000. By contrast, the

Team owner Charlie Comiskey had baseball's tightest purse strings but after the scandal broke, he opened his wallet to the tune of $1,500 for each of his players who wasn't involved in the scandal.

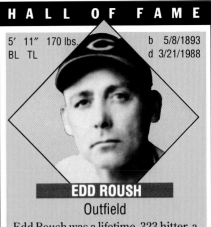
Edd Roush was a lifetime .323 hitter, a brilliant and acrobatic center fielder, and nobody's fool. He was intelligent and independent enough to make baseball work for him instead of the other way around.

Roush didn't like spring training, so he regularly engineered salary disputes that were resolved just in time for the regular season. Then he'd go out, hit .350 or so, catch everything in sight, and repeat the formula the next year. "All that fella has to do is wash his hands, adjust his cap, and he's in shape to hit," said Reds manager Pat Moran.

Even during a game, Roush played to suit himself. Once, when he decided Moran's argument with an umpire had gone on too long, he lay down in center field and, with his glove for a pillow, fell asleep. When awakened by Heinie Groh, who had run out to center from his post at third base, Roush was promptly ejected.

From 1916 to 1931, Roush swung the heaviest—48 ounces—and one of the most effective bats in the NL. He won batting titles in two of his first three years with the Reds, 1917 and 1919, and was an outstanding baserunner, with 29 career inside-the-park home runs. Roush played a very shallow center field, and used his speed and agility to chase down long drives. Roush retired after the 1931 season. He came back to the Reds as a coach in 1938, but retired after a year. He didn't need the work anyway; he was independently wealthy from shrewd investments in blue-chip stocks.

Reds were paying Heinie Groh $8,000; Jake Daubert, $9,000; and Edd Roush, $10,000.

Comiskey did other little things, such as paying $3-a-day meal money on the road while other clubs paid $4. And cute tricks, too, such as promising Cicotte a $10,000 bonus if he won 30 games in 1917, then—with the pennant in hand—benching him after he reached 28, ostensibly to rest up for the Series. The argument can be—and has been—made that Comiskey's niggardliness caused the resentful players to cast about for ways of getting the money they felt they deserved. Eliot Asinof, in his book *Eight Men Out,* claims that the players, not the gamblers, made the first overtures. Chick Gandil, he learned, looked up Joseph "Sport" Sullivan, a front man for the deal, and said in unminced words, "I think we can put it in the bag."

The other knock against Comiskey is that he knew what was going on during the Series—gambler friends told him, and so did other people in the know—but for some reason, after telling Heydler of Kid Gleason's suspicions, he chose to cover up rather than clamp down. He was still covering a year later. Rumors persisted, and newspapermen began to write more openly, enough to earn the Chicago franchise new nicknames: subtle souls liked "Opposite Sox" and "Dirty Sox," but for pungency and punch nothing beat "Black Sox."

In August 1920 the White Sox blew three games to Boston in so obvious a manner that second baseman Eddie Collins went to Comiskey in person to complain. He could no longer look the other way.

In the meantime, AL president Ban Johnson had conducted his own investigation to protect the fair name of baseball. If it happened to embarrass his onetime crony from Chicago, so much the better. Johnson gave a Cook

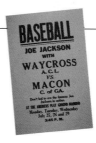

Aftermath of a Scandal

They were at the peak of their careers when they were banned from baseball for life. Of the eight White Sox expelled from the game by Commissioner Landis for their roles in the 1919 World Series gambling scandal, only 36-year-old pitcher Eddie Cicotte was beyond his best baseball years, and even he had a solid 1920 season with 21 wins. The other players ranged in age from 26 to 33, and several were coming off their best seasons ever. All of them faced an abrupt end to their careers in the major leagues.

Chick Gandil, the slick-fielding first baseman, was the players' ringleader and paymaster in the game-fixing scheme. The 1919 season was his last as a major league player; he sat out the 1920 season in a salary dispute. Gandil continued playing ball for a few years in "outlaw" leagues—those not sanctioned by organized baseball—and then settled down as a plumber in northern California. Four months before his death in 1970, he said of the scandal, "I'll go to my grave with a clear conscience."

Shoeless Joe Jackson, the brilliant left fielder who was a favorite of Chicago fans, hit .375 in the 1919 Series and followed that performance, at age 33, with one of his best seasons in 1920. Jackson played under assumed names in outlaw leagues with Swede Risberg, Gandil and Cicotte for several years, then in 1924 sued White Sox owner Charles Comiskey for $18,000 in back pay from a three-year contract he signed before the 1920 season. The jury awarded Jackson $16,711.04, but the judge set aside the verdict and dismissed the case, saying that Jackson had perjured himself by recanting his 1920 confession to a grand jury. In 1929 he moved to Greenville, South Carolina, where he ran a dry cleaning business and played semipro ball. In 1933 Greenville gained a minor league franchise, and Jackson was offered the job of player-manager, but Commissioner Landis denied his application.

Jackson, a local hero in Greenville, later ran a successful liquor store, and died in 1951, a player with a great record, but no plaque in Cooperstown.

Eddie Cicotte, master of the shineball, was one of the primary conspirators and the first to crack before the grand jury. Like Jackson, Cicotte played in outlaw leagues under assumed names for several years, then returned to his farm near Detroit. He became a state game warden and a security guard. Cicotte died in 1969.

Buck Weaver was the best third baseman in baseball in 1920. The 30-year-old Weaver hit .333 and struck out just 23 times in 630 at-bats in 1920. He turned down Gandil's offer to take part in the game-fixing scheme, then went on to hit .324 and play errorless ball in the 1919 Series. Though he refused to participate in the fix, he was banned for life for not revealing the plot. Weaver sued the White Sox for the remaining two years' salary in his contract, and got an out-of-court settlement from Comiskey. But his repeated appeals for reinstatement were denied. He stayed in Chicago, played semipro ball, and wound up as a racetrack clerk. In 1945 Happy Chandler replaced Landis as commissioner, and Weaver thought he saw an opportunity to do what he wanted most: to clear his name. But despite a recommendation for leniency from Judge Hugo Friend, who had presided over the 1921 trial of the Black Sox players, Chandler denied Weaver's appeal, as did his successor, Ford Frick. Weaver died in Chicago in 1956.

Happy Felsch, the great defensive center fielder, had turned in a star-quality season in 1920. At 29, Felsch had career highs of .338, 40 doubles, 15 triples, 14 home runs and 115 RBI in what became his last season. Felsch returned to his home in Milwaukee, where he ran a bar and raised six children. He died in 1964.

Swede Risberg, shortstop, had his best season in 1920. After playing ball for several more

Ty Cobb called Shoeless Joe Jackson (below, left) "the finest natural hitter in the history of the game." But when Jackson was banned from baseball in 1921, he returned to his native South Carolina and became a local celebrity. A few months before his death in 1951, he still looked natural with a bat in his hands as he helped out a player in a local textile league.

Arnold Rothstein (above) and Abe Attell were two of the main gambling figures in the Black Sox scandal. In an argument in front of Lindy's restaurant in New York, Attell said, "Rothstein, you're gonna die with your shoes on!" In 1928 Rothstein was shot and killed during a poker game.

years in outlaw leagues, Risberg became a dairy farmer in Minnesota. Eventually, he moved to Oregon, where he owned a tavern. Risberg outlived the other seven Black Sox and died in 1975.

Lefty Williams won 23 games in 1919, and then did a great job of throwing the Series by losing three times and posting a 6.61 ERA. Williams ran a poolroom in Chicago for a while, then moved to California, where he opened a garden shop. He died in 1959.

Fred McMullin was the utility infielder who overheard a conversation about the fix, demanded to be cut in on the action, then batted just twice—and was 1 for 2—in the Series. McMullin played on a semipro team with five other Black Sox in 1921, then lived in obscurity until his death in Los Angeles in 1952.

And what of the gamblers who made the fix possible? Former major leaguer Bill Burns, the man Cicotte alledgedly contacted with the idea of the fix, returned to Chicago for the trial, gave a Texas address and said his occupation was "fishing." Joseph Sullivan, the front man contacted by Chick Gandil, was not indicted, and disappeared from the public eye. Former boxer Billy Maharg, another contact man, testified at the 1921 trial and claimed he was an autoworker. Former boxer Abe Attell, who had apparently handled the placement of bets, was not indicted. Attell was arrested several times in the 1920s for liquor violations, then after Prohibition ran a bar that attracted sports fans. In 1961, at the age of 78, he publicly professed his innocence and blamed the whole scandal on Arnold Rothstein.

County grand jury a laundry list of gamblers' names to look up. On September 24, 1920, subpoenas went out for, among others, "Sleepy Bill" Burns, a former major leaguer living on the shady side of the street; Abe Attell, one-time featherweight boxing champion; and Arnold Rothstein, racetrack owner and celebrity gambler.

The wheels fell off the wagon three days later when the Philadelphia *North American* published an interview with an ex-boxer named Billy Maharg. He had been working for Bill Burns, Maharg said, and had served as the go-between who brought the players and the gamblers together.

With only three days of the 1920 season left to play, with his team only one game behind, and with the walls tumbling down around him, Comiskey did what he had to do. He wired the eight culprits that they were indefinitely suspended, and ended by saying, "Until there is finality to this investigation, it is due the public that I take this action, even though it cost Chicago the pennant." He meant it. Only two regular White Sox starters, Eddie Collins and Shano Collins, were still in uniform. Yankee owner Jake Ruppert and other club owners not in the running offered him "your choice of players" to finish the season. Comiskey refused with thanks.

The Cleveland Indians won the 1920 AL pennant, and the right to take on the Brooklyn Robins. It was a quiet Series, surprisingly well attended but not very exciting, until Game 5. Then Bill Wambsganss, Cleveland second baseman, made a play for the history books. In the top of the fifth, the Robins had runners on first and second, no outs. The next batter, pitcher Clarence Mitchell, ripped what looked like a sure line drive single to right. The runners took off. Wambsganss ran, leaped, speared the ball in

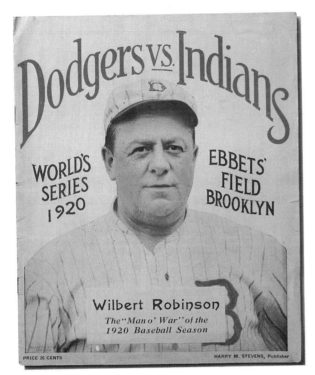

Brooklyn manager Wilbert Robinson led his Robins into the 1920 World Series against the Indians amid the courtroom drama of the Black Sox scandal, and scored only eight runs—a record low—in losing to Cleveland.

5′ 11″ 166 lbs. b 7/13/1889
BR TR d 3/20/1984

STAN COVELESKI
Pitcher

The 1920 World Series was a pretty lively affair, producing the first grand slam, the first home run by a pitcher, and the only unassisted triple play in World Series history. Its one constant was Stan Coveleski's spitball.

In 1920, Coveleski, one of 32 pitchers authorized by the commissioner to throw the spitball, turned in the greatest Series pitching performance since Christy Mathewson threw three shutouts in 1905. Coveleski won three games, allowing just 15 hits, two walks, and two runs in 27 innings as the Indians beat the Brooklyn Robins five games to two.

Born Stanislaus Kowalewski, he left school after fourth grade to work in the coal mines in his hometown of Shamokin, Pennsylvania. His brother Harry became a major league pitcher in 1907, and Stan followed suit five years later. Brought up by the Philadelphia Athletics late in the 1912 season, Coveleski shut out Detroit in his first major league start. His ability to control the spitball—something few pitchers could do—led to four straight 20-win seasons with Cleveland from 1918 to 1921. Coveleski once pitched seven innings without throwing a called ball; he allowed an average of one home run every 46 innings in his career.

The Indians traded Coveleski to Washington in 1925, and he went 20–5 to help the Senators win their second straight AL pennant. Called "The Greased Pole" by *The New York Times*, Coveleski was elected to the National Baseball Hall of Fame.

flight, kicked the bag at second and whirled to slap the tag on the runner coming from first, who had stopped dead in his tracks, dumbfounded. It was the first unassisted triple play in World Series history, and it seemed to take the starch out of the Dodgers. The Indians took the Series, five games to two.

Up in Chicago, Eddie Cicotte had been singing for the grand jury, and Felsch, Jackson and Williams soon joined the chorus. Public feeling against the players was so strong that they were afraid to leave the courtroom without guards, but it was the confession of Shoeless Joe Jackson that broke the hearts of fans.

Shoeless Joe was a country boy from South Carolina; one day in the minors he played in his socks to ease the pressure on a blister, and fans hung a name on him. He couldn't read or write, but he could play baseball. His career batting average, .356, is the third highest ever. He hit over .370 four times, once over .400, but never won a batting title because Ty Cobb or George Sisler always edged him out. He was so good he found it difficult to be bad. In the 1919 Series, which he admitted trying to throw, he batted .375 and fielded flawlessly. Joe was a popular hero, and some people said his performance in the Series proved that he had agreed to the fix just to get the money so he could retire to his farm. In other words, cheating the fixers at their own game somehow made it all right.

When Joe Jackson was called to testify, the enormity of what he had done must have dawned on him. He covered his face with his hands as he walked through the horde of news photographers into the courtroom. But when he had finished testifying, after almost two hours, he walked out erect and smiling, and announced, "I got a big load off my chest. I'm feeling

6′ 2″ 180 lbs.   b 9/6/1888
BR TR   d 9/25/1976

RED FABER
Pitcher

Red Faber wasn't one of the White Sox players who took bribes to fix the 1919 World Series, but that doesn't mean he didn't suffer as a result of the scandal. On the strength of a good fastball and a better spitball, Faber earned 254 lifetime wins, but he might have topped 300 had the scandal not cost the White Sox most of their talent late in the 1920 season. Faber stayed with Chicago for his entire 20-year career—Walter Johnson and Ted Lyons are the only pitchers to serve longer with one team—but in his 14 post-scandal seasons the Sox finished over .500 only twice.

A master of control, Faber won 24 games in 1915, his second year in the majors. In 1917 he led Chicago to a world championship with three World Series wins. Faber missed the 1919 Series because of an injury, but came back strong in 1920 with 23 wins for the White Sox, who finished the season in second place.

In 1921 Faber turned in another stellar year. His 25 wins accounted for 40 percent of the seventh-place White Sox' wins, and at 2.48, his was the only ERA under 3.00 in the AL. He won 21 more games in 1922 along with his second straight ERA title. From 1920 to 1922, Faber averaged 334 innings a season, and the work began to take its toll. Though he remained a consistent 10- to 15-game winner, his strikeout totals fell and his ERA rose throughout the rest of the 1920s and the early 1930s. Faber pitched through 1933 with the White Sox, winning 38 games after he turned 40.

Shoeless Joe Jackson (right) was a lot more at ease on a ballfield than he was in a courtroom. Illinois Assistant State Attorney Hartley Replogle (left) tried to protect Joe Jackson from reporters after his confession, but Jackson wanted to talk.

better." The poignant scene that happened next became the myth that baseball fans still remember. When Shoeless Joe walked out of the courthouse, a crowd of boys clustered about him. There were some newsmen, too. One of the boys cried out, "It ain't true, Joe, is it?" And Joe murmured, with his head down, "Yes, I guess it is, boys." The reporters described the scene as they remembered it, and the version that symbolized the whole sorry mess to the baseball fans of America is the one that has lived: a small boy in short pants tugging at the sleeve of the great ballplayer and pleading, with tears in his eyes, "Say it ain't so, Joe."

The grand jury returned indictments for fraud in October 1920, but before the case could come to trial a new state's attorney took office, and somewhere along the line all the papers in the case, including the players' confessions, disappeared. It is generally believed that the Chicago underworld had struck a deal with selected members of the former prosecutor's staff, especially when some of those staff members later turned up as attorneys for the players. In the midst of all this skulduggery, the players repudiated their confessions. Without evidence of any kind, the indictments had to be dismissed.

But Ban Johnson, perhaps aware of the fact that the owners were becoming disenchanted with his stewardship of the American League, refused to let the matter drop. He traveled thousands of miles, following new leads, digging up new evidence, rebuilding the case. He scoured the mountains of northern Mexico looking for Bill Burns, brought him back to Chicago as a state's witness, and got the case reopened. But to no avail. On August 2, 1921, after hearing evidence for a month, the jury brought in a verdict of not

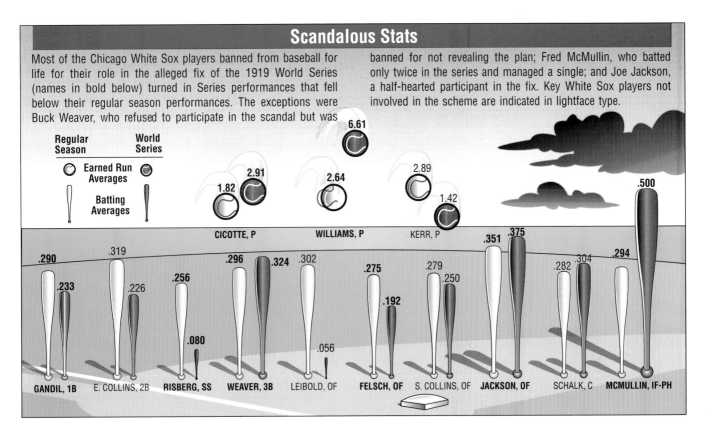

Scandalous Stats

Most of the Chicago White Sox players banned from baseball for life for their role in the alleged fix of the 1919 World Series (names in bold below) turned in Series performances that fell below their regular season performances. The exceptions were Buck Weaver, who refused to participate in the scandal but was banned for not revealing the plan; Fred McMullin, who batted only twice in the series and managed a single; and Joe Jackson, a half-hearted participant in the fix. Key White Sox players not involved in the scheme are indicated in lightface type.

Regular Season / World Series

Earned Run Averages

Batting Averages

CICOTTE, P 1.82 2.91
WILLIAMS, P 6.61 2.64
KERR, P 2.89 1.42

GANDIL, 1B .290 .233
E. COLLINS, 2B .319 .226
RISBERG, SS .256 .080
WEAVER, 3B .296 .324
LEIBOLD, OF .302 .056
FELSCH, OF .275 .192
S. COLLINS, OF .279 .250
JACKSON, OF .351 .375
SCHALK, C .282 .304
MCMULLIN, IF-PH .294 .500

guilty. That night, the Black Sox celebrated the acquittal with a hilarious party in an Italian restaurant on Chicago's West Side. By strange coincidence, the jurors also held a party that night in the same restaurant. There was no prearrangement, it was said, and although their private rooms adjoined, the two parties kept strictly to themselves.

The celebration didn't last long. The very next day the eight players were tried, convicted and sentenced by baseball's own tribunal. Until the time of the Black Sox scandal, professional baseball had been run by the three-man National Baseball Commission, which had managed to hang most of the sport's dirty laundry in the cellar to dry, away from prying eyes. But by the time the Dirty Sox blew the doors and windows out, the club owners, fearing for the game's survival, had installed a new ruler, Judge Kenesaw Mountain Landis.

Commissioner Landis issued a statement the day after the Sox were acquitted that left no doubt about which way the wind emanating from the new office was going to blow: "Regardless of the verdict of juries, no player that entertains proposals or promises to throw a game, no player that sits in a conference with a bunch of crooked players and gamblers where the ways and means of throwing games are discussed, and does not promptly tell his club about it, will ever again play professional baseball."

So much for the Chicago Eight, including third baseman Buck Weaver, who did not agree to the fix, received no money, and in fact played a stellar Series, hitting .324 and fielding his position magnificently. When 20,000 Chicagoans signed a petition seeking Weaver's reinstatement, Landis had him into his office, listened to him admit that he had attended the fix meeting,

The Boston Daily Globe

BOSTON, WEDNESDAY MORNING, SEPTEMBER 29, 1920—TWENTY PAGES — TWO CENTS

ODD FELLOWS POUR IN FOR BIG PARADE TODAY

Expect 40,000 in Line—Display of Fireworks Tonight

Oliver Elected Grand Sire and Judge Eastin Deputy—Next Session To Be in Toronto

ALL SAFE, SAYS ALLEN; CONFIDENCE RETURNS

Commissioner Takes Over Fidelity's Affairs

McKnight Leaves Dorchester Trust; Tremont Reports Normal Business

TWO WHITE SOX STARS ADMIT THROWING BIG 1919 SERIES

Cicotte Confesses to Finding $10,000 Under His Pillow Before Games With Reds---Jackson Says He Received $5000

EIGHT ALLEGED BASEBALL CROOKS

JOE JACKSON — EDDIE CICOTTE — CHIC GANDIL — CLAUDE WILLIAMS — SWEDE RISBERG — FRED McMULLIN — 'HAP' FELSCH — 'BUCK' WEAVER

SEVEN WHITE SOX AND AN EX-MEMBER OF TEAM ("CHICK" GANDIL) ACCUSED IN BASEBALL SCANDAL

Eight Indicted, Others Being Weaver, McMullin, Williams, Risberg, Felsch, Gandil

Comiskey Suspends Players-- Abe Attell Named as Head Of Gambling Clique

Special Dispatch to the Globe

CHICAGO, Sept 28—The eight suspected players on the Chicago American League team's roster were indicted today, charged with "conspiracy to commit an illegal act," in a word to allow the Cincinnati team of the National League to win the world's championship in 1919 for a money consideration. Two players, Edward V. Cicotte, pitcher, and Joseph Jackson, outfielder, have confessed.

They told the Grand Jury of the combination among the leading players who gambled on the World's Championship, and the good name of the generous owner of the team for $100,000.

Pres Charles A. Comiskey of the White Sox acted like a Brutus by suspending all the players, though a pennant and a World's Championship are not beyond his grasp. He did this early in the day. The play-

ers named in the indictments are:

ARNOLD GANDIL, formerly first baseman, who did not return to the team this season and is on the Pacific Coast.

EDWARD V. CICOTTE, veteran pitcher.

CLAUDE P. WILLIAMS, pitcher.

FREDERICK McMULLIN, substitute infielder.

JOSEPH FELSCH, center field.

OSCAR FELSCH, left field.

GEORGE WEAVER, third base.

CHARLES RISBERG, shortstop.

The punishment if found guilty is a term from one to five years in the penitentiary or a fine of $10,000.

Cicotte Betrays All

In the midst of this wholesale corruption it is cheering to know that Eddie Collins, John Collins, Faber, Schalk and others come through unstained.

and then said, coldly, "You knew everything that was going on; and if you did not so inform your club, I hold you as guilty as the actual plotters and the men who took money for throwing the Series."

And what did the Cincinnati Reds—Heinie Groh, Edd Roush, Greasy Neale, Jake Daubert, Dutch Ruether and Hod Eller, pretty fair ballplayers in their own right—what did they think of all this and the shadow it cast over their 1919 world championship?

"Rumors were flying all over the place," said Edd Roush diplomatically. "But nobody knew anything for sure."

"Maybe the Sox did throw it," Heinie Groh grudgingly admitted. "I don't know. Maybe they did and maybe they didn't."

It remained for tough Jimmy Ring, who pitched one Series win and took one loss, to put into plain English what the Reds really thought. "They played like horseshit," he said. "But we would have beaten them anyway." ◗❙◖

Despite regular-season infighting and their World Series conspiracy, the 1919 White Sox were an impressive collection of talent. They led the AL in runs scored, batting average, stolen bases and fewest walks allowed, and were second in double plays, shutouts, fewest errors committed and fewest runs allowed.

The Commission is Dead, Long Live the Commissioner

Early in 1903—after several years of court battles, ticket price wars and roster raiding—NL president Harry Clay Pulliam and August "Garry" Herrmann, Cincinnati Reds owner, sat down with AL president Ban Johnson and his crony Charlie Comiskey, owner of the Chicago White Sox.

In just two days of negotiating, the four set up the "National Agreement," which endured without change for 50 years: major league baseball was to consist of two leagues of eight teams each, with common rules of play and nonconflicting schedules. The agreement also provided for player contracts that included a "reserve clause," which gave clubs the exclusive rights to a player's services. Until the mid-seventies, when a series of arbitration and court rulings allowed players to act as free agents, clubs had the legal power to retain, trade or sell players at will.

Responsibility for making the agreement work was lodged in a National Baseball Commission, with Herrmann as chairman and the two league presidents as members. Since NL presidents frequently came and went, the real power on the commission, the "Supreme Court of Baseball," was wielded by Herrmann and Johnson, who, although in different leagues, formed a natural bloc based on a lifelong friendship.

Autocratic and despotic, the burly, boozing Johnson ruled the AL with an iron fist, hurling suspensions and directives like thunderbolts from on high. In 1910, despite previous clashes with Comiskey, Johnson was able to secure a 20-year term as the league's president at an annual salary of $25,000. He held on when Comiskey later tried to give him the boot. In 1914 several court cases challenged Ban Johnson's high-handed suspensions and blacklists. More trouble came in 1915, when the new Federal League challenged the reserve clause, accusing major league clubs and the National Commission of conspiring to restrain trade in violation of antitrust laws. The suit was heard in the Federal District Court of Northern Illinois, presided over by a gaunt, 48-year-old judge who was frequently seen at home games of the White Sox and the Cubs: Kenesaw Mountain Landis.

Landis had already made a name for himself in the press by slapping a whopping $29 million fine on Standard Oil of Indiana. It didn't matter that the decision was later reversed; the judge had become a national figure.

Born in Ohio in 1866, named after the Georgia battlefield where his father had been wounded in the Civil War, the featherweight jurist—5' 7" and 125 pounds—was a heavyweight on the bench. He was also unwilling to jeopardize America's national institution. "Do you realize," he said, "that a decision in this case may tear down the very foundations of this game, so loved by thousands?"

Instead of reaching a decision, Landis deliberated. He deliberated all winter, all spring, all summer, and far into the fall. Finally, what he had been waiting for happened: the Federal League began to fold. In an out-of-court settlement, renegade players had their major league eligibility restored, and all lawsuits were dropped.

The settlement was costly, but major league magnates, recognizing what Landis had done for them, hailed him as a hero—especially AL owners, who had been growing increasingly disenchanted

AL president Ban Johnson (far left) and Reds owner August Herrmann (far right) served on the National Commission which ruled baseball for its entire 17-year tenure. NL president Tom Lynch (center)—a former umpire—lasted just four years, angering owners with his steadfast support for umpires in disputes with players and managers.

with Ban Johnson and his tyrannies. After Johnson sneeringly called Landis a "showboat," the AL power brokers responded with a campaign to dissolve the National Commission.

On the surface, most AL owners remained faithful to their czar, but a minority started cutting away his power base—the unforgiving Comiskey, Yankee owners Jake Ruppert and Til Huston, and Red Sox owner Harry Frazee, who was on Johnson's hit list for permitting gambling in his park.

At the 1919 fall meeting of team owners, a move to abolish baseball's Supreme Court nearly succeeded; chief justice Johnson was in serious trouble. A year later, the Black Sox scandal made it clear that something had to be done to save the reputation of the game. And who better to take the helm than Judge Landis? Landis demanded complete control without interference from the owners, and on November 12, 1920, he was unanimously elected to the new post of baseball commissioner, at a reported salary of $50,000 a year.

So it was done. Exit the National Commission. Enter a new commissioner of baseball—an event, umpire Bill Klem remembered later, "that turned Johnson into a screaming harridan."

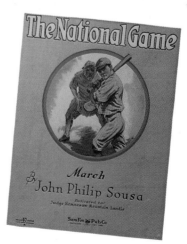

In the 1920s baseball marched to the beat of Commissioner Landis' drum, and John Philip Sousa provided the melody.

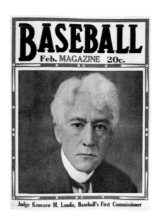

A Competent Despot

"The game needed a touch of class and distinction at the moment, and somebody said, 'Get that old guy who sits behind first base all the time. He's out there every day, anyhow.' So they offered him a season's pass and he jumped at it."

—*Will Rogers*

n August 16, 1920, a sultry, steaming day at the Polo Grounds—the New York City stadium where the Giants and Yankees took turns playing home games—Yankee pitcher Carl Mays was on the mound facing the Indians. In the top of the fifth, with the score 3–0 in favor of Cleveland, shortstop Ray Chapman stepped up to the plate. A great bunter and probably the fastest man in the American League, Chapman usually crowded the plate. He took a ball and then a strike. With a 1–1 count, Yankee catcher Muddy Ruel signaled for a low fastball.

At the top of his windup, Mays saw Chapman shift his feet into a drag-bunt position. Mays changed his delivery to a dust-off pitch—a smoking submarine fastball; high and inside. A batter has perhaps half a second to pick up and react to a fastball coming his way. Chapman, whose head was almost over the plate, never moved.

There was a sharp *crack* as the ball dribbled out between first base and the pitcher's mound. Somebody—the reporting gets fuzzy—either Ruel, Aaron Ward at third, or Mays himself—fielded the ball and fired it to Wally Pipp at first. Pipp, making what he thought was the putout, cocked his arm to start the ball around the infield, then suddenly pulled up as he glanced toward home. Every head in the park, it is said, swung in the same direction.

Chapman, after taking two steps toward first, had fallen in a heap. Ruel and Cleveland player-manager Tris Speaker, the on-deck batter, helped

Cleveland shortstop Ray Chapman (opposite, center) was one of the game's most gifted and popular players. In 1920 he was hitting .303 and the Indians were on their way to a pennant when Chapman was killed by a ball pitched by Yankee Carl Mays.

Howard Ehmke was a submarine-style pitcher who hit a lot of batters. In fact, Ehmke, who pitched from 1915 to 1930, hit 137 batters, seventh on the all-time list. Carl Mays, whose fastball killed Ray Chapman, is not among the top ten.

Claude Hendrix had a turbulent career during the scandal-plagued 1920s. Hendrix reportedly agreed to fix a game he was to pitch for the Cubs against the last-place Phillies on August 31, 1920. Cubs' president Bill Veeck found out about the fix, and at 31, Hendrix' career was over.

Chapman to his feet. He tried to walk but slumped unconscious, bleeding from both ears.

A doctor raced down from the stands to give first aid. Indian players carried Chapman to the clubhouse, and he was taken to nearby St. Lawrence Hospital. By five o'clock the next morning, Ray Chapman was dead, the first and only major leaguer killed by a baseball.

Carl Mays, a tough competitor, continued to pitch until lifted in the eighth for a pinch hitter. He lost the game—the winning run, ironically, coming across as a result of the hit batter. He learned of Chapman's death the next day, and insisted he had not thrown with intent to hit him.

Most of the players on top of the play agreed that Chapman had made no attempt to get out of the way. But Mays had a reputation as a headhunter, and even though other pitchers were ahead of him in the number of batters hit, he was vilified by the fans and pilloried in the press. Undaunted, Carl Mays pitched nine more years with considerable success, and by the time he hung up his spikes in 1929 he had compiled the kind of numbers that should have made him a serious candidate for induction into the Hall of Fame. He never made it.

Bitterly, in later life, he said, "I won over two hundred big league games, but no one today remembers that. When they think of me, I'm the guy who killed Chapman with a fastball." But Fred Lieb, New York newspaperman who served on the Hall of Fame's Veterans Committee for more than a decade, said that had nothing to do with the vote. "The question mark," said Lieb, "has been his performance in the Series of 1921."

Carl Mays' submarine delivery tailed in on right-handed batters, especially those who crowded the plate, like Ray Chapman. Mays always maintained Chapman stepped into the pitch that killed him.

League Park

Cleveland's League Park was truly one of baseball's most intimate stadiums. A block of seats along the third-base line jutted so close to the visitors' dugout that fans could harass visiting players, and while the screen in right field was 40 feet high, the foul pole was a cozy 290 feet from home plate.

Only its ticket booths and a portion of its left field stands remain today as part of a municipal park, but League Park is still remembered as the home of some of the game's greatest stars, including Cy Young, Napoleon Lajoie, Joe Jackson, Tris Speaker and Bob Feller.

Young, baseball's winningest pitcher, threw League Park's first strike on May 1, 1891, as the Cleveland team, then called the Spiders, beat Cincinnati before a capacity crowd of 9,000. The wooden stadium was located at the junction of two streetcar lines and was built by Spiders owner Frank Robison, who happened to own a local streetcar company.

Cleveland joined the new American League in 1901, and in 1903 became known as the Naps in honor of Napoleon Lajoie, their new acquisition, who had made a name for himself with Philadelphia. On October 2, 1908, in a League Park duel, Cleveland's Addie Joss pitched the second perfect game in the AL's short history, beating Chicago's Ed Walsh, 1–0.

After the 1909 season, the wooden stadium was torn down and replaced. Baseball's fourth concrete-and-steel structure, the new League Park was described by *Baseball Magazine* as "magnificent . . . one of the finest additions yet made to the equipment of the National Game." In order to discourage cheap home runs to right field, club president Ernest Barnard piled a 20-foot screen atop the 20-foot fence in right to finish the project.

Despite stars like Lajoie and Jackson, Cleveland struggled in its new park. The tide turned in 1916. The stadium was renamed Dunn Field after new owner Jack Dunn, and three players—center fielder Tris Speaker and pitchers Jim Bagby and Stan Coveleski—arrived to put the Cleveland Indians on the map. Speaker was a .344 lifetime hitter whose speed and daring in the park's spacious center field delighted fans and frustrated opponents. Bagby and Coveleski were hard-throwing pitchers about to reach their prime.

In 1920 it all came together for the Indians. Bagby won 31 games, Coveleski won 24, Speaker hit .388, and star shortstop Ray Chapman anchored the infield. And when the White Sox lost eight key players, suspended late in the season because of the 1919 World Series fix, the Indians captured the flag with a 51–27 home record. Dunn Field continued to be the Indians' good-luck charm in the World Series against Brooklyn. After Brooklyn won two of three in Ebbets Field, the Series returned to Cleveland, where the Indians' pitching and fielding took over. In the next four games—all before overflow crowds—the Indians wrapped up the Series, five games to two.

In 1928 Dunn was gone and the stadium became League Park once more. Babe Ruth hit his 500th career home run over the screen in right on August 11, 1929, but in the summer of 1932 the Indians began playing in the new 70,000-seat Municipal Stadium. Because League Park was smaller and cheaper to operate, it hosted the Indians' weekday games from 1934 through 1946, including rookie Bob Feller's 17-strikeout performance against the Athletics on September 13, 1936.

New Indians president Bill Veeck closed the park in 1947, two years after League Park hosted its last world champion, the Cleveland Buckeyes, who won the Negro World Series in 1945.

Ladies' Day at League Park (left); the stadium's new teepees (below) were put up in 1946, but were an attraction for only one year as the Indians moved all their games to Municipal Stadium in 1947; even after seats were added in left and center field in 1920, League Park remained one of baseball's smallest stadiums, with a capacity of under 30,000.

League Park

Lexington Avenue and
East 66th Street
Cleveland, Ohio

Built 1891
Rebuilt 1910
Demolished 1950

Cleveland Spiders, NL
1891–1899
Cleveland Indians, AL
1900–1946

Seating Capacity 21,414

Style
Grass surface, asymmet-
rical, steel and concrete

Height of Outfield Fences
Left field foul pole: 5 feet
Left center field: 10 feet
Dead center field: 35 feet
Right center field: 22 feet
Right field foul pole: 40 feet

Dugouts
Home: 1st base
Visitors: 3rd base

Bullpens
Outfield: foul territory
Home: right field foul line
Visitors: left field
 foul line

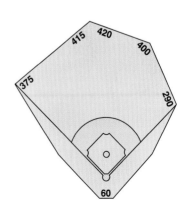

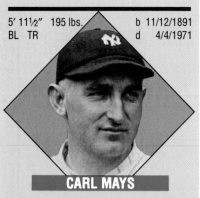

5′ 11½″ 195 lbs.   b 11/12/1891
BL TR   d   4/4/1971

CARL MAYS

Pitcher

Carl Mays, someone once said, had the temperament of a man with a permanent toothache. Even before a pitch he threw struck and killed Cleveland shortstop Ray Chapman, Mays was one of baseball's least liked players. But he was a great pitcher, and didn't much care what other people thought of him. He once praised another pitcher by saying, "This fellow has no friends and doesn't want any friends. That's why he's a great pitcher."

Mays broke into the majors with the Red Sox in 1915, and by the following year was an established star. He used a submarine-style delivery, with his hand almost scraping the ground. He had a great sinking fastball, and a will to win that was second to none. "Whatever criticism you can make about Mays," said teammate Everett Scott, "he has more guts than any other pitcher I ever saw."

Mays went 22-9 with a 1.74 ERA in 1917, then won 21 more in 1918. He wound up with the Yankees late in 1919, and paid the club big dividends over the next two seasons: he won 53 games, 26 in 1920 and 27 in 1921. But Mays and Yankee manager Miller Huggins did not get along, and Huggins traded Mays to Cincinnati in 1924, where he went 20–9 while the Yankees sank to second place. He retired after the 1929 season with Hall of Fame numbers—208 wins, a .623 winning percentage, a 2.92 ERA—but died in 1971 without a plaque in Cooperstown bearing his name.

Judge Landis (above, left) watched his first World Series as commissioner in 1921. In Game 2 he sat next to Mrs. Clark Griffith (above, right), wife of the Washington Senators' owner.

That was the first New York "Subway Series," featuring John McGraw's Giants—back in the hunt for the world championship after humiliating failures in 1911, 1912, 1913 and 1917—against their parvenu tenants, the Yankees, who had the audacity to outdraw the Giants in their own ballpark for the second year in a row.

The Giants had ridden to the pennant on a magnificent late-summer surge from 7½ games back, set in motion by a five-game sweep of the front-running Pirates. The Yankees were riding on the back of Babe Ruth, who was on his way to a colossal year—59 home runs, 171 runs batted in, and a .378 batting average.

Mays started the 1921 Series for the Yanks, pitched a five-hitter, and beat Shufflin' Phil Douglas, 3–0. Waite Hoyt duplicated that score for the Yankees in Game 2 with a two-hitter. The Giants came back with a vengeance, 13–5, then Mays and Douglas locked horns again in Game 4. It was a tight contest for seven innings, Mays virtually untouchable, the Yankees ahead on the Babe's first World Series homer. But suddenly the Giants touched Mays, piling up four runs in the eighth and ninth for the victory that evened the Series.

Late that night, a prominent Broadway actor was ushered into the presence of Judge Landis, the new commissioner of baseball. Landis listened as the actor delivered a disquieting story: Mays had been offered a substantial sum by persons unnamed, in cash, to let up enough in close games to ensure a Giants' win. At the start of the eighth inning that afternoon, the actor asserted, Mays' wife, sitting in the grandstand, wiped her face with a white handkerchief—the signal to her husband that the money had been handed over.

Giants catcher Frank Snyder scored the tying run on Dave Bancroft's single in the fourth inning of Game 6 of the 1921 World Series. Scoring behind Snyder was pitcher Jesse Barnes, who also had a remarkable run on the mound in that Series. Barnes won Game 3 with seven innings of four-hit relief, then replaced starter Fred Toney in the first inning of Game 6 and allowed just four hits in $8\frac{1}{3}$ innings for his second Series win.

It was a wild tale, the stuff of bad melodrama. But the Black Sox scandal was still an open wound, and Landis had shown little patience with other suspected miscreants. Despite the lateness of the hour, he immediately alerted his detective agency and launched a full investigation. Nothing was uncovered, either to incriminate Mays in any way or to corroborate the actor's story, but the shadow of doubt clung to the star-crossed pitcher for the rest of his life.

Carl Mays, a humorless and tough-minded fellow by nature, seemed to attract controversy the way a dog attracts fleas. On July 13, 1919, Mays—famous for his submarine delivery—was pitching for the Red Sox against Chicago. After two innings, victimized by four unearned runs, struck in the back of the head by a throw from catcher Wally Schang trying to nab a baserunner, and fuming over the lack of support all season that had collared him with a 5–11 record, the tempestuous Mr. Mays stalked angrily into the visitors' clubhouse, got dressed, and caught a train back to Boston, where he packed a fresh bag, hopped in his Marmon roadster, and headed for Pennsylvania to do some fishing.

There follows enough drama to make an afternoon soap opera: Boston threatens to trade Mays; AL president Ban Johnson orders no trade until Mays returns to his club; Yankee owners Jacob Ruppert and Til Huston locate the sulking pitcher by telephone and get a commitment from him to join the New York Yankees, beating out a number of other clubs hot on the maverick pitcher's trail.

Boston owner Harry Frazee, strapped as usual for cash, agrees to trade Mays to the Yankees for $40,000 and two players. But Ban Johnson flies into

As baseball commissioner, Judge Landis frowned upon players fraternizing with known gamblers and mobsters. When he saw this photograph of Cubs' catcher Gabby Hartnett (left) chatting with Al Capone (right), he responded by forbidding players from talking with fans either before or during games.

a rage, immediately suspends Mays, and nullifies the trade. Dark rumors hit that the AL czar, for reasons of his own, wants Mays to go to Cleveland.

Ruppert and Huston go to court, shocking the old guard, which believes in baseball solving its own problems away from the limelight. Judge Robert F. Wagner, father of the future mayor of New York City, issues an injunction restraining Johnson and the league from interfering with Mays' right to pitch for the Yankees. Pitch he did: on August 7 Mays won his first game as a Yankee, and went on to rack up 11 consecutive complete games, finishing the 1919 season with a 9–3 record for New York.

The action behind the scenes went even worse for Johnson. The league was hopelessly split on the Mays issue, beset by inconclusive meetings and nagging legal actions. Then the Yankee colonels dropped a bombshell—a $500,000 suit claiming that Johnson was trying to drive them out of baseball. This prompted a final kill-or-cure meeting of AL team owners, lasting until the wee hours of the morning and teetering on the brink of physical combat more than once. For Ban Johnson, the settlement was the beginning of the end. He kept his title as president of the American League but was stripped of most of his powers. By the following season, the baton of power had been passed to Judge Landis, the newly elected commissioner of baseball.

The year 1921 ended the nine-game World Series. It was Landis' first season as high potentate of baseball, and after sitting with fitting ceremony through eight games as the Giants took the championship, five games to three, he called for restoration of the seven-game formula, complaining testily that a nine-game Series "overtaxes the patience of the public."

Postseason barnstorming tours were a great way for players—especially stars like Lou Gehrig (far left) and Babe Ruth, shown here with USC football coach Howard Jones—to make a few extra bucks. But barnstorming by World Series participants was banned, and when Ruth appeared ready to ignore the rule in 1921, Judge Landis threatened to suspend him. The Babe wasn't impressed. "Aw, tell the old guy to go jump in a lake," he said. Landis made good his threat, and Ruth sat out the first six weeks of the 1922 season.

Although trick pitches and dirty balls were banned after Ray Chapman's tragic death in 1920, beanings were far from extinct. In 1926 Cardinal outfielder Chick Hafey was beaned several times, and as a result he became one of a very few major leaguers to wear glasses. The glasses helped Hafey, and in 1927 his batting average rose 58 points to .329.

Other things were overtaxing the patience of the commissioner, especially the flood of "him too" squealings and countersquealings that had been surfacing, in some strange form of catharsis, since the Black Sox debacle primed the pump. Since so much of the finger pointing involved games played before 1919, the commissioner's office wearily established a five-year statute of limitations on charges of dishonest play.

L andis quickly earned a reputation for swift judgment. According to historian Donald Honig, "Landis, whose stern features suggested Old Testament authority and inflexible integrity—he looked and acted like a third-rate thespian impersonating a judge—became baseball's unforgiving arbiter of its integrity...a frown from the judge was almost as good as getting the rope."

Banishment from professional ball for a player, owner or manager involved in a fixed game had been established with the founding of major league baseball in the 1870s. Landis simply carried out such sentences with fanatic zeal. And with easy money available from gamblers and other sharp elements in the 1920s, temptation was everywhere an underpaid baseball player cared to look. As late as 1943 he barred Bill Cox, an owner of the Phillies, from baseball for life for betting on his own team. No complete record has ever been compiled of all the bad apples in baseball's barrel, but Bill James, in his *Historical Baseball Abstract,* lists 38 major leaguers who were involved in scandals in the decade between 1917 and 1927. Of that number, 20 were banned for life or branded as *personae non gratae* because of issues related to the integrity of the game. One, Rube Benton, was reinstated, probably because he helped to unclothe the Black Sox malefactors. Four retired players

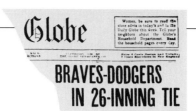
The Longest Game

Brooklyn's Leon Cadore and Boston's Joe Oeschger locked up in a pitchers' duel on April 20, 1920. They went 11 innings before anyone scored—and they were just getting loose. On May 1 these two pitchers went at each other longer than anyone else ever has in a single game. For 26 innings—the last 20 of them scoreless—they traded possession of the mound, and by the time darkness dropped its curtain on baseball's longest one-day run, no one had won. The game ended in a 1–1 tie.

Rain fell in Boston most of that Saturday morning. But it stopped and the game got under way at Braves Field at 3 p.m. The Dodgers, who went on to win the NL pennant, started the day at 8–4, one-half game behind the first-place Reds. The Braves, who lost 90 games and finished seventh, were in sixth place at 4–5.

The Dodgers got their run in the fifth, thanks in part to Oeschger's clumsy glove work. Ernie Krueger walked to open the inning, and Cadore hit a hard grounder back to the mound. Oeschger fumbled the ball, and with it any chance of forcing Krueger at second. Ivy Olson then lined an RBI single over shortstop Rabbit Maranville's head.

Boston got its run in the sixth on a triple off the scoreboard by Walt Cruise and a single by Tony Boeckel. From there it was all zeros, but hardly dull. The Braves had a golden opportunity to win the game in the ninth, but with the bases loaded and one out, second baseman Charlie Pick grounded into an inning-ending double play.

It was Oeschger's turn to sweat in the 17th, as the Dodgers loaded the bases with one out. He got Rowdy Elliott to hit a sharp grounder back to the mound and forced Zack Wheat out at home. Boston catcher Hank Gowdy threw wide to first trying for a double play, prompting Ed Konetchy to round third and head for home. First baseman Walter Holke recovered quickly, but his throw home was wide to Gowdy's right. Gowdy managed to catch the ball, dive headlong for the plate, and tag Konetchy out with the ball in his bare hand. That was the last scoring threat of the game.

Cadore, relying mainly on his curveball, allowed only 15 hits. Oeschger had a lively fastball that day, gave up just nine hits, and said he didn't get tired until the 18th inning. He claims he threw about 250 pitches, fewer than ten pitches an inning. The game was played at a grueling pace—26 innings in 3 hours 50 minutes, an average of one inning every nine minutes. By comparison, the 25-inning game in 1974 between the Mets and the Cardinals lasted 7 hours 23 minutes.

The contest pushed players, and sportswriters, to the limit. *The New York Times* said: "In the matter of thrills, the oldest living man can remember nothing like it, nor can he find anything in his granddad's diary worthy of comparison." Even the scorers got punchy. The *Times* credits each pitcher with three walks and Cadore with eight strikeouts to Oeschger's four. The *Boston Globe* was more democratic, crediting each pitcher with four walks and seven strikeouts. The game had a dramatic effect on the players' 1920 batting averages and ERAs. For example, Boston's Charlie Pick wound up hitting .274 for the season. Take away his 0 for 11 against Cadore that day and his average would be .282. Remove the game from Cadore's 1920 stats and his ERA rises from 2.62 to 2.88. Boston's Oeschger wound up the season with a 3.46 ERA, but it would have been 3.75 without his part in the marathon.

Cadore went on to win a career-high 15 games that season for the NL champion Dodgers, while Oeschger probably wanted to stay as far away from the Dodgers as possible. A year and a day before baseball's longest game, Oeschger had battled Brooklyn's Burleigh Grimes for 20 innings. The result? A tie, 9–9.

Brooklyn's Leon Cadore (top) lasted all 26 innings on May 1, 1920, but later that season, in his only career World Series start—Game 4 of the 1920 Series against Cleveland—he was knocked out in the second. The 26-inning game was a high point for Boston's Joe Oeschger (above), but his roller coaster career continued with 20 wins in 1921 followed by 21 losses in 1922. The Boston Globe chronicled the game via cartoon (left).

THE POWER
OF OFFICE

The game of baseball has undergone drastic changes since Kenesaw Mountain Landis became its first commissioner in 1921, but the powers of the office have remained largely the same. The commissioner is a one-man judicial system ruling over all those involved in professional baseball. He is prosecutor, judge and jury, and has wide powers to condemn and punish anyone whose actions he deems contrary to the best interests of baseball.

Though he is hired and paid by club owners, the commissioner's power extends over them, as it did when Commissioner Bowie Kuhn suspended New York Yankee owner George Steinbrenner in 1974 for making illegal contributions to Richard Nixon's presidential campaign. Commissioners have also supported the players against the owners, as when Albert B. "Happy" Chandler—who succeeded Landis in 1945—pushed to establish a minimum wage, a pension plan and limits on salary cuts for players.

The commissioner mediates conflicts between the leagues, and may play an advisory role in labor disputes between players and owners. The World Series also falls under the commissioner's jurisdiction.

The length of his term is established by the owners at the time of his election, but must be at least three years. His election requires the votes of three-fourths of the owners, and must include five from each league. He may be reelected by a simple majority vote, with a minimum of five votes from each league.

Detroit's Ty Cobb (right) and George Burns (left) were among a bunch of players who, in 1927, escaped close scrutiny of their alleged game-fixing and gambling activities. Public sentiment was with Cobb, and Judge Landis ended the investigation.

were implicated and never again invited to old-timer affairs. One player was banned for life and two others for stipulated periods for matters not having to do with the integrity of the game. The other accused players were either cleared of the charges against them or allowed to stay in the game for lack of hard evidence.

Several cases had elements that would have been funny had Landis' justice been less severe. Shufflin' Phil Douglas, after McGraw chewed him out once too often, penned a fantastic letter to the St. Louis Cardinals inviting them to bribe him to desert the Giants, so he wouldn't have to help McGraw win the pennant. It cost Douglas his career.

Lee Magee, born Leopold Hoernschemeyer, was proof that some people can't do anything right. With the Reds in 1918, he and teammate Hal Chase each made a $500 bargain with a gambler for Cincinnati to lose a game against the Boston Braves. The game was tied in the 13th inning when Magee came to bat. He tapped an easy grounder that hit a rough spot in the infield, bounced up, and broke the nose of Johnny Rawlings, the Boston shortstop. The luckless Magee had no choice but to take first base. The next batter, Edd Roush, slammed a home run, sending Magee across the plate with the winning tally, $500 poorer.

At least one case had all the earmarks of a miscarriage of justice. Ray Fisher, pitching for the Reds near the end of his career, was asked to accept a hefty, and to his mind uncalled-for, pay cut for the 1921 season. He opted to seek a job as baseball coach with the University of Michigan instead, and received permission from manager Pat Moran to visit Ann Arbor to pursue the matter. It was announced in the press that the Reds had put him on the voluntarily retired list. But Reds' owner Garry Herrmann, in a fit of pique, accused

Fisher of violating his contract and switched his name to Cincinnati's ineligible list. Fisher appealed to Landis and got the back of the commissioner's hand. It was a time of roiled waters in baseball and a lot of subtle little influences were at work under the surface. But the plain truth seems to be that Ray Fisher was callously run out of baseball for life by his team's owner and the game's new lord high executioner—the former out of spite and the latter because he needed the powerful Cincinnati owner's support in his own running feud with Ban Johnson.

"Landis had remarkable charisma; he stood out in any gathering," commented Fred Lieb. "He had many of the foibles of the ordinary man. He was vain, egotistical, domineering, and a show-off. He swore like a trooper, chewed tobacco, and was fond of bourbon whiskey. Some writers doubted his sincerity, thinking it contradictory that a man who could drink bootleg liquor behind the scenes would sentence a man for twenty years for violation of the prohibition amendment and the Volstead Act, as Landis had done. To understand the seeming contradiction you had to understand that Landis on the bench was a totally different man from Landis in the golf clubhouse."

This may seem a harsh judgment on the good judge, who in legend has been painted as the sainted savior of baseball, the righteous hand of God that came down from on high to smite villainy wherever it showed its evil head, and with cool detachment and surgical precision removed all excrescences from the pure body of the game. And in truth, you could say he did do some of that. But although he played up his physical attributes—his stern, granite-jawed visage, his piercing eagle eyes, his carefully tended halo of silver hair —to fit the popular mental image of a Moses, if not the Almighty, the fact remains that Kenesaw Mountain Landis was a man whose wife called him

For 24 years baseball's first commissioner, Kenesaw Mountain Landis (opposite), threw bolts of his justice across the baseball landscape. Sportswriter Heywood Broun wrote of him: "His career typifies the heights to which dramatic talent may carry a man in America if only he has the foresight not to go on the stage."

The Seven Czars of Baseball

The National Commission, founded in 1903, consisted of August Herrmann, owner of the Cincinnati Reds, and the two league presidents. In 1920, the triumvirate gave way to a single commissioner, who is still baseball's lone watchdog.

Name	Previous Occupation	Years as Commissioner
Kenesaw Mountain Landis	Federal Judge	1921–1944
Albert B. "Happy" Chandler	U.S. Senator	1945–1951
Ford C. Frick	Sportswriter; President, National League	1951–1965
William D. "Spike" Eckert	Lieutenant General, U.S. Air Force	1965–1968
Bowie Kuhn	Attorney	1969–1984
Peter V. Ueberroth	Business Executive	1984–1989
A. Bartlett Giamatti	President, Yale University; President, National League	1989–

Not the type to join children at a knothole in a ballpark fence, Landis nevertheless posed (above) for the popular weekly magazine Saturday Evening Post. *To him, baseball was more morality play than sport. "Baseball has got to be better in its morality than any other business," he said.*

"Squire," and who positively *hated* to lose even 25 cents in a golf game. He was a mortal man, with as much clay between his toes as the rest of us.

Landis not only played his role like a polished actor, he worked to make himself an institution. He stayed in his exalted post, much to the frustration of baseball owners, until his death in 1944. But as much as he reveled in his own power, he championed the rights of the individual player and stood for the nobility of the game. As Robert Smith put it, "Landis appointed himself spokesman for the ballplayer, and turned a ballplayer's skeptical eye on every suggestion for 'improving the game' that the magnates brought forth. Landis worked on the assumption that practically every 'improvement' an owner could think of was going to be paid for by the hired hands; and he went just as far as his sometimes doubtful power permitted him in forcing a fair shake for the small-salaried player. After he had been in power a few seasons, the baseball magnates began to mutter about him. Had it really been necessary, they wondered, to give the old bird all *that* power?" ◗

The Last of the Spitballers

Call them the soggy seventeen. Their ranks include such distinguished Hall of Famers as Burleigh Grimes, Stan Coveleski and Red Faber, as well as such sub-.500 forgettables as Dana Fillingim, Clarence Mitchell and Marvin Goodwin. But the 17 pitchers who were allowed to throw the spitball after the pitch was banned constitute as distinctive a group of players as the game has ever produced.

The demise of the spitball began after the 1919 season, when owners voted to limit each team to two legal spitball pitchers. Then, after popular Cleveland shortstop Ray Chapman was struck and killed by a dirty ball he probably didn't see, the Rules Committee outlawed the application of all foreign substances by pitchers. But since there were 17 active pitchers for whom the spitball was a primary weapon, a grandfather clause was inserted, allowing them to throw the pitch for the rest of their careers.

For the record, in the NL they were Grimes and Mitchell of Brooklyn, Bill Doak and Goodwin of St. Louis, Fillingim and Dick Rudolph of Boston, Phil Douglas of New York, and Ray Fisher of Cincinnati. The nine AL spitballers were Coveleski and Ray Caldwell of Cleveland, Doc Ayers and Hub Leonard of Detroit, Urban Shocker and Allen Sothoron of St. Louis, Faber of Chicago, Jack Quinn of New York, and Allan Russell of Boston.

Grimes was the most successful and the most colorful of the bunch. He saw his first spitter at the age of ten, and threw the majors' last legal one 31 years later. Most spitballers relied on chewing tobacco, but Grimes chewed bark from slippery elm trees in order to produce the moisture needed for his spitter. "Come spring the bark would get nice and loose and you could slice it free without any trouble," he said. Like a lot of spitball pitchers, Grimes kept batters guessing by going to his mouth before every pitch, spitball or not. Unlike most, Grimes had a solid array of pitches besides the spitter, including a fastball, a curve, a slider, a change, a screwball, and a devastating brushback pitch. Grimes won 20 or more games five times in the 1920s, and won 270 games in his career. He played for seven different teams, including two stints with the Cardinals and three with the Pirates.

Coveleski's major league career probably would have ended at three games had he not discovered the spitter. After a "dry" tryout with the Athletics in 1912, Coveleski spent three years in the minors before finding the pitch that earned him 215 career wins. He used alum, a chemical compound, to induce salivation, and could make the pitch break three ways.

The longevity of spitballers like Grimes and Quinn—who didn't leave the majors until he was 50—shows that the pitch, while tough to control, is easy on the arm. As further proof, two legal spitballers—Urban Shocker and Bill Doak—were among the last pitchers in baseball to post two complete-game wins in one day.

Douglas may have had the best stuff of the whole bunch, but he also had a drinking problem, and wound up banned from baseball for life after offering—in a letter to St. Louis outfielder Les Mann—to desert the Giants during their 1922 pennant race with the Cardinals. No less a hitter than Rabbit Maranville whined that Douglas shouldn't be allowed to throw the spitter: "He's 6' 4", has a fastball you can hardly see, a curveball and a change-of-pace. What does he need of a spitball?"

And while the spitter was banned after the 1920 season, pitchers still find ways to get one across. One hitter, frustrated with his inability to catch up with Nolan Ryan's fastball, turned Maranville's complaint around and asked, "Why doesn't he just throw the spitter like everyone else?"

Clarence Mitchell needed more than a legal spitball to give hitters cause for concern. In 18 seasons with six teams, he posted a 4.12 ERA and walked more batters than he struck out.

In 1932, at the age of 43, Red Faber (far left) could still show hitters— and other White Sox pitchers like Sad Sam Jones—how his spitball worked. Without much offensive support, however, Faber's 3.74 ERA in 1932 yielded a 2–11 won-loss record. Urban Shocker (above) began his career with the 1916 Yankees, then won 20 or more games four times with the Browns before returning to pinstripes in 1925.

Dunnie's Babe

"Landis was often referred to as the 'savior of base-ball.' Uh, uh. The savior of baseball was already on hand before Landis arrived, an ignorant, uncouth, but marvelously talented man named George Herman 'Babe' Ruth."

—*Glenn Dickey*

Momentous changes usually occur gradually: life on this planet evolved over eons; the Roman Empire took several centuries to die; the peace on Earth envisioned two thousand years ago still hasn't materialized. Babe Ruth, on the other hand, changed the face of baseball in one season. Until Ruth, the name of the game was "inside" baseball—get a man on, sacrifice, steal a base, squeeze the runner home; play for that one run and rely on your pitchers and fielders to protect it. Then Ruth of the Red Sox, the best left-handed pitcher in baseball, now an outfielder, stepped to the plate and with one swing of his big bat matched that scratched-out run and added up to three more if there happened to be runners on the bases.

Purists hated it. Brute strength, they sneered. No finesse, no matching of wits, no appreciation for the finer points of the game, the things that make baseball a chess match on the grand scale. They likened Mrs. Ruth's boy to a baboon, a gorilla and worse.

But the purists were a minority. Other fans, some who wouldn't know a double play from a double cross, came out to the ballparks in droves when Ruth came to town. "People in every big city in the land," wrote Robert Smith in *Baseball,* "suddenly discovered that baseball could be as exciting, in its summery way, as all-night drinking and dancing, airplanes, fast automobiles, and reckless gambling on the Stock Exchange. The Babe became almost a symbol of the age, and his fame was for a time surely unmatched by any figure

Babe Ruth (opposite) took a natural gift, and with it, forever changed baseball. "A rabbit didn't have to think to know what to do to dodge a dog. The same kind of instinct told Babe Ruth what to do and where to be," said teammate Sammy Vick.

For the most part, Ruth reveled in his fame, and rarely failed to live up to his reputation for good humor and generosity. "He was a parade all by himself, a burst of dazzle and jingle," wrote sportswriter Jimmy Cannon.

Though his 1920 baseball card identified him as a pitcher, Ruth's transformation to a position player was complete as soon as he was sold to the Yankees. Ruth pitched just one game that season, but more than made up for his absence from the mound with the highest season slugging percentage ever, .847. In 1921 he slumped to .846.

in sports or out. He became the Bambino and the Bimbo, in tune with some of the popular songs of the day. Newspapers almost everywhere ran daily charts of his home run record."

Smith is not talking here of Ruth's 60 glorious blasts in 1927. This was 1919; the "modern" American League record for homers in one season was 16, set by Ralph "Socks" Seybold of the Philadelphia Athletics in 1902. The National League mark was 24, punched out by Gavvy Cravath of the Phillies in 1915. The pre-1900 record was thought to be 25, by Buck Freeman of the 1899 Washington Senators, until a delver into dusty files discovered that in 1884 Edward Nagle Williamson of the Chicago Colts had belted 25 balls into the right field seats of the Congress Street grounds—barely 215 feet away—plus two more on the road. Williamson's magical year was a fluke, just as a scratch infield single is the same as a line drive on the score sheet. But the record was 27, and that was Babe's target.

He hit two in one game for the first time on July 5, then added two a week later to bring his total to 11, equaling his 1918 mark. By the end of the month he was dead even with Seybold at 16. In mid-August, following a two-week home run drought that tantalized sportswriters and fans alike, he hit number 17 to set a new modern American League record. Then he got hot. By Labor Day he was at 23, just a whisker away from tying Cravath's modern major league record.

In Boston, the Red Sox management announced that, as an added attraction, Ruth would pitch the first game of the holiday doubleheader. Fans jammed Fenway Park, overflowing into a roped-off area below the right field bleachers. They spent almost as much on action pictures of the Babe as they did for hot dogs and peanuts. His name was on everybody's lips, and when he

That Ruth, shown here at the age of three, survived to play baseball was something of a long shot. He was one of eight children, only two of whom survived infancy.

5′ 9″ 180 lbs.	b 6/10/1886
BL TL	d 4/20/1978

MOE SOLOMON
Outfield

He was supposed to be the next Babe Ruth. Moses Solomon was playing on a Class C club in Hutchinson, Kansas, in 1923 when he hit 49 home runs—more than anyone had ever hit in the minor leagues.

Solomon's slugging feat caught the eye of John McGraw, who was looking for a savior. McGraw's New York Giants were taking a pounding at the box office at the hands of the Yankees and Babe Ruth, baseball's finest drawing card. McGraw figured he could compete with the Yankees and their Sultan of Swat if he could come up with a slugger to attract more fans—especially those from the growing Jewish population in the Bronx and upper Manhattan, near the Polo Grounds. Solomon, who was Jewish and a New York native, looked like the ticket. The 22-year-old outfielder was given $4,500 to join the Giants in 1923. He came up to the majors amidst high expectations and much hype by New York's sporting press, who referred to him as the Rabbi of Swat.

Moe Solomon's major league career lasted exactly two games. He hit .375—3 for 8—but his play in the outfield was dreadful. According to writer Howard Lavelle, "He was a hazard on defense, not for himself, but for the risk he imposed on teammates." Solomon was promptly sent back to the minors. He had hit more homers in 1923 than he did in the rest of his career, which ended in 1930, when Solomon retired to a lucrative career in real estate.

came out on the field to warm up, a mighty roar rose to the heavens. During the first game, he sent a line drive screaming into the right field bleachers. The ball caromed back into the teeming throng on the grass. The umpire, seeing only the mad scramble for the ball behind the ropes, ruled the hit a ground-rule triple. The eyewitnesses in the bleachers changed their home run roar into a howl of protest. Massachusetts National Guardsmen, handling the duties of the striking Boston police, carried a hastily scribbled petition from the bleacherites down to the umpire. He showed no interest.

But all's well that ends with the home team on top. Babe won the first game, 2-1, driving in one Sox run with his triple and scoring the other a moment later. In the second game, playing left field, he slammed another drive into the right field seats that the bleacherites immediately surrounded and smothered. Officially, Babe Ruth had tied the modern home run record, but everybody in the right field bleachers that day knew better.

No matter. A week later he hit numbers 25 and 26. Williamson's doomed record dangled just out of reach for 11 frustrating days until Babe finally surmounted it with two landmark drives on succeeding days, one over Fenway's left field wall and the other over the roof of the Polo Grounds in New York. In keeping with his penchant for showmanship, Babe hit his 29th on the last weekend of the season, in Washington. It was his first of the season there, and it gave him at least one home run in every city in the league, something else no one had ever done before.

The sports world was agog. America had a new national hero. By the time the postwar decade ended, Babe Ruth had established himself as the greatest baseball player ever, bar none. The game of baseball America had played for more than half a century would never be the same again, and the

Being Mrs. Babe Ruth was never easy, but it got even tougher for Helen Woodford Ruth when Babe was hit with a $50,000 paternity suit by 19-year-old Dolores Dixon in 1925. Shortly thereafter, this portrait of the Babe as family man—with Helen and three-year-old adopted daughter Dorothy— appeared. The lawsuit was dropped, but Babe's image as a carouser persisted.

Rumors that the Babe (opposite, left) was adopted are put to rest by this 1916 Christmas photograph of George and his father, George Sr. (opposite, right), in the family-owned Baltimore saloon.

Pied Piper who was leading it into the golden era of the twenties hadn't even reached his stride yet.

Forget the stories you may have heard that his name was really Erhardt or Gerhardt, that he was part black, that he had been a foundling raised in an orphanage. He was born George Herman Ruth on February 7, 1894, or perhaps February 6, 1895—records and tradition collide here—to Katherine, née Schamberger, and George Herman Ruth, Sr., of Pennsylvania Dutch stock transplanted south to Baltimore.

Little George, as he was called, didn't receive much parental guidance. His mother was sick much of the time, and Big George was busy running his saloon all day and most of the night. The boy grew up tough in the streets and alleys, eschewing school, chewing tobacco, drinking booze, baiting storekeepers and cops, stealing whatever he could, and sassing his mother and father in both English and German. "I was a bum when I was a kid," he told one writer.

In 1902, when Little George was eight, he took the first of several long trolley rides out to St. Mary's Industrial School for Boys. Run by the Xaverian Brothers, the Home, as it was called, was part orphanage, part reform school, and part vocational school for youngsters from broken or out-of-luck homes. George arrived bearing the label "incorrigible," but that may have been applied, his sister Mamie maintained, because he refused to go to school, a statement seemingly borne out by the fact that he could neither read nor write when he reached St. Mary's.

He learned both skills as an "inmate" of the Home—he was in and out several times. He also developed a case of hero worship for Brother

It was at St. Mary's Industrial School that Ruth (back row, far left) — sent there by an overworked father and sickly mother — played on his first Red Sox championship team, this one sometime around 1910.

Though the picture of Ruth often recalled is one of an overstuffed torso balanced on spindly legs, in his early years (opposite) he was well-muscled with prodigious wrists and forearms.

Matthias, the prefect of discipline. Matthias, a huge man at 6′ 6″ and more than 250 pounds, introduced the young waterfront hellraiser to baseball, standing at one end of the yard and hitting out tremendous one-handed fungoes for the boys to chase and catch. Recognizing George's latent ability, he spent hours hitting the eager boy one grounder after another. "I could hit the first time I picked up the bat," Ruth said, "but Brother Matthias made me a fielder."

George was primarily a catcher at St. Mary's—a left-handed one using the school's right-handed glove. He also pitched and could do a creditable job at just about any position in the field. When he was 19, a strapping young buck standing 6′ 2″ and weighing about 190, he caught the eye of Jack Dunn, the owner-manager of the International League Baltimore Orioles.

He was "paroled" to Dunn, who signed him at the eye-popping salary of $100 a month for the six-month 1914 season and put him on a train for the Orioles' spring training camp in Fayetteville, North Carolina. The new rookie was so woefully unsophisticated that veteran Oriole ballplayers referred to him as "Dunnie's Babe," and half the nickname stuck. The press and public picked it up later, but many big league ballplayers followed the lead of Oriole third baseman Jumping Joe Dugan and simply called him "Jidge," a New England version of George.

By early July, Dunn's Orioles had opened a commanding lead in the International League race, with Ruth contributing 14 wins as a starting pitcher. But the short-lived Federal League had set up shop in Baltimore with a team called the Terrapins, and a minor league club like the Orioles, no matter how

Rape of the Red Sox

Fans of the Boston Red Sox have become enured to suffering. The Red Sox have gone without a world championship longer than any other existing team—more than 70 years—and during that time their fans have experienced some of baseball's most heartbreaking moments. But it wasn't always that way.

The Boston Red Sox were on top of the baseball world on September 11, 1918. Carl Mays pitched a three-hitter to give the Sox their fourth world championship in seven years. But over the next five years, the Red Sox toppled and the baseball world was turned upside down.

Red Sox owner Harry Frazee was continually beset by financial losses as a result of his uncanny ability to produce flop after flop on the Broadway stage. To offset his losses, he started wheeling and dealing with Yankee owner Jacob Ruppert. Frazee sold to Ruppert a group of players that formed the foundation of what became one of baseball's greatest dynasties—the New York Yankees of the 1920s. In 1923 the Yankees won 98 games in the regular season, and 76 of those wins were shared by four pitchers—Bullet Joe Bush, Sad Sam Jones, Waite Hoyt and Herb Pennock—all of whom came to New York by way of Boston's Fenway Park. Half of the Yankee starting infield—shortstop Everett Scott and third baseman Jumping Joe Dugan—came to New York courtesy of Frazee, as did starting catcher Wally Schang. Of the 24 players on the Yankees' 1923 roster, 11 had come from the Red Sox.

But the one that really hurt, Frazee's most heinous act in what became known as the Rape of the Red Sox, was the sale of Babe Ruth to the Yankees for $100,000 on the day after Christmas, 1919. Ruth had just completed an unprecedented season, including a record 29 home runs, but he was demanding a huge salary increase, and Frazee

was in big financial trouble. Ruppert, as always, was waiting to bail Frazee out by buying up premium goods at bargain-basement prices. Frazee was so deep in debt that in addition to the $100,000 purchase price for Ruth, Ruppert lent Frazee $300,000 and took a mortgage on Fenway Park.

Ruppert had the deepest pockets in baseball, and as Frazee's musical comedies continued to lose money, the Yankee owner continued to bolster his lineup. Baseball historian Donald Honig wrote, "A good year in Boston was virtual assurance of a career in New York."

The Rape of the Red Sox began innocently enough at the end of the 1918 season, when Frazee sold outfielder Duffy Lewis and pitcher Ernie Shore—both of whom were returning from service in World War I—to the Yankees. Midway through the 1919 season, Frazee dealt Carl Mays to Ruppert for two bad pitchers and $40,000, and while AL president Ban Johnson tried to nix the deal, Ruppert would not be denied. Mays became an immediate star in New York, going 9–3 in the second half of the 1919 season, then following that up with 53 wins and 20 losses over the next two seasons.

Since the cash deals seemed to be working well for Ruppert and his Yankees, he asked manager Miller Huggins what he needed to win. Huggins said he needed Ruth. At first, Ruppert balked at Frazee's asking price of $100,000, calling it crazy. "Frazee's crazy, all right," Huggins said. "He's crazy to let you have Babe for so little." Ruth led the Yankees to third place in 1920, and attendance more than doubled. Hoyt and Schang came to New York at the end of the 1920 season; Bush, Scott and Jones came a year later; Dugan came in July of 1922; and Pennock and George Pipgras—who pitched in the 1927, 1928 and 1932 World Series—came in January of 1923. The Dugan deal helped the Yankees hold off the St.

In 1916 Carl Mays (far left), Ernie Shore (center) and Babe Ruth (right) combined for 57 regular-season wins and for three more in Boston's World Series win over Brooklyn. The trio won 59 more in 1917, but then one by one were sold to Jake Ruppert's well-financed Yankees. Shore went in 1918, Mays in 1919, and Ruth in 1920.

Waite Hoyt was 10–12 in his first two seasons with the Red Sox, but his talent didn't escape the eyes of Yankee general manager Ed Barrow. In a 12-inning loss to New York in 1919, Hoyt allowed no baserunners between the first and 12th innings. On December 15, 1920, Hoyt became a Yankee.

Louis Browns in the 1922 pennant race, but Dugan's change of uniform late in the season so enraged the Browns' fans that Commissioner Landis established June 15 of each season as the trading deadline.

By 1923 the Red Sox were firmly planted in the AL's cellar, and Frazee, having done about as much damage as he could, sold the team after a record-low attendance of 229,668. Amazingly, in 1925 he produced the hit musical *No, No, Nanette!* and recouped most of his losses. But the Red Sox weren't as lucky. Nine years and six managers later, the team was still in shambles. In 1934 attendance was down to 182,150. The once-proud Sox lost 111 games and finished 64 games behind the first-place Yankees.

"They talk about the Yankee dynasty," said Ernie Shore, who was one of the Frazee-Ruppert deals, "but I still think of it as a Red Sox dynasty in Yankee uniforms."

Ruth's skillful baserunning—like his fielding ability—was almost completely obscured by his power. But he was an aggressive baserunner, as he showed in Game 1 of the 1923 World Series when he earned a triple with a nice hook slide to elude the tag by the Giants' Heinie Groh. Ruth had 13 triples and 17 stolen bases that season.

good, couldn't compete as a drawing card. With only a couple of hundred fans moving through the turnstiles and no help from organized baseball, Dunn had only one option.

In a week he sold seven of his eight starters and two of his three best pitchers. Ruth went to the Boston Red Sox, much to the dismay of John McGraw, who thought he would be a great draw in New York with the Giants. He split two starts, and after idling on the bench for a month was sent down to Providence, where he helped the Grays win the International League pennant, compiling a total record for 1914 of 22 wins and 9 losses. In a game in Toronto he also hit his first professional home run—the only one he struck as a minor leaguer.

He was called back up to the Red Sox in September, and made the major leagues his home for the next 22 years. All in all, it had been quite a year for the 19-year-old kid fresh out of semi-reform school.

Over the next few years, young George established himself as the best left-handed pitcher in the American League. In 1915 he was among the AL won/lost leaders with 18 and 8, a .692 winning percentage. In 1916 he posted a league-leading 1.75 ERA—14 points lower than that of the great Walter Johnson—and a 23-12 record for a .657 winning percentage. His nine shutouts set an AL mark for southpaws that stood for 62 years until Ron Guidry of the Yankees tied it in 1978.

In 1917 Ruth had a 24-13 season but decided that he wanted to quit pitching and change to the outfield, so he could play every day. Boston manager Ed Barrow was vehemently opposed to the move. The Red Sox were fighting for the pennant, and Barrow needed Ruth's arm on the mound.

The Roaring Twenties

In 1921 Babe Ruth had what was arguably the greatest season ever for a hitter, but the Babe wasn't the only player running up huge numbers in the 1920s. Skyrocketing batting and slugging averages were the norm, and the era's great hitters—including some whose prime was past or lay before them—cashed in. Below are some of the best single-season performances of the decade.

PLAYER	YEARS PLAYED	BEST 1920s SEASON	BA	SA	2B	3B	HR	RBI	R
Babe Ruth	1914–35	1921	.378	**.846**	44	16	**59**	**171**	**177**
Ty Cobb	1905–28	1922	.401	.565	42	16	4	99	99
Jimmie Foxx	1925–45	1929	.354	.625	23	9	33	117	123
Lou Gehrig	1923–39	1927	.373	.765	**52**	18	47	**175**	149
Rogers Hornsby	1915–37	1922	**.401**	**.722**	**46**	14	**42**	**152**	**141**
Al Simmons	1924–44	1929	.365	.642	41	9	34	**157**	114
George Sisler	1915–30	1920	**.407**	.632	49	18	19	122	137
Tris Speaker	1907–28	1923	.380	.610	**59**	11	17	**130**	133

Boldface indicates league leader.

Player and manager squabbled, but when Ruth threatened to jump the Sox and play for a wartime shipyard team, they compromised: Babe could play outfield and bat cleanup for three days, but on the fourth day he had to pitch.

It was a good compromise. The Red Sox won the pennant, and although Ruth's record dropped to 13-7, seven of his wins came in the last month of the war-shortened season. He won two more games as Boston beat the Cubs in the World Series, four games to two. His performance in that Series and the one in 1916, when the Sox took Brooklyn four games to one, earned Ruth a string of 29⅔ consecutive scoreless innings, breaking the record of 28⅓ set years earlier by Christy Mathewson. That record lasted until 1962, when another lefty, Whitey Ford, racked up 33⅔ scoreless innings in World Series play.

On top of all that, Babe hit .300 for the year, and tied for fourth in RBI and first in home runs with 11. And even though he came to bat far fewer times than did Ty Cobb, Tris Speaker, George Sisler, Frank "Home Run" Baker and the other big-name hitters, he had more extra-base hits than any of them. He was, in a word, spectacular, and the darling of the Red Sox fans.

The love affair between Babe and Boston lasted through the memorable 1919 season, when he came into his own as a slugger, broke all the existing records and was widely proclaimed the Home Run King. But it turned to ashes one morning in 1920 when Red Sox fans awoke to learn that their boy had been sold...to the hated New York Yankees.

Harry Frazee's interests went beyond proprietorship of the Red Sox. He was also a New York theater owner and producer, whose shows were invariably panned by critics. Frazee regularly bounced in and out of debt, so when cash was short he sold whatever property he could. The Red Sox roster

Ruth called baseball "the only real game in the world," and was happy to play it in its purest form—sandlot—before its purest audience—kids. "He had the happy faculty of wearing the world as a loose garment," wrote sportswriter Tom Meany.

was fair game: Ernie Shore, Duffy Lewis, Dutch Leonard, Carl Mays—and now the Babe! It was too much! But there was more, much more, to follow, for the Rape of the Red Sox, as it came to be called, had just begun.

One newspaper ran a cartoon showing Boston's Public Library and Faneuil Hall draped with "for sale" signs; it would be interesting to know what the artist would have drawn had he known that part of the deal was a $300,000 loan to Frazee from the Yankee colonels, Ruppert and Huston, who held a mortgage on Fenway Park. For his part, Ruth, barnstorming in California, reacted in the usual business-first fashion of sports idols. He sent a wire to Boston saying, "Will not play anywhere else. My heart is in Boston," even while haggling over salary with the Yankee brass.

The Bambino was made for New York—and New York certainly was made for him. Crowds swarmed into the Polo Grounds to see him play; even Colonel Ruppert, notorious for shunning public gatherings, came to the park to see the sweet, lethal swing—and its even sweeter results—that had the goggle-eyed Gotham press corps salivating in their search for colorful adjectives. Babe didn't disappoint them. In 1920 he clouted an unbelievable 54 round-trippers and batted .376 to help move the pennant-starved Yankees into an exciting three-cornered battle with the White Sox and the eventual winners, the Indians.

He topped that in 1921 with what may have been the best overall year any hitter has ever had: 204 hits, 44 doubles, 16 triples, an astonishing 59 home runs, 177 runs, 171 runs batted in, 144 walks and a .378 batting average. If walks had been counted as base hits, as they were the year before the turn of the century, he would have hit .509! By way of perspective, consider

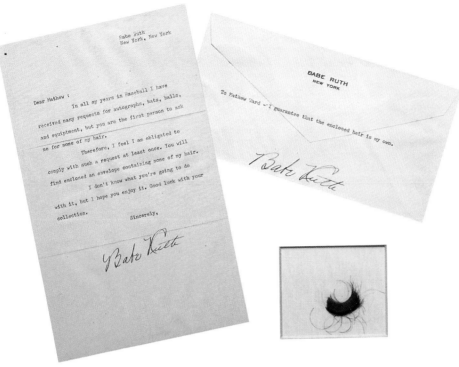

Ruth was deluged with requests from fans for all sorts of memorabilia, but apparently Mathew Ward was the first to ask for a lock of the Babe's hair. As usual, the Babe complied.

this: the Babe's 1927 season, when he homered 60 times to set what some people still consider the ultimate record, was only the eighth best of his career in terms of batting average.

As that career continued on its spectacular course, people began to forget what a great pitcher he had been. His hitting also overshadowed the fact that he was a natural at the other aspects of the game. He rarely made an error of judgment, and until he put on the potbelly that became as much a trademark as his smiling moonface, he was an alert, aggressive baserunner. And, thanks to Brother Matthias, he was a surprisingly graceful fielder.

But people didn't pack the stands to see him field or run the bases. They came to see him hit, and everywhere he went around the league someone could show you exactly where one of his monster home runs had landed, or sailed out of the park.

Charismatic, crude but lovable, and a showman at heart, he became the most popular player baseball has ever known. Wherever he turned, he saw his picture, heard his name. People rushed up just to look at him or touch his clothes. He took to eating meals in his hotel room to escape the crowds. But he liked it when dirty-faced boys waited for him after a game to get his autograph, perhaps because they reminded him of himself. He was rarely too busy for them, or for a visit to a hospital ward to promise a sick boy or girl that he'd poke a long one in the next game, "Just for you, keed." He also liked the gifts that came showering down, all sorts of things, from pets and clothes to a spanking new touring car with BABE RUTH emblazoned on the side—not to mention good, hard cash just for the use of his name.

It wouldn't be accurate to say that all the adulation went to Babe's head and changed him. The potential for his excesses—and he was guilty of

Ruth's legendary fondness for kids was well documented in stories like the famous hospital visit during which he promised a home run to an ailing youngster. Paul Gallico wrote about that visit in The New York Times: "The door opened and it was God himself who walked into the room, straight from His glittering throne. . . . God with a flat nose and little piggy eyes and a big grin, and a fat, black cigar sticking out of the side of it."

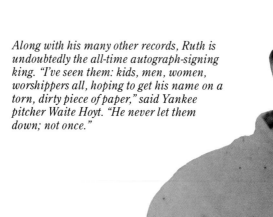

Along with his many other records, Ruth is undoubtedly the all-time autograph-signing king. "I've seen them: kids, men, women, worshippers all, hoping to get his name on a torn, dirty piece of paper," said Yankee pitcher Waite Hoyt. "He never let them down; not once."

Watches featuring the Babe's smiling face were hot items among Yankee fans, who wore them to the ballpark as good-luck charms.

many—was always there. But his overindulgences were magnified by his star status, and he was able to afford them because of his star's earnings—a peak of $80,000 a year at a time when other top ballplayers had to be content with around $15,000. The salary of the President of the United States also suffered by comparison, and when Babe heard that, he pointed out, logically enough, "I had a better year."

Cocktail party analysts characterized Babe as emotionally stunted because he never got enough of childhood's three staples—food, attention and affection. And in truth, he had gargantuan appetites in all of those areas. In the early days, other players would gather at the dinner table and watch in awe as he waved his fork and made three steaks disappear, or maybe a platter of lamb chops, or a roast chicken or two. His prodigious consumption of hot dogs and soda pop between innings is woven deep in baseball legend, and his capacity for alcohol, despite Prohibition, kept the party going night after night to dawn after dawn.

On occasion, of course, the piper called in his dance tickets. On the way back north in the spring of 1925, the Babe collapsed with a fever and horrendous pains in the stomach. He was hoisted through a Pullman car window and trundled off to the hospital, and rumors began to fly. When it turned out that he wasn't dead after all, but "merely" suffering from a gastrointestinal problem, reaction set in. Assuming the cause was an overgorging of hot dogs, W. O. McGeehan wrote a colorful story headlined "The Bellyache Heard 'Round the World." Other newsmen and some players whispered that the real problem was venereal disease. But, Babe proudly displayed a long, vivid scar below his rib cage, and the whisperers had to concede that abdominal surgery was hardly a standard procedure for a dose of the clap.

Still, people familiar with the habits of George Herman Ruth, tomcat, could be forgiven for leaping to conclusions. Everywhere Babe went were women eager to know him better, and he rarely turned down an opportunity. The best insight into Babe's active nightlife came from his sometime roommate Ping Bodie, who, when asked what it was like sharing quarters with the great Babe Ruth, said, "I don't room with Babe. I room with his suitcase."

Babe married Helen Woodford, a woman from Boston, after his rookie season, and she stood by him until the situation became unbearable. They were separated in 1926, and in 1929 she died in a fire. He then married Claire Hodgson, a beautiful dark-haired widow, who managed to give him a veneer of civilization. But underneath he was still as incorrigible as the eight-year-old who had been sent to St. Mary's by his parents.

On June 13, 1948, the Yankees celebrated the 25th anniversary of Yankee Stadium, "The House That Ruth Built." The loudspeakers sang out his name, the crowd roared, but the figure on the field wasn't the Babe of memory—the barrel-chested strongman on dancer's legs who trotted in from right field with almost mincing steps and never passed second base without stepping on the bag. This Babe was too small, a crumbling wreck of a man who used a bat as a cane to walk to home plate and croak out a few words.

On August 16, 1948, Babe died of throat cancer. He made it to Yankee Stadium one last time, lying in state for a day and a half as thousands of fans paid their respects. Thousands more filled St. Patrick's Cathedral for the funeral mass and packed the streets outside on an uncomfortably humid, rainy day. On the way out, one of the honorary pallbearers, Jumping Joe Dugan, whispered, "I sure would like to have a big glass of cold beer."

"So would the Babe," Waite Hoyt whispered back. ❶

The sight of Ruth at the plate rattled even the most confident of pitchers. "I have seen hundreds of ballplayers at the plate," wrote Paul Gallico, "and none of them managed to convey the message of impending doom to a pitcher that Babe Ruth did with the cock of his head, the position of his legs, and the little gentle waving of the bat, feathered in his two big paws."

Earle Combs

Yankee manager Miller Huggins gave Earle Combs his nickname. In 1925, Combs' first complete season with the Yankees, Huggins told his leadoff man, "We'll call you 'The Waiter.' When you get on first base, you wait for Ruth or Gehrig or one of the other fellows to send you the rest of the way around."

Combs did just that, becoming the table setter for the duo that feasted on pitchers like no other in baseball history. Beginning in 1925, after an injury-shortened rookie season, the triggerman of Murderers' Row had at least 179 hits and 113 runs scored for eight straight years.

Combs performed in the shadow of Ruth, Gehrig and the "other fellows" that played for the Yankees, but he was quite familiar to those in the know, like Cleveland pitcher George Uhle. "Ruth and Gehrig and the rest of them are tough enough. . . . But, inning in and inning out, game in and game out, the toughest man on the Yankee lineup to pitch to is Combs," Uhle said.

And in 1927 longtime AL umpire Billy Evans, a frequent contributor to the New York *Telegram,* wrote: "To my way of thinking, there is no better lead-off man in the majors than Earle Combs, the Yankees' brilliant center fielder. . . . The fact that Combs gets on often is a very important factor in the Yankees' success."

Combs, born in Pebworth, Kentucky, in 1899, graduated from Eastern Kentucky State Normal School, taught in an elementary school, and played semipro ball before spending two years in the minors. Besides being well educated, he was one of the game's true gentlemen—didn't drink, didn't swear.

He played 24 games his rookie year, then suffered a broken ankle that Ruth said cost New York the pennant. It was the first of three serious injuries in his career.

The next season Combs began to fully display his acute batting eye, proficient bunting and fleetness afoot. His speed was an asset both on the bases, where he led the AL in triples three times, and in the field, where he patrolled Yankee Stadium's spacious center field, covering so much ground, many said, he made Ruth look above-average over in right.

On May 18, 1927, a day after the Yankees won a game in Detroit, James R. Harrison reported in *The New York Times:* "Bob 'Fats' Fothergill whaled a terrific drive toward deep center. Crash, not to say, wham! But Combs dashed back and made one of the dizziest catches ever seen in these or any parts."

Combs continued his acrobatic and reckless play without injury until July 24, 1934, when he crashed full-speed into the concrete outfield wall in St. Louis' Sportsman's Park, and was knocked unconscious with a fractured skull. Doctors feared for his life; he was hospitalized for two months.

"You see, I'm made of tough stuff," said the tougher-than-concrete Combs from his hospital bed. "They said I was through in 1924 when I broke my ankle. I fooled them once and I believe I will do it again." He returned as a player-coach in 1935 and batted .282 until a broken collarbone left him a full-time coach. His first assignment was to tutor his replacement, Joe DiMaggio.

Combs also coached for the Browns, Red Sox and Phillies from 1947 to 1954. He then returned home and served as Kentucky's banking commissioner.

On July 27, 1970, Combs was inducted into the Hall of Fame. "When I heard I'd been named, it was like a bullet shot between my eyes," he said that day in Cooperstown. "It was the last thing I expected. I thought the Hall of Fame was for superstars, not just for average players like I was."

EARLE COMBS

Outfield
New York Yankees 1924–1935
Hall of Fame 1970

GAMES	**1,454**
AT-BATS	**5,748**
BATTING AVERAGE	
Career	**.325**
Season High	**.356**
SLUGGING AVERAGE	
Career	**.462**
Season High	**.523**
HITS	
Career	**1,866**
Season High	**231**
DOUBLES	
Career	**309**
Season High	**36**
TRIPLES	
Career	**154**
Season High	**23**
HOME RUNS	
Career	**58**
Season High	**9**
TOTAL BASES	**2,657**
EXTRA-BASE HITS	**521**
RUNS BATTED IN	
Career	**629**
Season High	**82**
RUNS	
Career	**1,186**
Season High	**143**
WORLD SERIES	**1926-1928,1932**

Thunder at the Plate

"The way they play today, it's as if two golfers decided to forget all about the course—with its doglegs, sand traps, roughs, and putting greens—and instead just went out to see who could hit the ball the farthest at a driving range."

—*Ty Cobb*

By the time the last huzzah of the 1919 season had echoed, the game that had been Ty Cobb's was well on its way to becoming the game that was Babe Ruth's. The Babe's 29 round-trippers that year provided a catalyst for a number of other elements changing the chemistry of baseball. A livelier ball, for example. Noting what Ruth had done to the home run record in 1919, people came to the conclusion that the American League had juiced up the ball. The powers that be answered indignantly that they had done nothing of the kind—give the credit or blame to better-quality yarn, better workmanship and changes in batting styles.

There might have been a germ of truth in the last argument, for the rabbit had first been injected in the ball almost a decade before. Ben Shibe, who backed Connie Mack in ownership of the Philadelphia Athletics and who had built the first concrete-and-steel ballpark, was one of baseball's great innovators. In 1909 he invented a cork-center baseball that had far more resiliency than the old dead ball. The Reach Company produced it for the American League, and Spalding followed suit for the National League. In 1910 the new ball was used in some regular-season games and in the World Series. The following year, however, it saw action in all games, with spectacular batting results. In the American League, 35 players batted over .300, Cobb and Shoeless Joe Jackson leading the pack at .420 and .408, respectively. In the National League, the *league* batting average climbed to

Ty Cobb and Joe Jackson (opposite) set standards of excellence at the plate that the sluggers of the lively-ball era never eclipsed. The dominant hitter of the dead-ball era, Cobb (left) owns the best batting average of all time. Jackson ranks third.

From 1906 to 1930, second baseman Eddie Collins (right) was a constant in the rapidly changing game of baseball. The speedy Collins hit .340 or better ten times, and in three separate decades.

Pittsburgh outfielder Max Carey was the quintessential slap-and-run-like-hell hitter in the 1910s, but four of his six .300-plus seasons came in the 1920s. He also won ten NL stolen-base crowns, and in 1922 was successful on 51 of 53 steal attempts.

.260, and the only pitcher with an earned run average under 2.00 was the New York Giants' Christy Mathewson.

Cobb, unquestionably the finest player in either league, came back with a .410 year in 1912—the fourth and last time anyone hit over .400 between 1900 and 1920—but otherwise the hitting barrage declined as pitchers reasserted their traditional control over the game, even though the cork-center ball remained in play.

There are a couple of ways to explain this seeming anomaly. For one thing, this was the heyday of the spitball, invented or rediscovered around the turn of the century by George Hildebrand, minor league outfielder and longtime American League umpire. Hurlers like Mathewson mastered the fadeaway—an early screwball—and other trick pitches.

Another reason was that teams were still locked into the dead-ball mind-set: playing for a run at a time, bunting instead of powdering the ball, stealing bases, working the hit-and-run and the sacrifice fly. Home runs, even though they came with greater frequency because of the lively ball, were still exceptions to mainline baseball strategy—stupendous yet serendipitous events that were appreciated but were never a part of the grand strategy.

So, aside from a momentary blip on the charts, the first decade of the lively ball had little effect on how baseball was played, or on the number of fans who made their way into ballparks. The old game was still the only game in town. For that and any number of other reasons—among them a dispiriting war in Europe—attendance for the last seven years of that decade was down, seriously down.

Cleveland center fielder Tris Speaker was rejuvenated by the lively ball. A career .344 hitter, Speaker dipped to .296 in 1919, but in 1920 his average soared to .388 and he led the league with 50 doubles.

Then along came Babe Ruth. His quest for the home run fired the imagination of fans all over the country. They flocked to ballparks to see him swing when the Boston Red Sox were in town, and it didn't take long for the baseball brain trust to add two and two and come up with dollar signs. If the fans needed big hits and big innings to keep the turnstiles spinning merrily, then that's what they would get. Did baseball magnates therefore conspire to add a little more jackrabbit to the ball for the 1920 season? They denied it, and so did the manufacturers, but a lot of people remained unconvinced.

"They fixed up a ball," wrote sportswriter Ring Lardner in disgust, "that if you don't miss it entirely it will clear the fence." To which historian Donald Honig added: "With the ball now so live it was almost possible to detect a pulsebeat between the seams, and with the pitchers unable to quickly adjust to the new style of play, it became a hitter's game, and the decade of the 1920s became the most glorious hitting circus in baseball history."

From the pitcher's point of view, the problem was considerably more than an inability to adjust. For most of its history—except for a period in its formative years when the batter had the right to tell the pitcher where he wanted the ball thrown—organized baseball had weighted the game in favor of the pitcher. That philosophy led to the tight, tense pitchers' battles of "inside" baseball, as well as the development of a magician's box of trick pitches designed to baffle the batter. Then, in the winter of 1919-1920, the owners took another giant step toward giving the game back to the hitters by outlawing all pitches that involved tampering with the ball—roughing it up with sandpaper or emery or loading it up with spit, tobacco juice or even resin. The penalty for violating this rule was a ten-day suspension.

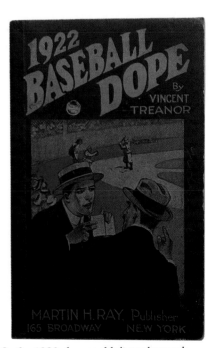

In the 1920s fans couldn't read enough about the decade's great hitting feats. In 1922 the story was whole teams with batting averages over .300. The NL had three, the AL just two. But the St. Louis Browns, led by George Sisler's .420, topped all major league clubs with a .313 team average.

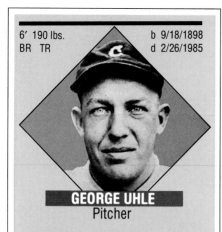

6' 190 lbs.   b 9/18/1898
BR TR   d 2/26/1985

GEORGE UHLE
Pitcher

In 1923 George Uhle did everything but sell popcorn for the Cleveland Indians. He led the AL with 26 wins, pitched more innings—357 ⅔—than anyone else until Bob Feller's 371 in 1946, and hit .361. But the Indians finished third in the standings, and the Most Valuable Player Award went to a guy named Ruth.

Most of the time, however, Uhle got the better of the Babe. "The hardest pitching nut I had to crack was a guy named George Uhle," Ruth once said.

Uhle, who compiled 200 wins with mostly mediocre teams from 1919 to 1936, went 10–5 as a rookie with Cleveland in 1919. Strong and solid, Uhle had a balanced repertoire of fastball, curve and change-up. He once pitched 20 innings in a 6–5 win over Chicago, a game in which he also got five hits. Uhle also claimed credit for inventing the slider—while playing catch with Harry Heilmann.

Throughout his career, Uhle posted great numbers at the plate and on the mound. On April 28, 1921, he drove in six runs against Detroit, including a grand slam. He led the AL with five shutouts in 1922, and his brilliant 1923 season included 52 hits, a record for pitchers that still stands.

In 1926 he led the AL with 27 wins, a .711 winning percentage and 32 complete games, and beat the AL champion Yankees six times. Often used as a pinch hitter, Uhle hit over .300 six times in his career. And his lifetime .288 batting average ranks second among pitchers—to Ruth.

The spitball Dutch Leonard was throwing in 1920 was legal—it just wasn't good enough anymore. Leonard's ERA, which had never been above 2.77 in his first seven years in the majors, rose to 4.33 when the lively ball entered play in 1920.

There were other reasons for banning the spitter. For one thing, fastidious fans found the way some hurlers splattered the ball disgusting, and it was an accepted but unproven fact that hot dog sales suffered on the days when certain spitballers were throwing. A more serious concern was the spitball pitcher's alleged inability to control what he threw, obviously a dangerous situation for batters. Of course, not everyone bought this criticism. "Dangerous?" contended Brooklyn's Burleigh Grimes, the best and longest lasting of the spitball artists. "It's easier to control than a knuckler. In 19 seasons I hit only one batter, Mel Ott, and he was leaning over the plate."

The spitball *is* more controllable than the knuckleball, old-timers will tell you, because its flight is predictable. When it is thrown properly, it breaks sharply down, much like a good overhand curve. That's why it was favored—and still is, unofficially—by pitchers with a good fastball but only a mediocre curve. It has the added advantage of being thrown with the same motion as the fastball, and it doesn't put strain on the arm as a curveball does. On the down side, infielders didn't like handling batted spitballs, not because they were overly squeamish but because the ball was often still loaded when they got it—and managers don't appreciate infielders throwing jug-handle curves to first base.

But there is no question that spitballs are tough on batters. Detroit Tiger outfielder "Wahoo Sam" Crawford complained about batting against "Big Ed" Walsh, who won 195 games with his spitball for the White Sox between 1904 and 1916: "I think the ball disintegrated on the way to the plate and the catcher put it back together again; I swear, when it went past the plate it was just the spit went by."

During the 1920 World Series, Cleveland's Stan Coveleski (left) used his legal spitter in three complete-game wins, allowing just five hits in each game. If more hitting was what the owners wanted, banning the spitball was definitely the way to go.

There were 17 spitballers in the big leagues when the rule was passed, and since the intent was not to deprive any player of making a living, all were exempted from the ban for as long as their careers lasted. In 1920 Grimes, who came to the Dodgers in the deal that sent Casey Stengel to Pittsburgh, won 23 games while losing only 11 for a .676 winning percentage, tops in the league. Like most spitballers, he played a cute psychological game, keeping the batter guessing by going through the motions of throwing the spitter on every pitch, even when planning to throw something else. Learning that some observant eye on the Phillies had noticed his hat moving when he actually spat on the ball, Grimes countered by wearing a larger cap that bobbed around all the time. He won 270 games over 19 years in the majors, good enough for a spot in the Hall of Fame. He was also the last major league pitcher to throw a legal spitball, for all the others had retired by the time he hung up his glove and wad of slippery elm in 1934. That was supposed to be the end of the spitter in the big leagues, but all it did, as Associated Press baseball editor Joe Reichler said years ago, "was go underground."

The saddest spitball tale belongs to Frank Shellenback, who broke in with the White Sox in 1918, but had the bad luck to be sent down during 1919, and so did not qualify under the new rule. Since the spitter was his main pitch, he never made it back to the majors. Stuck in the minor leagues, where the wet ball was still legal, he won more than 300 games, 295 of them in the tough Pacific Coast League, and very likely would have been a big league star if he hadn't been victimized by rotten timing.

After Ray Chapman was killed in 1920 by Carl Mays' dry, high and inside submarine pitch, baseball belatedly came to realize that simply banning doctored balls wasn't enough to provide a fair margin of safety. The background

Shufflin' Phil Douglas could have had a long, successful career if he'd stuck to throwing fastballs and spitballs. But Douglas' drinking problem got him bounced around to five teams in nine years, and though he had outstanding talent, he wound up his career just a .500 pitcher.

Cobb Hangs Up His Spikes

Usually it's boxers, not baseball players, who bounce in and out of retirement. But Ty Cobb was as much a fighter as he was a ballplayer, and he announced his retirement three times before he actually left the game.

At the end of the 1926 season—Cobb's sixth as player-manager—his Detroit Tigers wound up in sixth place. Cobb, approaching 40, had performed well at the plate and hit .339. But he had been criticized for causing dissension on the team and for making bad trades. He claimed he could not win with the players he had. On November 3, Cobb announced his retirement, both as manager and as player. "I hate to leave baseball," he said. "It is all I know." But when asked if he expected ever to play again, he said, "No. I have swung my last bat."

Detroit fans were stunned by the announcement. But when Cleveland manager Tris Speaker was fired a few weeks later, the story came out that both Cobb and Speaker were forced out of baseball because of allegations that they had conspired to fix a game late in the 1919 season. The charge came from Dutch Leonard, a pitcher who, in his time, had been released from both Detroit and Cleveland. While Cobb maintained he was innocent, AL president Ban Johnson said that "whether guilty or not he was through in the American League."

The game in question had been played seven years before, on September 26, 1919, between Cleveland and Detroit. Four players—Cleveland's Speaker and Smoky Joe Wood and Detroit's Cobb and Leonard—supposedly engineered a Tiger victory. The Tigers did win. But Cobb went 1 for 5 with a single, while Speaker had three hits, including two triples. Neither Wood nor Leonard played.

Public support for Cobb and Speaker was great, and even humorist Will Rogers defended them in his national column: "If they had been selling out all these years, I would like to have seen them play when they weren't selling!" On January 27, 1927, Commissioner Landis proclaimed their innocence. All of a sudden, just about every team wanted Cobb back. Cobb took time to go hunting.

Cobb didn't want to leave the game under a cloud, so when Athletics owner Connie Mack, whom he revered, offered him a record $70,000 and the chance to play for a pennant contender in 1927, Cobb agreed. At 40, Cobb played in 134 games, hit .357, drove in 93 runs, stole 22 bases, and even made an unassisted double play. But the A's finished second to the Yankees, and Mack said he could no longer afford Cobb's services.

Cobb received offers from several other teams, but didn't accept any of them. "I have been in harness long enough," he told reporters in January. But on March 1, 1928, he announced he had signed with the Athletics for one more year. While Cobb called the contract "highly satisfactory to me," it was understood that he had agreed to a hefty pay cut.

In 1928 Cobb proved his skills were still superior, as he hit .323, with 27 doubles in just 95 games. He even stole home one last time, extending his lifetime record to 50. On September 11 Cobb stood in the batter's box for the last time. He popped out to Yankee shortstop Mark Koenig. On September 17 the man with baseball's highest lifetime batting average—.367—finally called it quits. After 23 years in baseball, the time had come, Cobb said, "to get out of the game and play with my kids before they grow up and leave me. I prefer to retire while there still may remain some hits in my bat."

After 4,192 base hits, 6,361 putouts in the outfield, and who knows how many hook slides, Ty Cobb announced he would hang up his spikes for the last time. "It seemed like enough to me," he said.

5' 10½" 180 lbs.   b 8/30/1899
BR TR   d 2/11/1950

KIKI CUYLER
Outfield

When Hazen Shirley Cuyler joined the Pittsburgh Pirates at the end of the 1921 season, he brought with him all the tools of stardom—a fine bat, a great glove, a rifle arm, and speed to burn. He even brought his own nickname, which he earned in the minors from his ability to cover ground in the outfield. When teammates wanted him to take fly balls, calling "Hazen, Hazen" wasn't a viable option, so they shortened his last name and called "Cuy, Cuy."

By the end of 1924—his first full season—nearly everybody was calling Cuyler's name, for he had turned in one of the best rookie seasons of all time. Cuyler hit .354, stole 32 bases, and had 16 assists. Cuyler's line-drive power was well suited to the roomy power alleys of Pittsburgh's Forbes Field, and in 1925 his .357 average and 26 triples led the Pirates to the NL pennant. Cuyler then starred in the World Series against Washington. He won Game 2 with a two-run homer in the eighth, then won Game 7 with a two-run double off Walter Johnson.

But in the 1927 World Series, Cuyler could only watch as the Pirates were swept by the Yankees. Pirate manager Donie Bush benched him after Cuyler objected to being moved from third to second in the batting order and from center to left field to accommodate rookie Lloyd Waner. Cuyler was traded to the Cubs that winter. In the next seven years, he hit over .300 five times and helped the Cubs win two pennants.

Hack Wilson's fly ball swing was made for the lively ball and two of his home parks—Chicago's Wrigley Field and New York's Polo Grounds. In 1930 Wilson set the NL single-season home run record with 56, and the major league RBI mark with 190.

behind the pitcher also figured strongly in the equation. Modern-day batters may complain about the difficulty of picking up a pitched ball against a sea of white shirts in the center field bleachers. That's because today the ball is white. In earlier days, the problem was reversed. Center field usually ended against a dull blank wall or fence, and if there were center field bleachers, few fans of the time would even think of taking their jackets off. The ball was a dirty gray or brown blob. It started out white, of course, but that was when it was fresh, and fresh balls were a rarity. "We hardly ever saw a new baseball, a clean one," Giants outfielder Fred Snodgrass said. "If the ball went into the stands and the ushers couldn't get it back from the spectators, only then would the umpire throw out a new one."

A new ball got old faster than a snowman in July. First the pitchers worked it over with emery and sandpaper, frazzled the seams with a razor, drowned it in slippery elm and saliva, and rubbed it up good with dirt. Then the infielders, all of whom chewed tobacco or licorice, took over, spitting in their gloves and grinding the ball in the noisome pockets until it resembled a wet stone—and looked like a piece of the center field wall as it exploded toward the batter.

Difficulty picking out that dirty sphere from its dark background undoubtedly played a part in Ray Chapman's death. Recognizing that fact, baseball bolstered the ban on trick deliveries with a 1921 decision to keep only clean balls in play. Pitchers complained bitterly that the glossiness of new balls prevented them from getting a proper curveball grip. They sought permission to rub off the gloss with resin, but that was too much like a foot in the door. Instead, umpires began to "rub down" the game balls to get rid of

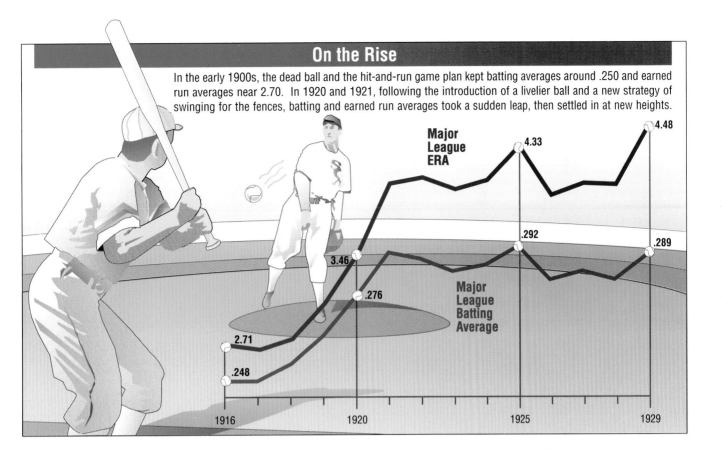

On the Rise

In the early 1900s, the dead ball and the hit-and-run game plan kept batting averages around .250 and earned run averages near 2.70. In 1920 and 1921, following the introduction of a livelier ball and a new strategy of swinging for the fences, batting and earned run averages took a sudden leap, then settled in at new heights.

Major League ERA

Major League Batting Average

4.33 · 4.48 · .292 · .289 · 3.46 · .276 · 2.71 · .248

1916 · 1920 · 1925 · 1929

the gloss, a practice that continues to this day. As far as hitters were concerned, another benefit of playing with clean baseballs was that they were considerably livelier than the battered, misshapen, soggy balls of the previous decades.

This triple-threat combination—the ban on the spitter and other trick pitches, the use and frequent replacement of a livelier ball, and the switch from Cobb's inside game to Ruth's outside-and-over-the-fence game—brought about the most sudden and dramatic change in baseball history. Batting averages spurted upward. For the 15 seasons preceding 1919, major league hitters averaged about .250; in 1920 the National League batted .270, and through the rest of the decade, the figure didn't go below .280 in either league. In 1922 the NL's composite batting average was .292, led by Pittsburgh's .308. During one memorable stretch, starting on July 29, the Pirates caught fire and embarked on a 13-game winning streak that brought them from sixth to third in the standings. The most remarkable part of this power run was a skein of five consecutive games during which, in every game, every man who batted for the Pirates—regular, part-timer, pitcher—had at least one hit! The team as a whole hammered out 100 hits in those five games, batting .446 with a magnificent .612 slugging average. Even the pitchers had 10 hits in 24 at-bats, including two doubles and a pair of homers, for a .417 batting average and a .750 slugging percentage.

Home run figures tell an even more vivid story. In 1918, admittedly a war-shortened season, NL batters managed 139 home runs; in 1921 they clouted 460; and by the end of the decade the total had risen dramatically to 892. What was happening can perhaps be best illustrated by the case of Hack Wilson, who started with the Giants in 1923, spent the bulk of his career with

While most other pitchers were running for cover in the slugging-happy 1920s, Eppa Rixey was turning his career around. Rixey's off-speed repertoire yielded a career average of just one homer every 48 innings, the best of his era.

Few people remember Detroit left fielder Bobby Veach because he played in the same outfield with Ty Cobb and Harry Heilmann. In 1921 the overlooked Veach hit .338, with 16 homers and 128 RBI—but Heilmann and Cobb hit .394 and .389, respectively.

the Cubs, and finished out with the Dodgers and Phillies. A squat powerhouse of a man at 5′ 6″ and 190 pounds, Hack enjoyed a number of fine seasons, topping them off in 1930 with a league-record 56 home runs and 190
runs batted in. Yet there are those who will tell you that, because of his up-
percut swing, Hack would have been a sure fly-out hitter without the juice in
the ball, and probably would have been doomed to spend most of his playing
days in the minor leagues.

For all that, the real thunder at the plate took place in the American
League, and not just in the larger-than-life persona of Babe Ruth. In
1921 four clubs batted over .300—and no one had even thought about
the designated hitter. The Detroit Tigers led the parade at .316, pummeling
out 1,724 hits, both all-time league highs. The Tigers, in turn, were led by
Harry Heilmann and his .394 average, the first of four .390-plus seasons that
line-drive-hitting Harry had in odd-numbered years through 1927.

But the list of hitters extraordinaire starts and ends with Ruth, who
overshadowed everybody else. Except, perhaps, Ty Cobb, who kept playing until 1928. At the age of 40, in the year before he retired from baseball
and in the year Ruth hit 60 homers, Cobb batted .357 and stole 22 bases. To
go with his 12 batting titles, Cobb had a lifetime average of .367 and a
slugging average of .513, figures that still look impressive compared with
Ruth's .342 and .690.

In 1922 Cobb hit at a stirring .401 rate, only to be buried by George
Sisler, who hit .420 for the St. Louis Browns. Sisler, who, like Ruth, had
started his career as a left-handed pitcher, sparkled when he switched
to first base. He banged out a lifetime batting average of .340, including

```
Phillies  .......  0  3  2  1  3  0  0  8  6—23
Chicago  ..·...  ¹ 10  0 14  0  1  0  0  x—26
```

The Highest Score

Three hours was an extraordinarily long time for a nine-inning baseball game in the 1920s. Brooklyn and Boston took 3 hours 50 minutes in 1920 to play 26 innings. But on August 25, 1922, the Chicago Cubs and the Philadelphia Phillies played a three-hour, nine-inning game.

Chicago sportswriter Frank Schreiber called the game "a comic opera arranged to the tune of base hits." There were 51 base hits, to be exact, still a major league record. And those 51 hits produced 49 runs, another major league record, and one winner—Chicago, 26–23.

The Phillies came into the game nestled in seventh place and with the league's worst pitching staff. But they could hit, paced by their .300-plus outfield of Cy Williams, Curt Walker and Cliff Lee. The Cubs were in third place, six games behind the front-running Giants, and were led by first baseman Ray Grimes and left fielder Hack Miller, who finished second and third in the batting race behind Rogers Hornsby.

The game started innocently enough, as Cub right-hander Tony Kaufmann pitched a scoreless first, and the best the Cubs could do off Phillies starter Jimmy Ring was a run-scoring single by Grimes. Center fielder Cliff Heathcote scored the run on his way to a perfect day: five for five with five runs scored and four RBI. The Phillies took the lead with a three-run second, helped by two Cub errors, but their pitching dam burst in the bottom of the inning. Punctuated by Miller's three-run homer to the deepest part of Wrigley Field, the Cubs scored ten times in the bottom of the second. Philadelphia pecked away for two in the third and one in the fourth, but the Cubs were reloading, and fired a record-breaking blast in the bottom of the fourth.

It went this way: Marty Callaghan, Miller and Marty Krug singled for one run. Inexplicably, with a six-run lead and no outs, Cub manager Bill Killefer had Bob O'Farrell lay down a sacrifice bunt. Turner Barber walked, and Heathcote's single scored two runs and sent Ring to the showers. Charlie Hollocher greeted reliever Lefty Weinert with a two-run double, and after a walk and a hit batsman, Callaghan's second single of the inning scored two more. Miller then hit his second three-run homer of the game, and after the Cubs reloaded the bases, Heathcote's double scored two, Hollocher scored another with a sacrifice fly, and Grimes doubled home the 14th Cub run of the inning. Callaghan, batting for a record-tying third time in the inning, struck out to end the carnage. Total damage: 14 runs on 11 hits, two Phillies' errors and two runners left on base. End of four, Cubs 25, Phillies 6.

It got sort of dull after that, until the Phillies tried to set a new record for the greatest comeback. They scored eight in the eighth and six more in the ninth, but Cub reliever Tiny Osborne came on to keep Chicago from blowing a 19-run lead.

Fifty years later, another Phillies team evened the score. Mike Schmidt's four home runs helped set the major league record for the greatest comeback, as the Phillies erased a 13–2 lead and went on to win, 18–16, on April 17, 1976. Who'd they beat? Who else—the Cubs.

a .407 in 1920 built on 257 base hits, still a single-season major league re-cord. Sisler then threatened his own record in 1922 with 246 hits, still the 8th-highest total ever.

Pitchers were generally miserable in that hit-happy decade as earned run averages ballooned. In 1920 Grover Cleveland Alexander led the NL with a 1.91 ERA; by 1929 the league's best was a fat 3.09 from New York's Bill Walker. But once the fans got a taste of boom-boom baseball, there was no turning back, and eventually the role of the pitcher had to change. When even spindly batters could hit the ball into the seats, pitchers learned to work much more carefully and could no longer coast through the low end of the batting order. Pitching hard for nine innings takes a lot out of the pitching arm, and a starting pitcher today who goes seven innings works at least as hard as the pitcher who went nine before the advent of the lively ball. The days of the iron-man throwers were numbered in the 1920s; therefore, the idea of relief pitching took root, and before long the bullpen became a much busier place.

Happy hitters, embattled pitchers—and ecstatic owners. With everybody going to the parks to see Babe Ruth in action, American League attendance in 1920 leaped to more than five million, beat-ing the previous high by a million and a half and beating the National League total by almost as much. Seven clubs established all-time attendance records, and the Yankees set a major league high of 1,289,422, almost 380,000 better than the 910,000 set by the Giants in 1908. This achievement becomes more impressive when you realize that no other club had ever drawn as high as 700,000, and that for most teams annual attendance was usually well under 500,000.

It was standing room only for the opener of the 1926 World Series between the Yankees and the Cardinals. A crowd of 61,658 packed Yankee Stadium ready for a slugfest, with Babe Ruth and Rogers Hornsby the main attractions, and instead saw New York's Herb Pennock outduel Bill Sherdel, 2–1.

By 1929 a new breed of hitter—powerful young sluggers like Philadelphia's Al Simmons (right) and Jimmie Foxx (far right)—had replaced slashing line-drive hitters like Ty Cobb and Joe Jackson as the game's premier offensive performers. In 1929 Simmons and Foxx combined for 67 homers and 274 RBI to lead the Philadelphia Athletics to the AL pennant.

The big story in the November 1923 issue of Baseball Magazine *was hitting. Remarkably, the game's two top hitters—Babe Ruth and Rogers Hornsby—each got on base more often than they were put out the following season. Hornsby hit .424 and Ruth .378, but pitchers walked them so often that their on-base percentages were .505 and .510, respectively.*

Attendance sagged in 1921, following revelations of the Black Sox scandal, but soon picked up again, with credit generally being given to Babe Ruth for saving the national game. New records for putting bottoms in the seats were established for four straight years starting in 1924, topping out in 1927 at 9.9 million. The New York Yankees, with major league baseball's largest stadium in the country's largest city and with the big bats of Murderers' Row, as might be expected, drew over a million almost every year during the decade. The Detroit Tigers hit seven figures in 1924. In 1927 the Chicago Cubs became the first National League team to draw more than a million paying customers, and they duplicated that gate in 1929.

During the magical year of 1920, the Giants also drew well. In fact, they also beat their old 1908 record, and together with the Yanks drew 2,219,031 to the Polo Grounds, almost a million more than ever before. But that was small consolation for tight-lipped Muggsy McGraw of the Giants, who couldn't stand playing second fiddle to anyone, and it wasn't long before Ruth and his Yankees were sent packing. ✦

Although Yankee Stadium became known as the House That Ruth Built, the Babe had his most productive seasons at the Polo Grounds (below). While he played there for only three seasons—1920 to 1922—Babe's career highs in triples, home run percentage, runs scored, RBI, and slugging percentage all came while he was playing at the Polo Grounds.

Harry Heilmann

The man could hit. Harry "Slug" Heilmann, a rock-hard 6′ 1″, 200-pound right-hander, delighted in terrifying 1920s pitchers with his screaming line drives. Indeed, Heilmann's "clothesline" drives left their mark, literally, on just about every outfield fence in the American League. Over a 17-year career, this Hall of Famer collected four AL batting titles and racked up a whopping lifetime batting average of .342. Considered one of the best right-handed batters of all time, Heilmann broke into the majors in 1914, hit over .300 for the first time in 1919, and surpassed that every year until he retired in 1932.

In 1913, 19-year-old Californian Harry Edwin Heilmann was working as a bookkeeper at a San Francisco biscuit company. When a friend asked him to fill in for an ailing third baseman on one of the San Joaquin Valley League teams, Heilmann jumped at the chance. The young accountant slapped out a game-winning double in the 11th inning—to the delight of both the crowd and a baseball scout who happened to be watching the game. The next day Heilmann signed with Portland in the Northwestern League. After a .305 season, he joined the Detroit Tigers in 1914.

Following a weak start and a return to the minors, Heilmann began his assault on the record books. With the introduction of the lively ball, the banning of the spitball, and some batting tips from Detroit manager Ty Cobb, Slug went on the warpath. Cobb helped Heilmann revise his stance, distributing more of his weight to his front foot and refining his swing. Remarkably, his average shot up 85 points in one season and he ended the 1921 season at .394: "I have given Ty Cobb credit for making me a successful batter."

With his combination of raw power and new-found finesse, Heilmann continued to drive pitchers to despair. Curiously, his hitting took on a cyclical nature, peaking in odd-numbered years, falling off in even years. After his .394 season, for example, Heilmann "slumped" to .356 in 1922. In 1923 he captured his second batting crown with an awe-inspiring .403 average but dropped to .346 the next year. Sure enough, in 1925 he returned to reclaim his crown with a .393 average.

In 1925 one sportswriter summed up the slugger's roller coaster stats: "Harry Heilmann, the fearsome Detroit slugger, has scaled the heights and plumbed the depths of batting levels to an almost unique degree." The next year, like clockwork, his average dropped to .367 and in 1927 rose to .398, only to fall 70 points in 1928.

While Heilmann's batting prowess is legendary, his fielding left something to be desired. As his nickname attests, Slug was anything but a speed merchant. In love with his batting but disenchanted with his outfield play, the Tigers made him a full-time first baseman in 1919. After leading AL first basemen in errors for two seasons, Heilmann returned to the outfield.

Nevertheless, as a hitter he had few equals in either power or moxie. Take, for example, his cool-headedness on the last day of the 1925 season as he battled Cleveland's Tris Speaker for the batting crown. After raising his average 50 points in the last month of the season, Heilmann trailed Speaker .38826 to .38927. With Speaker sitting on the bench because of leg trouble, Slug's performance was going to decide the crown. He went 3 for 6 in the first game of a doubleheader and boosted his average to .38947.

Heilmann's teammates congratulated him and advised him to sit out the last game to protect his crown. He wouldn't hear of it. "Don't worry about me," replied Heilmann with a wide grin, "I'm playing out the string." He went 3 for 3 and ended the season at .393—four points above Speaker.

HARRY HEILMANN

Outfield, First Base
Detroit Tigers 1914–1929
Cincinnati Reds 1930, 1932
Hall of Fame 1952

GAMES	**2,146**
AT-BATS	**7,787**
BATTING AVERAGE	
Career	**.342**
Season High	**.403**
BATTING TITLES	**1921,1923**
	1925,1927
SLUGGING AVERAGE	
Career	**.520**
Season High	**.632**
HITS	
Career	**2,660**
Season High	**237**
DOUBLES	
Career	**542**
Season High	**50**
TRIPLES	
Career	**151**
Season High	**16**
HOME RUNS	
Career	**183**
Season High	**21**
TOTAL BASES	**4,053**
EXTRA-BASE HITS	**876**
RUNS BATTED IN	
Career	**1,551**
Season High	**139**
RUNS	
Career	**1,291**
Season High	**121**

Mr. New York

John McGraw played baseball with the old Baltimore Orioles, the Cardinals and the Giants between 1891 and 1906. He batted .334 lifetime, stole 436 bases, and averaged nearly one run scored per game for over a thousand games. From the Birds' brilliant manager, Ned Hanlon—who perfected tactics that relied not on brawn but on speed, agility and alertness—John McGraw learned tricks that helped him change baseball from a boy's game to a man's art.

By playing the bunt, the squeeze play, the sacrifice, the stolen base, the Baltimore chop, and the hit-and-run, an Oriole trademark.

By playing with an intensity that accepted fair means or foul, a quick shoulder thrust to knock a passing runner off-stride, "accidentally" spiking the enemy baseman, holding onto the baserunner's belt when he tagged up to score on a fly to the outfield, even when, as happened on occasion, the runner unbuckled his belt and left the miscreant with the evidence of evil intent dangling from his hand.

By hiding an extra ball in the high outfield grass to use when the real ball got away from the defense, by raising the level of the third-base line to keep bunts from rolling foul, by sloping the first-base line to give the swift home-team runners a downhill start.

By sending the third-base coach dashing toward the plate when there was a runner on third, turning the opposing pitcher into a nervous wreck.

In 31 years as manager of the New York Giants, John McGraw (opposite) won a record ten NL pennants. "The game of ball is only fun for me when I'm out in front and winning," he said. "I don't care a bag of peanuts for the rest of the game."

McGraw was a loyal friend, a ferocious competitor, and a dangerous enemy. "I have seen McGraw go on to ballfields where he is as welcome as a man with black smallpox. He doesn't know what fear is," said pitcher Christy Mathewson.

McGraw played the game the same way he managed—aggressively and to win. In 1899, his first year as Baltimore's player-manager, McGraw hit .391, stole 73 bases, scored 140 runs, and walked 124 times for a .535 on-base percentage.

By baiting umpires, threatening them, intimidating them, sometimes coming to blows with them, inciting the home crowd against them, and generally never giving them a moment's peace.

By backing down from no one, including the league president.

John McGraw played and managed to win, whatever the cost.

When the decade of the twenties dawned, McGraw of the Giants was the dominant figure in baseball, an acknowledged genius, a strategist and tactician with an uncanny sense of the game. He hobnobbed with the great and would-be great, and counted so many friends around the National League that when the Giants were on the road he had to host wild and sometimes unruly cocktail parties in his hotel suite to greet them all. "He was a flamboyant personality," wrote Garry Schumacher, a newsman of the time. "He was Mr. New York, make no doubt about it."

But, like that city, he had a dark side. He was also Muggsy McGraw—although no one dared call him that in his hearing—the street fighter who went for the jugular, "the Little Napoleon," a five-foot seven-inch, terrible-tempered tyrant who ruled all he surveyed with an iron will and baseball's most vicious tongue. "He had the competitive instincts of a piranha," wrote historian Glenn Dickey. He was arrogant, dictatorial, insolent, sneering, bullying, belligerent, cocksure, eternally grouchy and endowed with a flame-throwing vocabulary beside which the word "obscene" paled. For such qualities, the fans, the New York City press, and many of his players idolized him. For the same reasons, he was hated throughout the league.

Still, McGraw was a mighty colossus towering over the game, not merely because of what he was, or what he was fancied to be, but because of

Travis "Stonewall" Jackson was John McGraw's type of shortstop, and played for him from 1922 to 1932. Jackson had great range, had the best arm of any shortstop in baseball, and was a great bunter. He was elected to the Hall of Fame in 1982.

what he had done. From 1903 through 1920, he led the Giants to six pennants and eight second places. It was a record no one else in baseball could match, not even the redoubtable Connie Mack. But it was only prologue—Al Jolson should have dedicated his 1920s hit "You Ain't Heard Nothin' Yet" to Muggsy and his Giants.

Coming off three of those second-place finishes in a row—1918 to the Cubs, 1919 to the Reds, and 1920 to the Brooklyn Robins, McGraw tinkered with his lineup in hopes of finding another pennant-winning combination. From the Phillies he acquired second baseman Johnny Rawlings, left fielder Irish Meusel, and a 31-year-old veteran named Charles Dillon Stengel. Casey, long an admirer of McGraw, was overjoyed to be going to the Giants. He raced up to Boston, where the Giants were playing the Braves, "before McGraw could change his mind." As he entered Braves Field through the outfield gate, oblivious to Giants pitcher Art Nehf standing nearby, Ol' Case went into a happy little jig, pounded his chest and chirped, "Wake up muscles! We're in New York, now!" They had fun with that one in the locker room.

The new Giants joined a team with a lineup loaded with future Hall of Famers: George Kelly, Dave Bancroft, Ross Youngs, and Frankie Frisch. The pitching didn't measure up, however, with only Nehf on a pace to win 20 games, and as the summer dwindled down the Giants were mired in second place again, seven and a half games behind the Pirates. On August 24 the Pittsburghers swashbuckled into the Polo Grounds for a five-game series, expecting to wrap up the pennant. The Giants swept that series, built up a head of steam, knocked the Buccaneers out of the race for good with three more victories at Forbes Field, and finished four games in front for McGraw's seventh National League pennant.

Dave "Beauty" Bancroft played with the Giants for only four years—1920 to 1923—but played on three pennant winners. Another of McGraw's Hall of Fame shortstops, Bancroft holds the all-time single-season record for total chances by a shortstop, 1,046 in 1922.

NINE INNINGS, NINE RALLIES

The game's outcome was no longer in doubt when the Giants came to bat in the top of the ninth. The two-time defending NL champs led the cellar-dwelling Phillies 21–8 on June 2, 1923, at Baker Bowl. But some fans hung around to see if the Giants could become the first team in the 20th century to score at least one run in each inning of a nine-inning game.

They did, but it wasn't easy, and it was 41 years before another team matched the Giants' feat. Several teams have scored in a game's first eight innings but, because they were ahead and at home, didn't bat in the ninth. Only the 1923 Giants and the 1964 Cardinals have scored in all nine.

The Giants scored an average of 5.6 runs per game in 1923; the Phillies' 5.30 team ERA was baseball's highest since the late 1800s. Ralph Head, who was 2–9 with a 6.66 ERA in his one-year major league career, was the Phillies' starting pitcher. New York roughed him up for four in the first on a three-run triple by Ross Youngs and a Phillie error. In four of the innings, the Giants scored just one run. But after Heinie Groh's two-out single scored Jimmy O'Connell in the third, the streak wasn't in real danger until the ninth.

Phillie reliever Jim Bishop—whose career record was 0-4—retired Bill Cunningham and Youngs to open the ninth. But George Kelly blasted a triple, and O'Connell, who already had four hits on the day, smashed his third double of the game, sending Kelly home and the Giants into the record books. It was their 23rd hit.

Manager-in-training Casey Stengel had his best and happiest years as a player in center field for McGraw in 1922 and 1923. "What I learned from McGraw I used with all my players," said Stengel, who won ten pennants in 25 years as a major league manager.

The Polo Grounds' other tenants, the Yankees, were winning their first AL flag, sparked by Babe Ruth's magnificent 59-homer year. The Subway Series was on. A case could be made that the World Series of 1921 was the greatest challenge of McGraw's career. He had been humiliated—but not humbled—in his last four attempts to capture the world championship. Now he was going head to head with the team that for the second year in a row had outdrawn the Giants in their own ballpark. Muggsy was ready.

Only 30,000 showed up for the opening game on the afternoon of October 5; newspaper reports of a sellout and heavy rains early in the day discouraged fans. Celebrities made it, however: show-biz stars like Flo Ziegfeld, Irving Berlin, Norma Talmadge, George M. Cohan; baseball legends like Monte Ward, Ned Hanlon, Harry Sinclair; even the governors of New York and New Jersey. Starting pitchers were Carl Mays for the Yanks and Phil Douglas for the Giants. The Giants were the "home" team that day, and as Shufflin' Phil started out to the mound to begin the first inning, McGraw called him back and pointed to the short right field wall. "Remember," he said, "don't give that big baboon anything but low curves." Douglas didn't have to ask Muggsy who he was talking about.

In the first inning, Ruth, batting third, singled home Elmer Miller from second. Shufflin' Phil then struck Ruth out twice, and Frankie Frisch got four hits, but there wasn't much else to cheer about, as the Yanks won, 3–0. In the second game the Giants became the "visitors." They put on their road uniforms, switched dugouts with the Yankees, and sent their ace, Art Nehf, to the mound. But young Waite Hoyt gave up only two hits in posting another 3–0 win for the Yankees.

It was a civil war in the 1921 World Series, as the Giants (above) fought the Yankees for supremacy at the Polo Grounds. McGraw's intimidating attitude gave his teams a unique stamp, even before they got to the dugout. "McGraw's very walk across the field in a hostile town was a challenge to the multitude," wrote Grantland Rice.

With their backs against the wall—no team had ever lost the first two games and gone on to win the Series—the Giants tied Game 3 at 4–4 in the third, then ripped the game apart with an eight-run seventh inning. They exploded for 20 hits, a World Series record, and won going away, 13–5.

In Game 4, Mays again facing Douglas, Babe gave the crowd what they came for, parking one in the right field bleachers for his first postseason homer, but the Giants won 4–2 and pulled even. The next day, in Game 5, Ruth astonished everyone by laying down a perfect bunt along the third-base line, beating it out for a single. That led to a rally and a 3–1 win for the Yanks, but an inflamed right elbow and a battered knee benched Ruth for the rest of the Series.

The Giants were down, three games to two, but stormed back in baseball's last best-of-nine Series to take Games 6 and 7. In Game 8, in the bottom of the ninth, the score 1–0, Yanks batting, Ruth limped up to the plate to pinch-hit for Wally Pipp. The crowd roared, but all Ruth could do was ground out to first. Aaron Ward wangled a walk. Then up to the plate strode Frank "Home Run" Baker, and cascading through the thoughts of longtime Giants rooters went memories of Merkle, Snodgrass, and the damage Baker had done to their team in 1911 and 1913. Baker worked the count from Nehf to 3 and 2, fouled off a couple, then smoked a line drive to right. Somehow second baseman Rawlings got in front of the ball, knocked it down, and from his knees threw to Kelly at first for the out. Ward—sure the ball was going through—galloped around second and headed for third. Kelly quickly made a perfect peg across the diamond. The ball and the charging Ward arrived almost simultaneously, and third baseman Frankie Frisch went sprawling. But when he hopped back to his feet the indomitable Fordham Flash was still

Catcher Frank Snyder, a mediocre hitter before he came to the Giants in 1919, hit .320 in 1921 and .343 in 1922.

Dazzy Vance

When Clarence Arthur "Dazzy" Vance kicked his leg a foot over his head and swung his powerful arm over the top, batters stood dazzled and confounded. For 11 seasons with the Brooklyn Dodgers, Vance dominated NL hitters with his "speedball." He led the NL in strikeouts every season from 1922 to 1928, and in 1924 he struck out almost twice as many batters as his closest competitor. But for all his speed, it was a curveball that clinched a spot for "The Dazzler" on the Dodger roster.

Vance had won 21 games in the minors in 1921, but the Dodgers were hesitant to gamble on a 29-year-old pitcher with a history of arm trouble. It was a worse deal than they thought: Vance lied about his age; he was actually 31. Brooklyn finally bought his contract only because the pitcher they wanted wasn't available.

In spring training the next year, Vance pitched against the St. Louis Browns. "With two strikes on the immortal George Sisler," Vance remembered, "I whipped over a curve and that great batter looked at it. Robbie [Brooklyn manager Wilbert Robinson] almost leaped out of the dugout shouting, 'What a curve! How that baby broke! Why didn't somebody tell me he could throw a curve?' . . . I always tell Sisler he put me in the big leagues." Vance won 18 games and led the league with 134 strikeouts and five shutouts in 1922, his first full season in the majors. In 1924 he was voted the first NL Most Valuable Player, beating slugger Rogers Hornsby and his .424 batting average. The MVP voters rewarded Vance's 28 wins, including 15 straight during the pennant race, and his 262 strikeouts—127 more than the second-best strikeout pitcher in the league. The Dodgers rewarded Vance with the highest contract in team history, a three-year deal for $50,000.

Only ten years before his MVP performance, it looked as if Vance's pitching career was over. His problems began in 1914 when Vance, then 23, hurt his right arm while wrestling. After an unsuccessful and painful debut with Pittsburgh the next year, he returned to Class A ball to win 17 games and a late-season trial with the Yankees. But after the season he hurt his arm in another wrestling match.

With broken dreams and a wounded arm, Vance hooked on with several minor league teams. He consulted doctors everywhere but found the best advice in his hometown in Nebraska. The family doctor diagnosed the problem as inflamed and strained cartilage in the elbow and prescribed a simple, old-fashioned treatment: rest. The doctor predicted that with proper rest Vance's arm would return to form in five years.

Dazzy kept pitching, though, saving his strength for when he needed it most. "For three years I had been staying on the payroll by extending my arm and pitching a good game every time they were ready to let me go," Vance said. Despite the troubles, the plan worked: in 1921 the arm regained its strength—as the doctor had promised.

Vance always remembered those painful years in the minors. "A sore arm cost me dearly," he told friends. "And I vowed that if I could help it, I would never suffer from another sore arm." As a result, he demanded four days rest between starts even though his colleagues pitched with two or three days between starts. When Brooklyn management complained about Dazzy's demands, he had a simple response: his record.

"Perhaps I didn't work every other day, but when the season was ended I generally pitched my full share of innings and games. What is more important, I won my full share of games. In other words, I did my work, a lot of work and good work, if I do say it myself. I was able to do this because I used my head. I always figured my head was given to me for some purpose besides merely to spread my ears apart."

In 1933 Vance (above, right, shown with former Brooklyn teammate Floyd "Babe" Herman) was 42 years old, but was still among baseball's best strikeout pitchers. Vance averaged 6.09 strikeouts per nine innings that season; only his 22-year-old Cardinal teammate, Dizzy Dean, did better—6.11.

DAZZY VANCE

Right-Handed Pitcher
Pittsburgh Pirates 1915
New York Yankees 1915, 1918
Brooklyn Dodgers 1922–1932, 1935
St. Louis Cardinals 1933–1934
Cincinnati Reds 1934
Hall of Fame 1955

GAMES	442
INNINGS	
Career	2,967
Season High	308$\frac{2}{3}$
WINS	
Career	197
Season High	28
LOSSES	
Career	140
Season High	15
WINNING PERCENTAGE	
Career	.585
Season High	.824
ERA	
Career	3.24
Season Low	2.09
GAMES STARTED	
Career	347
Season High	35
COMPLETE GAMES	
Career	216
Season High	30
SHUTOUTS	
Career	30
Season High	5
STRIKEOUTS	
Career	2,045
Season High	262
WALKS	
Career	840
Season High	100
NO-HITTER	1925
WORLD SERIES	1934
MOST VALUABLE PLAYER	1924

When the game was big, McGraw often turned to his littlest pitcher, Art Nehf. Though only 5′ 9″, Nehf was never bigger than in Game 8 of the 1921 World Series, in which he gave the Yankees just four hits in a 1–0 win.

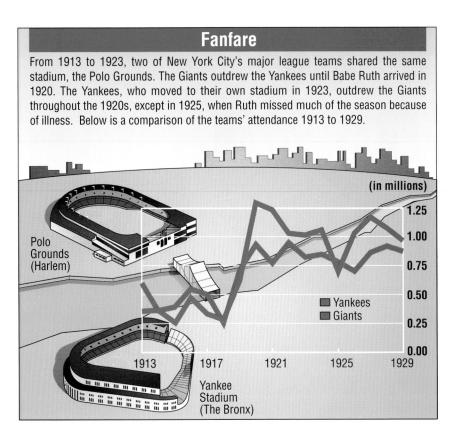

Fanfare

From 1913 to 1923, two of New York City's major league teams shared the same stadium, the Polo Grounds. The Giants outdrew the Yankees until Babe Ruth arrived in 1920. The Yankees, who moved to their own stadium in 1923, outdrew the Giants throughout the 1920s, except in 1925, when Ruth missed much of the season because of illness. Below is a comparison of the teams' attendance 1913 to 1929.

(in millions)

Polo Grounds (Harlem)

■ Yankees
■ Giants

1.25
1.00
0.75
0.50
0.25
0.00

1913   1917   1921   1925   1929

Yankee Stadium (The Bronx)

holding the ball. Double play, and the Giants had won their first world championship since 1905.

The victory was especially sweet for McGraw because his pitchers, led by Nehf, Douglas and Jesse Barnes, had held the heavy-hitting Yanks, possessors of a .300 team batting average for the season, to a .207 mark. Some sportswriters proclaimed that proof of the superiority of National League pitching. But a look at the record will show that the best pitching in the Series was done by Waite Hoyt in a losing cause. He pitched three complete games, winning two and losing one, and only two unearned runs crossed the plate—which equaled Christy Mathewson's 1905 performance of going 27 innings and coming out with an earned run average of 0.00.

Next season McGraw obtained Heinie Groh, considered the best third baseman in the league, from Cincinnati and shifted Frisch to second. As the 1922 season unfolded, baseball buffs argued hotly about whether the new Giants' combination of Groh, Bancroft, Frisch and Kelly was better than Connie Mack's $100,000 infield of 1911–1914—McInnis, Collins, Barry and Baker—or the 1906–1910 Cubs' fabled foursome of Steinfeldt, Tinker, Evers and Chance. Since the Giants had to ship George Burns to the Reds as part of the deal, the gap in center field could have made the debate less meaningful. But McGraw was still a master manipulator of players. To plug the big hole in center he pulled Stengel off the bench, and Casey responded with a solid game in the field and a batting average of .368.

More important in McGraw's list of problems was the state of his pitching staff. Fred Toney lost his stuff and went to Boston, along with $100,000, for the unproven Hughie McQuillan. Shufflin' Phil, with his bribe-me letter to

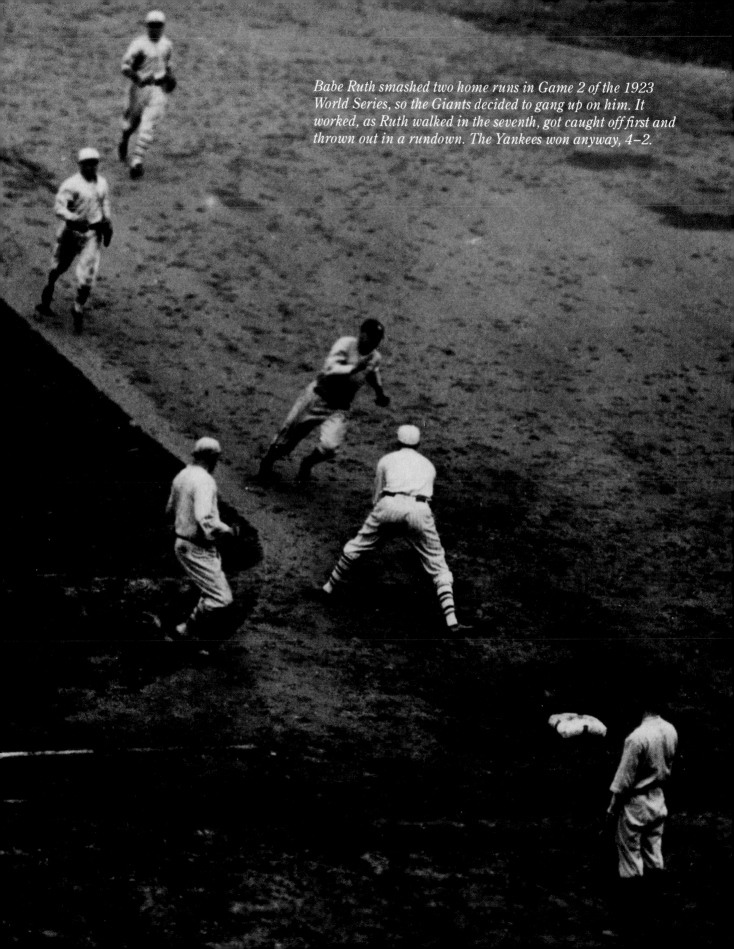

Babe Ruth smashed two home runs in Game 2 of the 1923 World Series, so the Giants decided to gang up on him. It worked, as Ruth walked in the seventh, got caught off first and thrown out in a rundown. The Yankees won anyway, 4–2.

After a disappointing regular season in 1922, Giants third baseman Heinie Groh and his trademark bottle bat opened up on the Yankees in tne World Series. Groh hit .474 and, with nine hits, led both teams as the Giants swept the Yankees.

The 1922 World Series, between the Giants and the Yankees, was the last ever to be played entirely in one stadium—the Polo Grounds. In 1923 the Yankees moved across the Harlem River to Yankee Stadium.

the Cardinals written in 100-proof alcohol, was kicked out of baseball forever by the austere Landis. But the luck that had been smiling on Muggsy held up. Rosy Ryan, 7–10 in 1921, posted a 17–12 record. Jack Scott, a lame-armed pitcher released by the Reds during spring training, showed up, nursed his wing along and played for the bonuses McGraw gave him when he won. He collected eight and missed only two. It was that kind of season. By the end of August, the Giants were firmly in first, and coasted to McGraw's eighth league championship, establishing him as the winningest manager in the history of the game.

For the second year in a row, it was a subway series, as the Yankees beat off a determined challenge from the St. Louis Browns by a one-game margin. In the pre-Series hoopla it became obvious that the Yanks, with a starting corps of Mays, Hoyt and Bob Shawkey, bolstered by the addition—from Boston, of course—of Bullet Joe Bush and Sam Jones, held a huge edge in pitching. Most of the betting, therefore, was not on who would win, but on how many home runs the Babe would hit.

The Giants, behind steady Art Nehf, sore-armed castoff Jack Scott and inexperienced Hughie McQuillan, swept the Series, four games to none. The closest the Yanks came was in Game 2, tied 3–3 in the tenth inning when umpires George Hildebrand and Bill Klem, noting how slowly the game was moving and convinced that it would not be possible to complete another full inning before dark, called off the action "on account of darkness." Since it was only 4:45, with perhaps 45 minutes of daylight left, the decision was greeted by the fans with screams of outrage. A jeering mob besieged Commissioner Landis and his wife in their box and followed them as they fled, feigning

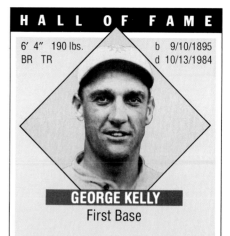

HALL OF FAME

6′ 4″ 190 lbs. b 9/10/1895
BR TR d 10/13/1984

GEORGE KELLY
First Base

John McGraw, who managed in the majors for 33 seasons, said George Kelly got "more important hits for me than any player I ever had."

Kelly's first three years in the majors hardly held Hall of Fame promise. In 144 at-bats from 1915 through 1917, the lanky first baseman hit an anemic .138, then went off for a year of military duty.

By 1920 he was the Giants' regular first baseman, and he rewarded McGraw's faith in him with 11 home runs and a league-leading 94 RBI. He was on his way to becoming one of the decade's most versatile and productive players.

Although he was overshadowed by the AL's Babe Ruth, Kelly was a first-rate power hitter in his own right. In 1921 he led the NL with 23 home runs, including three grand slams. Four times in his career he ranked among the league's top five in homers, and his ability in the clutch earned him five seasons of more than 100 RBI, including the Giants' four pennant-winning years, 1921 to 1924. On September 17, 1923, Kelly became the fourth player in the 20th century to hit three home runs in a game, and he repeated the feat in June 1924.

Kelly made the Hall of Fame as much for his glove and arm as for his bat. The 6′ 4″ Kelly, who earned the nickname "Highpockets," still holds the NL record for most putouts in a season.

The Meusel brothers—Giants' left fielder Irish and Yankees' right fielder Bob—wound up battling in three straight Subway Series in New York. Irish won the 1922 battle, as he scored the winning run (above) for the Giants in the eighth inning of Game 5.

dignity, across the playing field. Since the fans believed that calling the game was a ploy to milk an extra day's receipts from the Series, Landis announced that the gate for that day, over $100,000, would be donated to hospitals for disabled veterans.

The batting heroes of the 1922 Series were Giants Groh at .474 and Frisch at .471. And the Babe? McGraw ordered his moundsmen to pitch him low, slow and out of the strike zone. The result was Ruth's worst Series—no homers and just two hits, a single and a double, for an anemic average of .118.

The 1923 World Series was memorable on several counts. Once again it matched the Giants and the Yankees, but this time the subway took the fans to the Bronx as well as to Harlem. McGraw, in high dudgeon because the upstart American Leaguers were outdrawing his team, had booted them out of the Polo Grounds and told them to build a park of their own. Now he could look across the Harlem River from the quaint old Polo Grounds and see the magnificent new stadium that Jacob Ruppert had built for the Babe. The Yanks baptized their new home on April 18 before a sell-out crowd, with Ruth belting a three-run homer in the third, and from that point breezed to the pennant, 16 games ahead of Detroit.

On the south side of the river, the Giants took first place on opening day and never let go. They had to hustle to stay ahead of the Reds, however, who had three 20-game winners—Dolf Luque, Pete Donohue and Eppa Rixey. For his part, McGraw got his weak staff successfully through the season with a quick hook and a prayer, sometimes using five or six pitchers in a game.

Game 1 of the third Subway Series seesawed back and forth, with one spectacular play following another. In the seventh, with Jumping Joe Dugan on third and the score tied 4–4, Ruth hit a screamer to right. First baseman

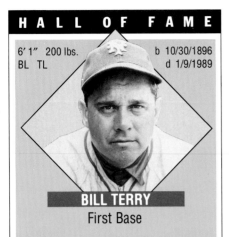

6′1″ 200 lbs.   b 10/30/1896
BL TL   d 1/9/1989

BILL TERRY
First Base

Bill Terry and John McGraw didn't see eye to eye on much. For McGraw, the game was his life; Terry saw baseball as a way to make money. When McGraw first offered Terry a chance to play with the Giants, his response was, "For how much?" Terry and McGraw wrangled over money throughout Terry's 14-year career as the Giants' first baseman, and they once went two years without speaking to each other. Yet when the time came for McGraw to hang up his cleats, his hand-picked successor was none other than Bill Terry.

When Terry reached the majors in 1924, the Giants already had a Hall of Famer at first base—George Kelly. Terry played sparingly during the 1924 season, but came alive in the World Series, hitting .429. In 1925 McGraw moved Kelly to second base to make room for Terry's 42-ounce bat, and Terry responded with a .319 average. He hit .310 or better every year from 1927 until his retirement as a player in 1936, and in 1930 hit .401. No National Leaguer has hit .400 since. He also drove in more than 100 runs six times, and his .341 lifetime batting average is 14th on the all-time list.

After he took over as Giants manager in 1932, Terry guided the team to three pennants in his ten-year tenure. In 1934 a writer asked him to evaluate the crosstown Brooklyn Dodgers, who at the time were a second-rate club. "Is Brooklyn still in the league?" was his reply. John McGraw would have been proud.

With two out in the top of the ninth inning of Game 1 of the 1923 World Series, Casey Stengel drove a Joe Bush pitch into the deepest part of Yankee Stadium's left center field alley. Stengel barely beat Bob Meusel's throw, and his unforgettable inside-the-park homer gave the Giants a 5–4 win.

Kelly flew into the air, knocked the ball down, and from his knees threw Dugan out at the plate by a step. McGraw called it the best play he had ever seen in baseball, and not many who were there disagreed with him. Then, in the ninth, score still tied, came the *pièce de résistance*. With two out, Casey Stengel lined one up the alley. The ball rolled to the far reaches of Yankee Stadium's left center field wall and Ol' Case, 34 years old and bowlegged, was off on a trip that took him around the bases, one shoe flapping, into immortality. An inside-the-park homer was rare enough in dead-ball baseball, but for an aging hustler to pull it off with the new lively ball was more than the fans could stand, and Damon Runyon's account of the heroic scramble in the New York *American* made Stengel a household word.

The Yanks evened it in Game 2 as the Babe poled out a pair, but in Game 3 in Yankee Stadium it was Stengel's day again. In the seventh inning of the scoreless game, Casey, who had been taking a terrible riding from Yankee players and fans since the appearance of Runyon's article, drove the ball deep into the right field seats. This time Stengel trotted slowly around the bases, grinning widely, savoring the moment—with his thumb pressed to his nose and fingers wiggling. Giants fans enjoyed the moment almost as much as Casey did, but Colonel Ruppert was upset. In the lobby of the Hotel Commodore after the game he complained stuffily to Commissioner Landis about actions "not a credit to baseball." Landis, who in the past had come down hard on player obscenity on the field, listened but did nothing. Later, he explained, "A fellow who wins two games with home runs has a right to feel a little playful, especially if he's a Stengel."

Casey's heroics were the high-water mark for the Giants that year, for the embattled Yankees came back to win the next three games and their first

world championship. The Series was a triumph for Ruth, too. He clouted three home runs and batted .368. For the losing Giants, Frankie Frisch had another spectacular Series, garnering ten hits and another .400 average.

Never one to play a pat hand, McGraw traded Stengel and Dave Bancroft over the winter, installed second-year man Travis Jackson as his regular at shortstop, and brought up two talented rookie infielders from Toledo, Fred Lindstrom and Bill Terry. All have plaques in the Hall of Fame.

Still dominant, the Giants led through most of the 1924 campaign, McGraw working his usual magic with a weak pitching staff. The Robins made a run at the gold in August and September on the arms of Dazzy Vance, who was having the best year of his career—28–6 and a 2.16 ERA—and Burleigh Grimes, the master of the spitter, who was on his way to a 22–13 record. On September 22, the Giants' lead was down to a half game, but they swept three from the Pirates. With three games against the Phillies left to the season, their magic number was two. They won the first of those games; and the Robins lost to the Braves. New York, accustomed as it was to winners, went delirious over McGraw's record-shattering fourth straight pennant.

But even before the champagne corks stopped rolling on the speakeasy floors, an unsavory incident came to light that soured McGraw's great season and cast a shadow over the upcoming World Series. On the day of the pennant-clinching game, Phillies shortstop Heinie Sand was approached by Jimmy O'Connell, a kid outfielder from California replacing Stengel in center field. O'Connell offered Sand $500 not to "bear down too hard" in these last games. Sand, who had known O'Connell on the West Coast, reported the incident to his manager, Art Fletcher, who told John Heydler, president of the National League, who put in a call to Judge Landis.

The Giants finally had the Polo Grounds all to themselves in 1923, but didn't make the most of it. In the World Series against the Yankees that fall, McGraw's troops failed to hold the fort, losing all three home games, including the clincher in Game 6 before 34,172 fans (above).

The flap over an alleged game-fixing scheme late in the 1924 pennant race centered on Giants' coach Cozy Dolan (above), who was often called McGraw's "Man Friday." Dolan was banned from the game, although McGraw was never implicated.

Slugging first baseman Bill Terry was one of the few players who stood his ground when criticized by McGraw. The pair once went two years without speaking, but it was Terry who succeeded McGraw as the Giants' manager in 1932—at McGraw's request.

From top to bottom, the Giants' infield of first baseman George Kelly, third baseman Heinie Groh, shortstop Travis Jackson and second baseman Frankie Frisch was baseball's best in 1924. It was a solid group defensively, and only Groh hit below .300.

The commissioner immediately hot-footed it to New York and put O'Connell on the grill. The kid outfielder, the soul of naiveté, freely admitted the bribe attempt and explained that he had been put up to it by Cozy Dolan, a Giants coach and an old crony of McGraw's. The whole team, he said, was supposed to chip in and make up the $500 purse, and Frisch, Youngs and Kelly had all assured him it was a good idea and to go ahead with the plan.

Quizzed by Landis, the three flatly denied any knowledge of the affair. Cozy Dolan, who apparently had read about too many courtroom dramas, kept repeating "I don't remember" to every question from the commissioner, even those dealing with the most innocent details. Out of patience, Landis reached a snap decision: Frisch, Youngs and Kelly were exonerated on their word; Dolan and O'Connell were placed on the ineligible list—banned for life.

The judgment was announced just before the first World Series game of 1924, and almost halted the fall spectacle. Ban Johnson, president of the American League and no fan of the commissioner, was indignant over what looked to him like a whitewash. He called for a federal investigation, hoping to plant black eyes on Landis and McGraw, and at the same time dump a little dirt on the National League for a change.

The games went on as scheduled, however, and have since been ranked among the greatest ever played. It's a great story, but one that belongs to Walter Johnson and the Washington Senators. ◑

"There has been only one manager, and his name is John McGraw," said Connie Mack.

Frankie Frisch

His first major league start came in the heat of the 1919 pennant race between New York and league-leading Cincinnati. Giants manager John McGraw inserted Frankie Frisch into the lineup at second base for a doubleheader against the Reds. On the first play of the first game, Cincinnati's Morrie Rath sent a smash toward Frisch—a smash that took a bad hop. The ball caromed off Frisch's chest, but he artfully pounced on it and nipped the runner at first.

"That was all I had to see," McGraw said. "The average youngster, nervous anyhow at making his first start, would have given up on the play . . . . Frisch never quit on it. He'll be a great one."

Frisch fielded 13 chances cleanly during the critical doubleheader that September day. He also got a hit in each game and stole three bases in the nightcap as the Giants swept the doubleheader.

New York, in turn, lost both games the following day to the eventual pennant winner. Nonetheless, McGraw had found the man who later spearheaded the drive to four consecutive World Series appearances, the first in 1921.

"The Fordham Flash" was a diamond fireball: a spectacular fielder and a dynamic baserunner who often lost his cap on head-first slides.

Frisch was born September 9, 1898, to a wealthy manufacturer. His father wanted him in the family lace-linen business rather than in baseball. Frisch went on to Fordham College, where he captained the baseball, football and basketball teams.

After college, in 1919, when Frisch signed with the Giants, his father was reluctant to let his potential partner go. "Only for the summer," his father told him, "the linen business in the fall."

But Frisch returned to the Giants in 1920. He quickly became the leader on the field for McGraw, and eventually became the Giants' captain.

In 1921, his second full season, Frisch batted .341 with 211 hits and 100 RBI. He scored 121 runs and led the league with 49 stolen bases as New York captured the first of its four straight pennants. He also had become the pet of disciplinarian McGraw.

From 1921 through 1924, Frisch hit no less than .327 during the regular season, and hit at least .300 in each World Series, becoming the only player to bat .300 or better in four consecutive fall classics.

The Giants fell to second place in 1925 and to the second division a year later. In the summer of 1926, McGraw turned on the man who many felt was being groomed to succeed him as manager, and Frisch became the main target of continuous invective from his irascible manager.

"Finally I couldn't take it any more," Frisch said when things came to a head on a road trip to St. Louis. "I was the team captain in 1926 and he bawled me out about everything. My legs were in terrible shape. I had pulled muscles and spike wounds all over both legs, so I said 'Nuts to this' and left the club."

Frisch returned to the team in New York, but in the off-season, he was part of the deal of the decade. McGraw traded Frisch, along with pitcher Jimmy Ring, to the Cardinals for player-manager Rogers Hornsby, the 1925 NL MVP.

In his first year with the new club, Frisch set records at second base—1,037 chances, 641 assists—and led the league at his position with a .979 fielding percentage. In 1928 St. Louis won the pennant, the first of Frisch's four World Series appearances with the Cardinals.

Frisch's playing days ended in 1937. He managed St. Louis until late 1938, Pittsburgh from 1940 to 1946, and the Chicago Cubs from mid-1949 to 1951. He was elected to the Hall of Fame in 1947.

For a dollar, in 1924 kids could get Frankie Frisch's "Home Run King", mechanical baseball game created by the Fordham Flash himself and endorsed by some of his friends. In the photograph below, Frisch (far right) duels Giants pitcher Rosy Ryan. Former Giants manager Bill Mutrie and Giants pitcher Dinty Gearin observe the action.

My boy thinks the world of the Home Run King toy which you sent him—he plays with it by the hour.
Yours truly,
ART. N. NEHF
N. Y. Giants.

It will get a great reception from the Kids.
Rogers Hornsby,
Champion Batsman of the National League

It's the most amusing baseball toy that I have ever seen.
Christy Mathewson,
President Boston Braves

I cannot conceive any father neglecting to get a Home Run King for his boy.
Dazzy Vance,
Brooklyn Dodgers

DAD, GET YOUR BOY A FRANKIE FRISCH TOY! YOU'LL BOTH ENJOY IT

FRANKIE FRISCH

Second Base, Third Base, Shortstop
New York Giants 1919–1926
St. Louis Cardinals 1927–1937
Hall of Fame 1947

GAMES	**2,311**
AT-BATS	**9,112**
BATTING AVERAGE	
Career	**.316**
Season High	**.348**
SLUGGING AVERAGE	
Career	**.432**
Season High	**.520**
HITS	
Career	**2,880**
Season High	**223**
DOUBLES	
Career	**466**
Season High	**46**
TRIPLES	
Career	**138**
Season High	**17**
HOME RUNS	
Career	**105**
Season High	**12**
TOTAL BASES	**3,937**
EXTRA-BASE HITS	**709**
RUNS BATTED IN	
Career	**1,244**
Season High	**114**
RUNS	
Career	**1,532**
Season High	**121**
WORLD SERIES	**1921-1924,1928**
	1930-1931,1934
MOST VALUABLE PLAYER	**1931**

Frisch wasn't quite himself in the 1930 World Series against the Philadelphia A's. He was too late with this slide, and hit just .208 as the Cards lost in six games.

The Big Train

"You better come out here and get this pitcher. He throws a ball so fast nobody can see it and he strikes out everybody. He throws a ball so fast its like a little white bullet going down to the catcher and his control is so good that the catcher just holds up his glove, shuts his eyes, then picks the ball out of the pocket. He's a big 19-year-old fellow, like I told you before, and if you don't hurry up, someone will sign him and he will be the best pitcher that ever lived."

Traveling salesmen tend to be persistent. At least three major league managers during the hot summer of 1907—Hughie Jennings of the Detroit Tigers, Clark Griffith of the New York Highlanders and Pongo Joe Cantillon of the Washington Senators—had received letters and telegrams from a peripatetic drummer in the Rocky Mountain states touting some kid phenom in an Idaho semipro league.

Free-lance prospecting was common back then, before the days of organized scouting. Come up with a nugget and you might get a bonus or a job out of it. The three managers had heard it all before, but their situations were different. Jennings didn't need any help—his Tigers were pennant-bound. Griffith thought about it but waited too long. The Senators were the doormat of the league again, a condition so commonplace it gave rise to a classic baseball putdown: "Washington—first in war, first in peace, and last in the American League." Pongo Joe needed all the help he could get. He sent a catcher who was on the injured list, Cliff Blankenship, all the way out to Idaho to scout the kid phenom.

What Blankenship saw was a tall, skinny teenager with extremely long arms and a buggy-whip sidearm delivery. The kid lost the game, 1–0, on a teammate's error in the 12th inning, but what Blankenship also saw for 12 innings—or thought he saw—was a fastball so fast it just barely showed as a

In the 1920s—an age of new pitches and trick deliveries—Walter Johnson (opposite) showed that the fastball was still king. "He's got a gun concealed about his person," wrote Ring Lardner. "They can't tell me he throws them balls with his arm."

In 1911 Johnson looked like a harmless country boy, unless you had to hit against him. He completed 36 of 37 starts for the Senators and had a .658 winning percentage pitching for a team that won at a .416 clip.

In 1906, when 18-year-old Walter Johnson was playing for a team in Weiser, Idaho, he struck out everyone in sight. The "Weiser Wonder" averaged 15 strikeouts a game that season, and had a string of 75 consecutive scoreless innings.

blur. He scrounged up a piece of paper, wrote out a contract for $350 a month, threw in a $100 cash sweetener, and signed the kid then and there. The name scribbled on the contract was Walter Perry Johnson.

Johnson was born in Humboldt, Kansas, to a family of German-Dutch farmers who had arrived by wagon train, pulled up stakes for California and at last settled in Idaho. He was digging postholes for the Idaho Telephone Co. in 1907 when Blankenship took him on the long journey back to the nation's capital. Early in his career people began calling him "Big Swede," probably because of his name. When someone who knew better asked why he didn't set the ethnic record straight, Walter replied mildly, "They're good people, the Swedes. I wouldn't want to offend them." That will give you some idea of what Walter Johnson was like.

He was as green as the banks of the Potomac when he arrived in Washington, a gangly, unsophisticated country bumpkin who hiked back to the hotel in his uniform after his first game, not realizing there was a team bus. Outside the hotel, a stranger who had been at the game approached and said, "You're famous already, kid. See? They've named a hotel for you."

"I looked across the street," Johnson recalled years later with a chuckle, "and sure enough, there was a big illuminated sign that said 'Johnson Hotel.' Well, do you know, I was so green I actually believed the man!"

His first start was against the hard-hitting Tigers. "He was a rube out of the cornfields, and we licked our lips," said Ty Cobb. "I watched him take that easy windup—and then something went past me that made me flinch. The thing just hissed with danger. We couldn't touch him . . . there was only one answer left to his incredible, overpowering speed. We bunted. Sure enough, the boy hadn't handled many bunts. . . . We finally beat young

An excellent all-around athlete, Johnson fielded his position well. He ranks fifth all-time among pitchers in assists, fourth in total chances, and seventh in double plays.

Johnson, who didn't drink or smoke, let his face appear on a cigarette-company-sponsored baseball card in 1911.

Walter Johnson, 3–2, but every one of us knew we'd met the most powerful arm ever turned loose in a ball park."

Was Johnson as fast as old-timers remember him? Was he really faster than the likes of Bob Feller, Nolan Ryan, Lefty Grove, Bullet Joe Bush, Sandy Koufax and all the other hurlers of super smoke? No one can say for sure. Officially, Ryan has been timed at better than 100 mph and Feller at 98 mph, but not with devices of equal sophistication. And before Feller, there were no measuring devices, except for the human eye and a batter's experience. Earl Schenck Miers, in his book *Baseball,* reported, without offering sources, that "Walter Johnson . . . was said to be able to throw a ball at 117 miles per hour, though it was never measured."

Charley Gehringer, Detroit's great second baseman, remembered old-time Tiger catcher Del Baker saying that when Johnson was in his prime, "he threw the ball so hard you could hear it."

Sam Crawford, Tiger outfielder, said, "You hardly see the ball at all. But you *hear* it. *Swoosh,* and it smacks into the catcher's mitt. He had such an easy motion it looked like he was just playing catch . . . and then *swoosh,* and it was by you!"

Eddie Ainsmith, who caught Johnson in his early years, said, "If you tried to hit against him on a dark day, you were out of luck. I had all I could do to see the ball when he let fly."

Grantland Rice, dean of baseball writers, struggling to capture the essence of Johnson's style in a single colorful phrase, likened him to a runaway locomotive, the fastest thing he could think of, and called him "Big Train."

Johnson's long arms were perfect for throwing fastballs, and all the more prominent in his Sunday best. Detroit outfielder Davy Jones, who in 1907 was the first major league hitter Johnson faced, said Johnson had "absolutely the longest arms I ever saw."

Billy Evans, an umpire of the time, offered Johnson what may be the ultimate compliment to a pitcher. "Walter," he said, "is the only pitcher who ever made me close my eyes." But Billy was an ump with a soft spot.

The good news for American League batters was the fact that Johnson was an exceptionally gentle person who refused to throw at opposing players. "The beanball is one of the meanest things on earth," he said in 1925, "and no decent fellow would use it. The beanball pitcher is a potential murderer. If I were a batter and thought the pitcher really tried to bean me, I'd be inclined to wait for him outside the park with a baseball bat."

Johnson was so afraid he might kill or hurt a batter with his fastball that he wouldn't even pitch inside. Ty Cobb, canny and combative, boasted that he always dug in against Johnson once he learned that he wouldn't be brushed back, and "hit the outside pitch more often than I was entitled to."

Because of his temper and character, Johnson was loved throughout baseball as intensely as Cobb was hated. He was almost too kind and considerate to be believed. He was leaving for a movie with teammate Joe Judge one evening when a stranger tied him up in a long conversation. Why didn't he cut the guy off, Judge asked later.

"He said he knew my sister," Johnson explained.

"I didn't know you had a sister," said Judge.

"I don't," said Johnson.

Senators outfielder Clyde Milan, who roomed with Johnson for 14 years, recalled, "He not only had the greatest arm of all time, but the finest disposition you could imagine. He had some sort of phobia about young fellows breaking into baseball. He'd never embarrass them. If we had a

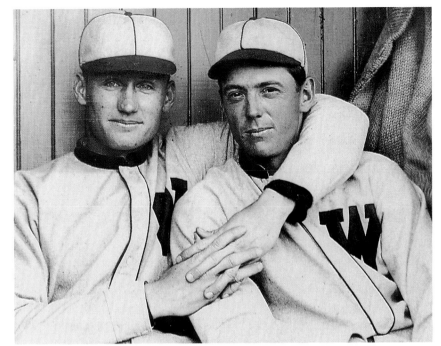

Johnson and center fielder Clyde Milan (above, right), who were both discovered by the same scout in 1907, roomed together for 14 seasons. Milan, one of baseball's greatest base stealers, retired from the Senators at the end of the 1922 season, two years shy of a World Series.

comfortable lead, he'd always lay in nice fat ones for rookies and let them hit it."

Wahoo Sam Crawford, a classic dead-ball thumper, said, "Walter Johnson and I were good friends, and once in a while he would sort of 'give' me a hit or two, just for old time's sake. But there was nothing he enjoyed more than fanning Ty Cobb. . . . Of course, if it was a close game all that was out the window. The friendship deal was off, then. Cobb never did figure out why I did so well against Walter, while he couldn't hit him with a ten-foot pole."

Although he labored for 21 years with a losing team, Johnson's total of 416 wins is by far the best in the American League, and ranks second in the majors only to Cy Young's 511. He won 20 or more games 12 times, and 30-plus games twice. In three seasons, he won 25 games with a team that finished seventh; he accounted for more than a third of the games won by the Senators in a season six times.

In his first full season, 1908, he won 14 games and pitched six shutouts, three of them in four days against the Highlanders. In all, he set a major league career record of 110 shutouts.

In 1910, when he was 22 years old, he won 25 games and struck out 313 batters as Washington finished seventh. That was the first of his 12 strikeout titles. His career total of 3,508 strikeouts stood as a record for more than half a century. From 1910 to 1919 he averaged 26 victories a year while the Senators were averaging only 76. For ten of his first 12 years, he allowed, on average, fewer than two earned runs a game. This was a virtue made by necessity, for the Senators were usually such a weak-hitting club that he was involved in 1–0 decisions 64 times. Still, he managed to win 38 of them. In 1912 Johnson won 16 consecutive games to set a league record. He had sole

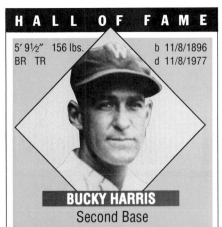

5′ 9½″ 156 lbs.
BR TR

b 11/8/1896
d 11/8/1977

BUCKY HARRIS
Second Base

In 1924 Clark Griffith, owner of the Washington Senators, called on his second baseman, 27-year-old Stanley "Bucky" Harris, to pilot his club. Harris responded by leading the Senators to the world championship, earning himself a second nickname—"Boy Wonder."

Going into 1924, Harris had only four full seasons of major league experience. He was a scrappy, intelligent player, and Griffith was convinced that Harris could bring out the best in his talented team. That season, Harris became the youngest manager to win a World Series.

In the 1924 Series, Harris starred in the field, at the plate and in the dugout. He set Series records for total chances and putouts by a second baseman. He hit .333 with two homers and seven RBI, including three RBI in the Senators' 4-3, 12-inning win in Game 7. And in Game 7 he used his pitchers skillfully, starting right-hander Curly Ogden so that Giants' manager John McGraw would put left-handed Bill Terry—who was 6 for 12 in the Series—in the lineup. After just two batters, Harris brought in lefty George Mogridge in order to get Terry out of the game. Harris finished the game with Walter Johnson, who shut out the Giants in the final four innings.

Harris led the Senators to another pennant in 1925. He managed for 29 seasons after that. Only Connie Mack and John McGraw won more games as managers than Harris. And in 29 years, he never brought a team in last.

Goose Goslin

Even though Goose Goslin had a lifetime batting average of .316, with a league-leading .379 in 1928, he thought he could have done better. "You know, I'd have probably had a lifetime batting average of close to .650 if it hadn't been for one thing. When I was up there at the plate, my left eye was pretty well blocked off from seeing the pitcher and the ball," said Goslin, a left-handed hitter. Why was he seeing with only one eye? "This here nose of mine. . . . What's wrong with figuring I'd have at least doubled that average if my left eye had been able to see what was going on?"

Besides being droll, and even a bit theatrical, the Goose was an intense player. He was a .300 hitter and a 100-RBI man 11 times, from 1921 to 1938. On three different occasions he hit three home runs in a game.

Goslin's powerful right arm—he was a pitcher in the minors—almost kept him from the batting title, or even from playing, in 1928, after consecutive seasons of .344, .334, .354 and .334. At the Senators' spring training field in Tampa, a high school track meet was in progress. Goslin playfully picked up a shot and threw it hard—just as he would a baseball.

The next day his arm was dead—and it stayed dead. Manager Bucky Harris needed Goslin's potent bat in the lineup, so every time a ball was hit to Goose in left field, the shortstop ran out toward Goslin to receive a lob.

On the final day of the season, with Washington playing in St. Louis, Goslin had a lead of one percentage point over the Browns' Heinie Manush, the 1926 batting champion. In his last at-bat, Goslin needed a hit, a walk, or anything but an out. No one had ever pinch-hit for the Goose, but with the batting title on the line, Goslin decided not to bat.

"You better watch out," teammate Joe Judge said in the dugout, "or they'll call you yellow." The proud Goslin strode to the plate, but quickly fell behind 0–2. "And then it came to me—get thrown out of the ballgame. I called him [home plate umpire Bill Guthrie] every name in the book. I stepped on his toes. I pushed him. I did everything."

Guthrie didn't buy the ploy. "Okay, are you ready to bat now? You're not getting thrown out no matter what you do . . . and you better be swinging, too. No bases on balls." Goslin swung. Single to right. Batting title by one point, .379 to .378.

Heinie Manush recalled, "Goose and I played on a pennant team for Washington five years later, but neither of us ever mentioned that game in St. Louis."

That pennant team, in 1933, was the third of five for Goslin. Washington lost that Series, and with Detroit in 1934, Goose played in another losing Series. Next October the Tigers faced the Cubs, and Goslin was a hero. His ninth-inning single scored Mickey Cochrane with the winning run in Game 6, giving Detroit its first Series title.

After two more years with the Tigers, Goslin returned to the Senators in 1938. During his 57th at-bat, Goslin swung and wrenched his back. "Come on out, Goose," said manager Harris, sending in a pinch hitter, "and rest up a bit."

Besides being the first time Goose ever had been pulled for a pinch hitter, it was his last time at bat. He made the Hall of Fame in 1968.

Hitting was easy for free-swinging, free-spirited Goose Goslin. "I truly loved those fastballs," he said. "Zip they'd come in, and whack— right back out they'd go."

GOOSE GOSLIN

Outfield
Washington Senators 1921–1930, 1933, 1938
St. Louis Browns 1930–1932
Detroit Tigers 1934–1937
Hall of Fame 1968

GAMES	2,287
AT-BATS	8,655
BATTING AVERAGE	
Career	.316
Season High	.379
BATTING TITLE	1928
SLUGGING AVERAGE	
Career	.500
Season High	.614
HITS	
Career	2,735
Season High	201
DOUBLES	
Career	500
Season High	42
TRIPLES	
Career	173
Season High	20
HOME RUNS	
Career	248
Season High	37
TOTAL BASES	4,325
EXTRA-BASE HITS	921
RUNS BATTED IN	
Career	1,609
Season High	138
RUNS	
Career	1,483
Season High	122
WORLD SERIES	1924-1925
	1933-1935

Goose Goslin's only hitless game of the 1925 World Series came in Game 2, when the Senators and Pirates wore black armbands in honor of Christy Mathewson—one of baseball's most beloved stars—who died hours after Game 1. Goslin hit .308 in the Series overall, but Pittsburgh won in seven.

Boston's Smoky Joe Wood (near right) and Johnson squared off in some memorable pitching duels, yet each claimed the other was the superior pitcher. Johnson said "there's no man alive that can throw harder than Joe Wood," while Wood countered by calling Johnson "the greatest pitcher who ever lived."

In the 1925 World Series, Senators center fielder Sam Rice batted leadoff against the Pirates and hit .364. But Washington couldn't overcome shortstop Roger Peckinpaugh's eight errors, and lost in seven.

possession of the record only a short while, however, for a little later in the season Boston's Smoky Joe Wood matched it. Strangely enough, the modern NL record for consecutive wins by a pitcher in a single season was also set that year when Rube Marquard of the Giants posted 19.

The high-water mark for the Big Train was the 1913 season, when he almost single-handedly hauled the Senators into the unaccustomed stratosphere of second place. He won 36 games and lost only seven that year for a league-leading .837 percentage. He completed 29 of those games, pitched 55 consecutive scoreless innings, tallied 243 strikeouts and 11 shutouts, and compiled a magnificent ERA of only 1.09—all league-leading figures.

In 1920 Johnson's string of 20-game seasons came to an end. He was sidelined with the only sore arm of his career and won a mere eight games while losing ten and pitching only 143 innings. He was 32 that year, and it looked as if the Big Train was heading for the scrapyard. He bounced back, winning 17, 15 and 17 again over the next three seasons, but for the first time he was giving up more hits than innings pitched, and his ERAs soared to 3.51, 2.99 and 3.54.—decent marks, but hardly vintage Walter Johnson.

In 1924 everyone expected a continuation of the Subway Series that had been running since 1921. The Giants did their part, taking an unprecedented fourth straight pennant for McGraw, but Babe Ruth and the Yankees got derailed somewhere along the line. Steaming into the station two games ahead of them were the heretofore hapless Washington Senators under their new wonder-boy manager, 27-year-old Bucky Harris. It was Washington's first pennant ever. And chugging along was the Big Train himself, 36 years old now, but with a 23-7 record, an ERA of 2.72, and leading the league again in strikeouts and shutouts. It was just like the old days, only better, because for

Going into the 1924 World Series, Giants manager John McGraw led the Senators' Bucky Harris in managing experience 25 years to one. The rookie won in seven.

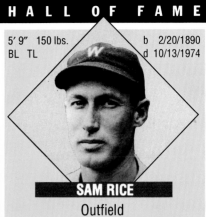

In April 1912, after several unsuccessful attempts to become a pro ballplayer, Sam Rice was devastated when his entire family—parents, siblings, wife and two children—was killed by a tornado. He rambled across the country working odd jobs, then joined the Navy, and in 1915, hooked up with the Washington Senators.

Rice became a complete player. A lifetime .322 hitter, he had a 20-year career that included hitting streaks of 31, 29 and 28 games, and six 200-hit seasons. He struck out just once every 33.7 at-bats, tenth on the all-time list.

Nicknamed "Man O'War" after the famed racehorse, Rice stole 351 bases in his career, including a league-leading 63 in 1920. His speed and strong throwing arm were well suited to the spacious power alleys of Washington's Griffith Stadium, and his 278 career assists rank 13th all time.

Rice is remembered for his controversial catch in Game 3 of the 1925 World Series against Pittsburgh. The Senators led 4-3 in the eighth when Rice leaped into the stands to catch a drive by Earl Smith. He disappeared among the fans, and ten seconds went by before he appeared with the ball. Umpire Cy Rigler ruled it a legal catch.

Rice retired in 1934, 13 hits short of the magic 3,000-hit mark. At the age of 70, he still hadn't been elected to the Hall of Fame, but he wasn't complaining. "Don't feel sorry for Sam Rice," he said. "If he deserved to be in there, he would be." Three years later, by a unanimous vote of the Veterans Committee, he was.

a change he played with some serious teammates. Goose Goslin batted .344 and knocked in 129 runs; Sam Rice hit .334, Joe Judge .324, and solid performances came from shortstop Roger Peckinpaugh, third sacker Ossie Bluege and catcher Muddy Ruel.

Washington went wild. While everyone was happy to see the Senators up from the doormat, most of the sentimental outpouring was for gentle, modest, humble, uncomplaining Walter Johnson, who had labored so tirelessly and so effectively for so many bitter seasons. The rest of the nation had a grin on its face, too, for the stench of the O'Connell-Dolan affair had rubbed off on the rest of the Giants, and fans almost everywhere were wearying of the New York stranglehold on their favorite sport. Besides, if anyone deserved a break from fate it was certainly good old Walter Johnson, a man who didn't drink, didn't smoke, and came closest to cussing when he ripped out a salty "Goodness gracious sakes alive!"

The Big Train had waited 18 summers for a chance to pitch in the World Series, but things did not go well for him in Game 1. Nervous and obviously not at his best, he gave up two runs in the 12th and lost, 4–3, to Art Nehf and a cast of seven future Hall of Famers.

Washington took Game 2 in another thriller. The Giants scored twice in the top of the ninth to tie the score at 3–3, only to have Peckinpaugh knock in the winning run with a two-bagger in the Senators' last at-bat.

With the action moving to New York, the Giants won Game 3, 6–4. Then Washington evened the Series, 7–4, on a big day at the plate by Goslin, who went 4 for 4 with a home run, and knocked in four runs. Johnson started Game 5, but his storied fastball was no mystery to the Giants. They whacked him for 13 hits and a 6–2 victory. With the New Yorkers now ahead in games,

Giants first baseman George Kelly led all players with seven runs scored in the 1924 World Series. The most dramatic was the tying run in the top of the ninth in Game 2. All 5' 9" and 150 pounds of Washington catcher Muddy Ruel went flying when the 6' 4", 190-pound Kelly came sliding in.

3–2, the odds were pretty big that old Walter Johnson had lost his chance to rack up a World Series win.

Back in the nation's capital, the Senators staved off elimination as curveballer Tom Zachary outpitched Nehf for his second victory, 2–1, with both Washington runs scoring on a clutch single in the fifth by manager Harris. Now the stage was set for the seventh game—and what a game!

Washington jumped off to the lead on a home run by Harris. The Giants tied the score in the sixth on a sacrifice fly by Irish Meusel, then picked up two more runs on errors by Judge at first and Bluege at short. McGraw's men were ahead 3–1 and smelling another world championship when destiny came careening out of the wings and took over the stage. In the bottom of the eighth the Senators had the bases loaded with two out. Harris slapped a ground ball down to third. It was an easy chance for 18-year-old Freddie Lindstrom, playing in his first Series. But the ball hit a pebble and bounced high over his head into left field. Two runs scored and the game was tied. Delirious Washington fans threw confetti, newspapers, their hats and even their coats onto the field. The game was held up until the commotion died down, and then McGraw sent Art Nehf in to put out the fire.

In the top of the ninth the crowd rose in riotous welcome as Walter Johnson emerged from the bullpen and began the long, dramatic walk to the mound. It wouldn't be accurate to say he was the Big Train of old, but neither had his epitaph been written. He was in trouble in the ninth as Frisch tripled with one out, but he struck out Long George Kelly and got Meusel on a grounder.

He was in trouble in the tenth, walking the first batter, but he struck out Travis Jackson, then closed out the inning by starting a snappy double play.

It was the Senators' first World Series, and fans turned out in record numbers for the 1924 Series opener at Washington's Griffith Stadium (opposite). Temporary bleachers in left field allowed 35,760 fans in, but also helped fly balls reach the seats as Giants Bill Terry and George Kelly both homered to left to spoil Walter Johnson's Series debut, 4–3.

The Giants outscored the Senators 27–26 overall in the 1924 World Series, but Muddy Ruel (far right) scored the run that really counted. It came in the 12th inning of Game 7—as Giants catcher Hank Gowdy watched in dismay—and won the Series for Washington.

After winning the 1924 World Series, things got pretty cushy for the Senators. But manager Bucky Harris didn't let them rest on their laurels, and Washington rode a late-season spurt to the 1925 pennant, finishing 8½ games ahead of second-place Philadelphia.

He was in trouble in the 11th—big trouble. Heinie Groh, pinch-hitting for Hughie McQuillan, singled. Lindstrom laid down a perfect sacrifice bunt to move Billy Southworth, running for Groh, to second with only one out. But Johnson got Frisch to flail three times at empty air, sent Ross Youngs to first on four intentional balls, and sent Kelly to the same place on three strikes, that making three outs and first being Kelly's position.

He was in trouble again in the 12th as Irish Meusel led off with a single to right, but he fanned Hack Wilson, got Jackson on a ground ball and Hank Gowdy on a fly.

In the bottom of the 12th, a remarkable sequence of events began to unfold, a dramatic scenario seemingly directed by some unseen hand. With one out, Muddy Ruel lifts an easy pop foul behind the plate. Giants catcher Gowdy, trying to line up the ball, circles and steps on his mask, losing both his footing and the ball. Accepting the heaven-sent reprieve, Ruel promptly lines a vicious double down the left field line.

With a storybook finish within reach—the chance to win his own game—Johnson comes to bat. It doesn't happen. He sends an easy grounder to Jackson at shortstop. But Jackson kicks the ball, and Johnson and Ruel are both safe at first and second. Earl McNeely steps into the batter's box and raps a sure double-play grounder to third. The hand reaches in again and does a one-two number on the kid third sacker. As Lindstrom crouches, the setting sun blinds him. And then, as if to make sure of what is about to happen, the ball once again hits a pebble—maybe the same one that did the dirty deed in the eighth inning—and hops like a thing possessed over the kid's head and into left field. Meusel comes in and fields the ball cleanly. But Ruel, running as he never ran before in his life, has crossed the plate with the winning run!

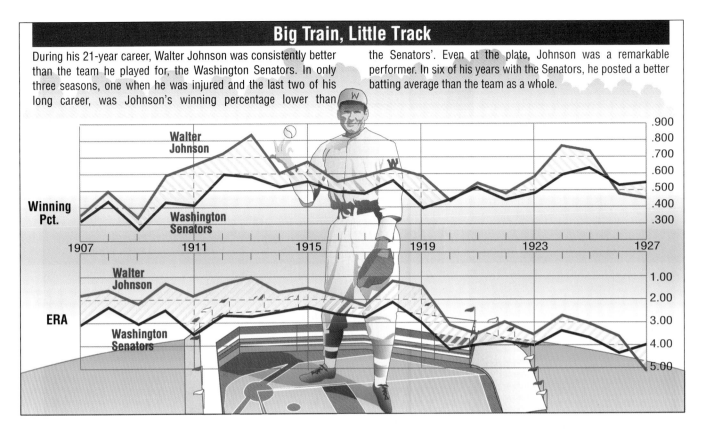

Big Train, Little Track

During his 21-year career, Walter Johnson was consistently better than the team he played for, the Washington Senators. In only three seasons, one when he was injured and the last two of his long career, was Johnson's winning percentage lower than the Senators'. Even at the plate, Johnson was a remarkable performer. In six of his years with the Senators, he posted a better batting average than the team as a whole.

Winning Pct.

Walter Johnson

Washington Senators

1907   1911   1915   1919   1923   1927

.900
.800
.700
.600
.500
.400
.300

ERA

Walter Johnson

Washington Senators

1.00
2.00
3.00
4.00
5.00

Was fate working for the beloved Walter Johnson, or against the hated John McGraw? That was Muggsy's last pennant year, and the second time in a dozen years that he had to swallow bitters as untimely errors snatched a championship from his grasp. On the other hand, the rest of the country had been rooting unashamedly for the old Big Train to come through, and the mellow feeling from dusty hamlet to big city was that the Series belonged to Johnson, then and forever, as a reward from On High.

If confirmation of that belief was necessary, it came after the game from losing pitcher Jack Bentley, who had a simple explanation for the series of weird events he had just been a party to. This is what he said: "The good Lord just couldn't bear to see a fine fellow like Walter Johnson lose again."

Washington drew an encore in 1925, the first and last time the team won pennants back to back. It was also Walter Johnson's 12th and last 20-game year, and the first time since teammate Bob Groom won 24 in 1912 that he was joined by another 20-game winner. The welcome addition was spitballing Stanley Coveleski, unloaded by the Indians. That pitching combination—a pair of old-timers—backed by some solid stickwork from the rest of the team, brought the Senators in 8½ games ahead of Connie Mack's rejuvenated Athletics.

In the National League, the hard-hitting Pirates broke McGraw's spell, squelching his hopes for a fifth consecutive flag. That was the year Pittsburgh compiled a team batting average of .307 with an awesome lineup: first baseman George Grantham, .326; shortstop Glenn Wright, .308; third baseman Pie Traynor, .320; catcher Earl Smith, .313; and outfielders Kiki Cuyler, .357, Max Carey, .343 and Clyde Barnhart, .325.

Teenager Fred Lindstrom played third base for the Giants in the 1924 World Series, because regular Heinie Groh had injured his knee late in the season. Groh watched from the bench as two bad-hop grounders bounced over Lindstrom's head to score the tying and winning runs in Game 7. "It was Fate, that's all," Groh said. "Fate and a pebble."

In 1924, when Walter Johnson finally got to pitch in a World Series, Senators' fans showed their appreciation by buying the Big Train his own Lincoln and presenting it to him before Game 1.

For a while during the 1925 World Series, it appeared that the force that had been operating for the Senators the year before—call it destiny, divine intervention, or lady luck—was still on the job. Johnson won the first game, 4–1, with a superb performance, allowing only five hits and striking out ten batters. He came back in Game 4 and pitched a six-hit shutout, winning 4–0 thanks to a three-run homer by Goslin and a solo blast by outfielder Joe Harris. That gave Washington a 3–1 edge in games, and no team had ever come back from that kind of deficit to win the Series. But that's when the juice ran out for Washington.

The Pirates took the next two games to even the Series. For the crucial seventh game, manager Bucky Harris went to his meal ticket, handing the ball to Johnson. The game was played in a steady downpour, but Commissioner Landis was reluctant to order a postponement, since it was already October 15 and more rain was forecast for the next day. Working from a mound so muddy it provided almost no footing, old Walter staggered into the eighth inning, hanging on like a bulldog to an early Washington lead. Then, with the skies already opened, Kiki Cuyler broke the Big Train's heart with a bases-loaded double, and the Pirates won, 9–7.

Perhaps it was just destiny evening things out. "We were still ahead seven to six," said Goose Goslin, "when Kiki Cuyler hit a ball . . . they called fair, and that won the game for Pittsburgh. It wasn't fair at all. It was foul by two feet. I know it was foul because the ball hit in the mud and stuck there. The umpires couldn't see it. It was too dark and foggy."

Harris should have gone to his bullpen when he saw Johnson being pummeled for 15 hits, 11 of them extra bases, but maybe it was the right thing to do to let the old war-horse go down giving it his best shot.

From 1930 to 1932 Johnson managed the Senators to three straight seasons with 92 or more wins but couldn't crack the dominance of the A's and Yankees. He went to Cleveland in 1933, and his replacement, Joe Cronin, led the Senators to their last pennant.

Johnson was elected to the Hall of Fame in 1936, then tried to politicize his fame with a run for the U.S. Congress as a Republican from Maryland in 1940. He lost.

"In 1925," wrote Glenn Dickey in *The History of American League Baseball,* a man who had called many a ball and strike on Johnson, umpire Billy Evans "was not assigned to the umpiring crew, so he was writing for a newspaper syndicate. As he left the press box that day, tears were streaming down his cheeks. Walter Johnson had that kind of effect on people."

The Senators finished above .500 in four of the next six years, although Walter Johnson's winning ways diminished. He closed out his 21st season for Washington in 1927, with five wins, six losses, and a broken leg—smashed by a batted ball. After an apprentice year managing Newark, New Jersey, in the International League, Johnson went back home to manage the Senators from 1929 to 1932. The best he could do was a second-place finish in 1930, the year his beloved wife Hazel died.

Johnson managed the Cleveland Indians for the better part of three seasons—1933 to 1935—but again failed to bring home a pennant winner. In 1936 he was named one of the five charter members of the Hall of Fame, and three years later ended his baseball career with a one-year stint as the radio voice of the only major league team he ever played for—the Washington Senators. ⏸

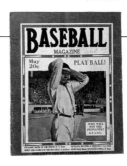

Relief at Hand

During the 1923 season, the Washington Senators won 75 games and finished in fourth place. In 1924 Washington fielded virtually the same team, yet won 92 games, the American League pennant and the World Series. The Senators did have a new manager in Bucky Harris, but on the field there was only one significant addition—Firpo Marberry, baseball's first great relief pitching specialist.

Although pitchers were once expected to play nine innings like everyone else, using a pitcher mainly in relief was far from new by 1924; it's just that no one had ever played the role quite as well as Marberry. Before 1924 Senators owner Clark Griffith had used relievers more than most. In 1923 Allan Russell pitched in relief 46 times, and led the AL with nine relief wins and nine saves.

In truth, the *save*—which, in broad terms, signifies that a relief pitcher has preserved an existing lead—didn't exist as a recognized statistic until 1960, when Chicago sportswriter Jerry Holtzman suggested that saves are a more accurate gauge of a reliever's performance than wins and losses. After the new statistic was adopted in 1961, saves in prior seasons were calculated retroactively.

In 1924, behind the three aging Senators' starters—Walter Johnson, George Mogridge and Joe Martina—Russell was less effective. The relief role fell to the hard-throwing Firpo Marberry, whom Griffith had found on a scouting trip to Arkansas the year before. His 11 wins, 3.09 ERA and record-setting 15 saves that year led the Senators to their first pennant.

Marberry had little more than a blazing fastball, but that was enough for a couple of innings late in the game. Games at Washington's Griffith Stadium began at 4:00 p.m., so by the time Marberry came in it was twilight and, for hitters, the toughest time of day. Marberry was the prototype of today's relief aces—hurlers with a one- or two-pitch repertoire that hitters can catch up with over the course of nine innings, but not in short stints. "He couldn't keep the pace through a whole game," Senators catcher Muddy Ruel said of Marberry. "He was invincible for two or three innings."

The Giants' John McGraw was another of the earliest managers to use specialists in relief. McGraw's Giants and Griffith's Senators led their respective leagues in saves on their way to pennants in 1924. Marberry continued his fireman duties in the World Series against the Giants that year, and saved two games. But in Game 7 Marberry gave way to Walter Johnson for the final four innings of the Senators' 12-inning win.

Marberry's performance had given other managers something to think about. He followed up his record-breaking 1924 season with 15 more saves in 1925, another pennant-winning season for Washington. All 55 of Marberry's appearances in 1925 were in relief, and then in 1926 he saved 22 games, breaking his own record.

In 1920 major league pitchers completed 57 percent of the games they started. By 1929 complete games were down to 48 percent. The relief revolution was building, and thanks largely to Marberry, what had been considered a fad early in the century was becoming an integral part of the game.

Senator owner-manager Clark Griffith (left) was an early believer in a well-rested pitching staff. In 1905, when Griffith managed the New York Highlanders, they were the first staff to pitch fewer than 100 complete games. In the 1920s, as owner of the Senators, Griffith had the best reliever the game had ever seen—Firpo Marberry (below). In 1926 Marberry's total of 22 individual saves was higher than any team's total.

Radio Waves

Harold Arlin, a 26-year-old Illinoisan, sat in a ground-level box seat on August 5, 1921, in Forbes Field, home of the Pittsburgh Pirates. He was surrounded by pieces of bulky equipment and was talking into what looked like an old fashioned telephone. The instrument had, in fact, started life as a telephone, but engineers at Pittsburgh station KDKA had converted it into a microphone. With it, Harold Arlin was describing the baseball game between the Pirates and the Philadelphia Phillies. The game ended with the Pirates winning, 8–5, and Arlin went into the record books for announcing the first radio broadcast of a baseball game.

This was not the first broadcast of a sports event. That happened on April 11, 1921, when Florent Gibson, sports editor of the Pittsburgh *Post,* described over KDKA the lightweight boxing match between Johnny Ray and Johnny Dundee at Pittsburgh's Motor Square Garden. But Arlin, a Westinghouse foreman during the day and a KDKA studio announcer at night, went on to other play-by-play triumphs—the Davis Cup tennis matches at the Allegheny Country Club and, in the fall, the football game between Pitt and West Virginia. Before long, Arlin was rewarded by KDKA with expanded responsibilities and a grand title: "the first full-time radio announcer in the world."

When KDKA, an offspring of Westinghouse Electric and Manufacturing Company, went on the air November 2, 1920, with its first broadcast—the

A painting celebrating the marriage of baseball and radio graced the May 1924 cover of Scientific American. *That year WMAQ in Chicago became the first station to air every home game of its teams, the White Sox and the Cubs.*

DAMON RUNYON

He was a war correspondent, a columnist, and an author of short stories, poetry and screenplays. But for 12 years, Damon Runyon, the man called by one writer "the prose laureate of the semi-literate American," wrote about baseball.

Runyon shunned the customary inning-by-inning narrative of game stories in favor of more colorful descriptions of the game's situations and personalities. He often buried the score of a game deep in the story, but his prose was so elegant that no one cared, and he was so popular that his byline ran above the story's headline.

While covering the 1919 World Series for the New York *American,* Runyon wrote that White Sox pitcher Dickie Kerr was "too small for a pitcher . . . too small for too much of anything, except, perhaps, a watch charm." He called Otis Crandall, a relief specialist with the Giants from 1908 to 1913, "the doctor of sick ballgames." The tag stuck, and Otis Crandall became Doc Crandall.

Runyon had his first stories published at 13. He joined the *American* in 1911, and for 12 years was a beat writer with the Giants and the Yankees. Perhaps his most famous piece of baseball writing was his description of Casey Stengel's romp around the bases on the way to his inside-the-park home run that won Game 1 of the 1923 World Series for the Giants. In 1923 Runyon wrote: "The baseball land teems with tales of the strange didoes cut by Casey Stengel."

With Harold Arlin's broadcast of a Pirate game over Pittsburgh station KDKA on August 5, 1921, baseball entered a new era. "No one had the foggiest idea, the slightest hint of an inkling, that what we'd started would take off like it did," he said.

Warren G. Harding-James M. Cox presidential election returns—radio was still very much a novelty. Station KQW in San Jose, California, made its first broadcast in 1909, and had a regular schedule by 1912. Station 2ZK of New Rochelle, New York, broadcast music regularly in 1916, and WWK in Detroit was on the airwaves early in the fall of 1920. Crystal sets were the order of the day. Listeners used bulky earphones to pick up the tinny sounds of the few programs being broadcast, suffering the pain of excessive static. Loudspeakers capable of enough volume for groups of people to hear had not yet come off the drawing boards.

Early broadcasters, like pioneers in any endeavor, were bedeviled by near-calamities that seem like slapstick comedy today. For its first six months, KDKA broadcast from a tent pitched on the roof of a Westinghouse plant in East Pittsburgh. One day a passing locomotive coughed up a cloud of pitch-black smoke that engulfed the studio and covered everything with soot, including, at the high point of her aria, a renowned and elegantly gowned soprano. One hot summer night, a tenor, reaching for the high C in his aria, inhaled a moth—swarms were attracted to the studio lights—and nearly choked. Broadcast baseball had its white-knuckle moments, too. "Sometimes the transmitter worked," Arlin pointed out, "and sometimes it didn't. And sometimes the crowd noise would drown us out."

Another near-calamity occurred when the Yankees were in Pittsburgh for an exhibition game and the great Babe Ruth agreed to say a few words to the radio audience. Arlin, sure he had thought of everything, handed the Babe the prepared text and introduced him. Ruth froze. "All of a sudden," Arlin said, "this big, talkative, garrulous guy—he can't say a word. He's struck mute. I mean, this radio thing was just so new. So I grab the speech

and now *I'm* Babe Ruth. I'm reading the script and there's the Babe, trying to compose himself, smoking a cigarette and leaning against the wall. And you know something? We pulled it off. I sign off and Babe Ruth hasn't made a sound." As icing on the cake, KDKA received letters praising the resonant fullness of the Bambino's voice.

In the beginning, Arlin noted, "our guys at KDKA didn't even think baseball would last on radio. I did it as a one shot project, a kind of addendum to events we'd already done . . . And, quite frankly, we didn't know what the reaction would be—whether we'd be talking into a total vacuum or whether somebody would actually hear us."

What no one realized fully at the time was that radio and sports—not just baseball—were made for each other. The postwar frenzy for entertainment was leading to the golden age of sports, and radio came along at just the right time. For years the nation's newspapers, once they realized the grip that sports had on the American psyche, had held sports fans captive. You want to know the scores? Who won the fight? Who hit the home run? Who passed to whom for a touchdown? How the Babe did yesterday? What the odds are on the race tomorrow? Who got traded and who got sent down and who's on the injured list and who's on first? Go down to the corner and buy the daily paper.

Now, all of a sudden, the sports fan had instant gratification. Here was KDKA in Pittsburgh again, using its imagination and broadcasting the day's baseball scores as they came in on teletype. And here was young David Sarnoff, general manager of the new Radio Corporation of America, with a dream: broadcasting a blow-by-blow account of the world's heavyweight title bout between champion Jack Dempsey—the Manassa

The comic strip featuring sportswriter Ring Lardner's Jack Keefe first appeared in the Milwaukee Journal *in 1922. Lardner created the satiric characterization of a smart-aleck ballplayer in short stories for the* Saturday Evening Post *in 1914. Later published as a novel,* You Know Me Al *is recognized as a baseball classic.*

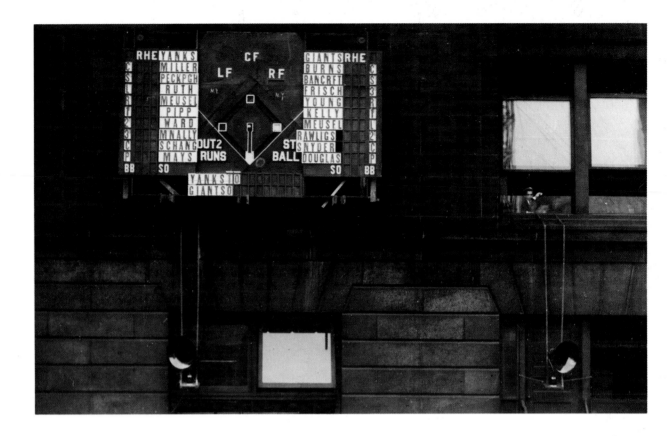

In 1921 most fans still were getting their baseball news from their local paper. In Cleveland, the Plain Dealer *kept fans on top of the game with an up-to-date scoreboard outside the newspaper's building.*

Mauler, more popular than the president of the United States—and Georges Carpentier, the glamorous French challenger. No backroom brawl, this, but a real *international* event!

The fight was scheduled for July 2, 1921, in the wooden bowl at Boyle's Thirty Acres in Jersey City, New Jersey, and Sarnoff had a problem—no equipment. He called in Major J. Andrew White, editor of a magazine named *Wireless Age.* White borrowed a transmitter that General Electric had just built for the Navy but hadn't yet delivered. He talked officials of the Lackawanna Railroad into stringing an aerial between their two experimental wireless towers in nearby Hoboken, New Jersey. He persuaded the railroad's Pullman porters to let him convert the galvanized shack they used for changing into their uniforms into a temporary studio. And he tapped two radio technicians, Harry Walker and J. O. Smith, to serve as his technical hands.

On the night of the fight, White sat at ringside, Sarnoff in the next chair, talking into a telephone. In Hoboken, Smith took down the information and then relayed the blow-by-blow description into the studio microphone. This was a time when "remotes," on-the-spot radio coverage, were almost unknown. Across the metropolitan area served by WJY Hoboken, approximately 300,000 crystal sets and one-tube receivers were tuned in, and it was Smith's voice the audience heard describing how the challenger broke his thumb against the champ's jaw, and how Dempsey's sledgehammer blows drove Carpentier into the canvas in the fourth round.

The first broadcast re-creation of a baseball game hit the airwaves the following October, when the Giants and the Yankees met in the Polo Grounds in the first Subway Series. Two East Coast stations—WJZ in Newark, New Jersey, and WBZ in Springfield, Massachusetts—had joined the

Westinghouse network, which linked KDKA by direct line to the Polo Grounds. In western Pennsylvania, KDKA's broadcast area, listeners caught the eminent columnist of the New York *Tribune,* Grantland Rice, earphones clamped to his head under the ever-present fedora, as he called the action into a microphone. Listeners in the Newark and Springfield areas, however, had to be satisfied with a re-creation.

This was, nonetheless, a historic event. The broadcast was set up by WJZ, operating from the roof of a factory in Newark out of a tin-shack studio furnished in storage-room style—moth-eaten rugs, nondescript chairs and tables, a rented phonograph, a battered piano, and lots of imagination. From the press box in the Polo Grounds, Newark *Call* reporter Sandy Hunt telephoned the plays to Thomas H. Cowan, WJZ's 37-year-old program supervisor. Cowan converted Hunt's report into a verbal play-by-play for his audience, working without scorecard, press guides, spotters, statistics, or any other aids of modern announcers. "Guys like Cowan . . . " said an admiring Ken Coleman, voice of the Red Sox in later years, "all they had were their ears and, even more than that, their brains. It put such an emphasis on imagination."

Radio, like that other technological marvel, the motorcar, was really catching on. A newspaper revealed in 1922 that "more than 3 million American homes now possess at least one radio." As the World Series approached that year, Charles W. Horn, chief engineer of WJZ, prevailed upon Western Union to lease its telegraph wires, establishing a link between Newark and the Polo Grounds. For the first time, World Series games were to be broadcast live to listeners in the New York metropolitan

The Golden Age of Sportswriting

Not for nothing was it called baseball's golden age. Baseball in the 1920s was, in many ways, baseball at its very best—hit-and-run hustlers going head to head with the new breed of power players.

It was a golden age for sportswriters, too. Before radio and television, before night games, there were two ways for fans to get their baseball. The fortunate few went to the games; the rest of the country read their newspapers. And what a choice they had. Sportswriting in the twenties was an art form unto itself, with a style and jargon that hasn't been equalled since.

Take the lyrical Damon Runyon, for example, who later made his way into the literary world with classics like "The Idyll of Miss Sarah Brown," which became the basis for the Broadway musical "Guys and Dolls."

It is the cool of the season.

There is much babble of the pennants. Who will win 'em? Why? No, no! Yes, yes!

It is all very bewildering, and confusing. One instinctively turns away to seek a sequestered spot to rest the fevered brain.

We wander in the backwash of the National League events, and suddenly come upon a restful picture. Here are the Boston Braves, sitting quietly in seventh place, and letting their feet dangle over into the cooling waters of the last hole.

Yes, sir, it is certainly soothing to find the Boston Braves after all this pennant chatter. It was very soothing to the Giants up at the Polo Grounds yesterday afternoon, when they got home from the pulling and hauling at Pittsburgh to find the Boston Braves.

It was like getting back to the old fireside of a Christmas eve to find the stockings stuffed full of candy and peanuts. The Giants casually beat the Boston Braves by a score of 7 to 2, and dated 'em up for another meeting over in Beanburg next week.

New York *American*,
September 4, 1920

Or Ring Lardner, famous for the exploits of bench-warmer Jack Keefe in his classic "You Know Me Al," covering the 1927 World Series in the New York World *for the city folks with his parody of down-home bumpkins:*

Jess Barnes pitched better than Bob at the start and not so good at finish. The way Jess pitched to Ruth did not seem to rouse unanimous enthusiasm amongst the bugs in the grandstand. Slow balls is what Jess feeds the Babe and the reason for same is because Babe dont hit slow balls out of the ball park. If Jess did not feed the Babe slow balls when he knows he cant hit slow balls so good, why that would make Jess a 1/2 wit and when he does feed the Babe slow balls, why it shows he is thinking. That is why the crowd hoots him for pitching slow balls, because the average baseball bug hates to see anybody think. It makes them jealous.

Well friends today is another day and may the best team win as I often say to Mother which is what I call the little woman when I am in a hurry and cant think of her name.

Paul Gallico, later famous as a novelist, like Lardner delighted in the use of sarcasm in his newspaper articles:

The jackrabbit ball is with us again. For the benefit of the uninformed, the jackrabbit ball is a baseball that the other side is slugging something scandalous. This felony is discovered annually by some ball team that has just been through a frightful shellacking. When the Yankees pasted the Washington Senators, 12–1 and 21–1, it was discovered suddenly that someone had sneaked the lively ball into the yard. No explanations were offered why it was that when the Yankees hit the ball it turned into a jackrabbit, while every time the Senators touched it up it was nothing but the good old-fashioned beanbag. The jackrabbitting was very onesided.

While the magnates swear that it is the same old baseball that our whiskered forefathers batted around, the inference is that at dead of night the under-secretary of the club owner sneaks to a private telephone, summons the manufacturer, and bids him pour a little strychnine or digitalis into the old apple to make its heart action quicken. The factory gets out the ball bearings, the block rubber, and the go-juice, and the home run epidemic follows. This is known as commercializing baseball and jeopardizing the lives and limbs of the players.

New York *Daily News,*
July 7, 1927

With Babe Ruth and the Yankees dominating the decade, that team made for good copy, and there was little a reader could do to escape it. Heywood Broun wallowed in purple prose lauding the Bambino in the 1923 World Series:

For the first time since coming to New York, Babe achieved his full brilliance in a World Series game. Before this he has varied between pretty good and simply awful, but yesterday he was magnificent.

Just before the game John McGraw remarked:

"Why shouldn't we pitch to Ruth? I've said before and I'll say again, we pitch to better hitters than Ruth in the National League."

Ere the sun had set on McGraw's rash and presumptuous words, the Babe had flashed across the sky fiery portents which should have been sufficient to strike terror and conviction into the hearts of all infidels. But John McGraw clung to his heresy with a courage worthy of a better cause.

In the fourth inning Ruth drove the ball completely out of the premises. McQuillan was pitching at the time, and the count was two balls and one strike. The strike was a fast ball shoulder-high, at which Ruth had lunged with almost comic ferocity and ineptitude.

Snyder peeked at the bench to get a signal from McGraw. Catching for the Giants must be a terrific strain on the neck muscles, for apparently it is etiquette to take the signals from the bench manager furtively. The catcher is supposed to pretend he is merely glancing around to see if the girl in the red hat is anywhere in the grandstand, although all the time his eyes are intent on McGraw.

Of course the nature of the code is secret, but this time McGraw scratched his nose to indicate: "Try another one of those shoulder-high fast ones on the Big Bum and let's see if we can't make him break his back again."

But Babe didn't break his back, for he had something solid to check his terrific swing. The ball started climbing from the moment it left the plate. It was a pop fly with a brand new gland and, although it flew high, it also flew far.

When last seen the ball was crossing the roof of the stand in deep right field at an altitude of 315 feet. We wonder whether new baseballs conversing in the original package ever remark: "Join Ruth and see the world."

New York *World,*
1923

Sometimes sportswriters were even moved to poetry. But unlike the others, who used the form to praise athletic prowess, Runyon claimed he needed it to save space:

The Sporting Ed. says, "Cut 'er short!
There's not much space to-day for sport.

"Between the ads,
Between the news.
All excess words I must refuse."

So short it is.
Quite short you see.
Two ball games at the old P.G.

The Pirates won.
The Giants won.
Scores: Three to one, and four to none.

The Sporting Ed. says:
"That'll do."
The box scores tell the rest to you.

New York *American,*
September 17, 1920

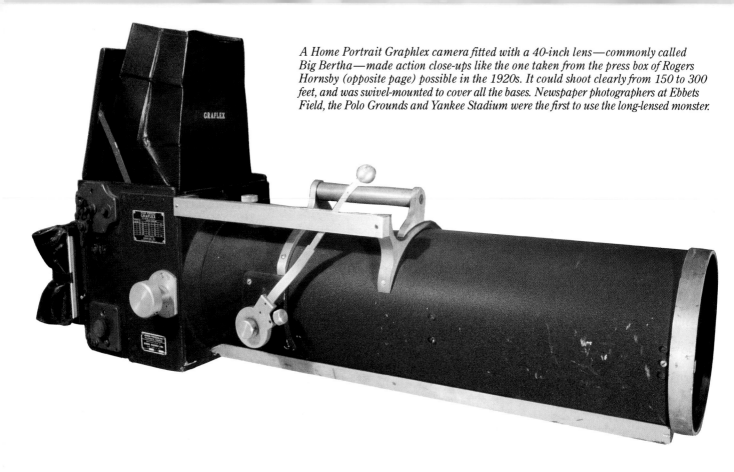

A Home Portrait Graphlex camera fitted with a 40-inch lens—commonly called *Big Bertha*—made action close-ups like the one taken from the press box of Rogers Hornsby (opposite page) possible in the 1920s. It could shoot clearly from 150 to 300 feet, and was swivel-mounted to cover all the bases. Newspaper photographers at Ebbets Field, the Polo Grounds and Yankee Stadium were the first to use the long-lensed monster.

area. If the public wasn't already agog, boldface advertisements in the newspapers fanned the flames:

> Hear the crowd roar at the World Series games with Radiola. Grantland Rice, famous sports editor of the New York *Tribune,* will describe every game personally, play by play, direct from the Polo Grounds. His story, word by word, as each exciting play is made by the Yankees or the Giants, will be broadcast from famous Radio Corporation-Westinghouse Station WJZ.
>
> There's an R.C.A. set for every home and every purse. As low as $25. Prepare for the big event by buying your R.C.A. set from your nearest dealer and ask him for the Radiola Score Sheet.

The historic first game was treated by the usually staid *New York Times* with similar flamboyant enthusiasm:

> Radio for the first time carried the opening game of the World Series, play-by-play, direct from the Polo Grounds to great crowds throughout the eastern section of the country. Through the broadcasting station WJZ, Grantland Rice related his story direct to an invisible audience, estimated to be five million, while WGY at Schenectady and WBZ at Springfield, Mass., relayed every play of the contest.
>
> In place of the scorecards and megaphones of the past, amplifiers connected to radio instruments gave all the details and sidelights to thousands of enthusiasts unable to get into the Polo

Grounds. Not only could the voice of the official radio observer be heard, but the voice of the umpire on the field announcing the batteries for the day mingled with the voice of a boy selling ice cream cones.

The clamor of the 40,000 baseball fans inside the Polo Grounds made radio listeners feel as if they were in the grandstand. The cheers which greeted Babe Ruth when he strode to the plate could be heard throughout the land. And as he struck the ball, the shouts that followed indicated whether the Babe had fanned or got a hit even before the radio announcer could tell what had happened.

Radio was a marvel, no doubt about it, and more than one shrewd businessman was cudgeling his brain to come up with a way to make money from it. The idea of selling air time for advertising hadn't yet arrived. Most stations were offshoots of companies like Westinghouse, RCA, General Electric and AT&T, which were in the business of manufacturing, among other things, radios. The main object of the stations, therefore, was to stimulate the sale of radio sets. They succeeded admirably, and for a period the manufacturers had trouble meeting the demand.

The first sets weren't exactly cheap, either. Westinghouse produced the first "popular-priced" home radio receiver in 1921: the price—not including headset or loudspeaker—was $60. Better technology brought prices down over the next few years, and the number of dedicated listeners and broadcasting stations boomed. By 1927 it was estimated that every third home in the country had a radio, and with a market like that sitting out there,

A native Bostonian, Fred Hoey became the voice of both Boston teams—the Red Sox and the Braves—in 1925. Boston baseball was mediocre, but Hoey became a star. Ken Coleman, a later voice of the Red Sox, said, "On the air, Fred was *Boston baseball."*

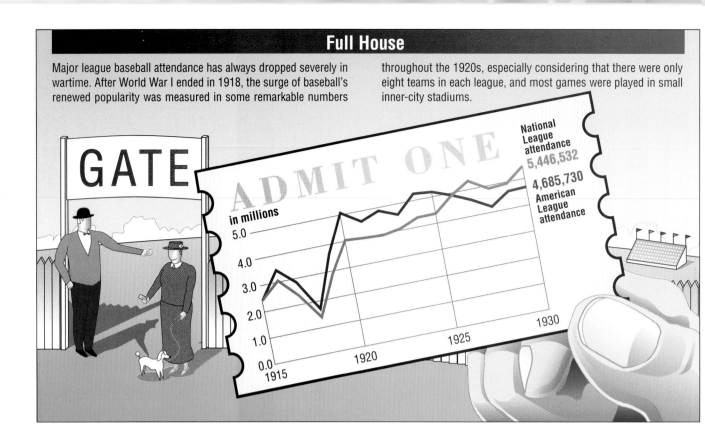

Full House

Major league baseball attendance has always dropped severely in wartime. After World War I ended in 1918, the surge of baseball's renewed popularity was measured in some remarkable numbers throughout the 1920s, especially considering that there were only eight teams in each league, and most games were played in small inner-city stadiums.

the brain cudgelers found a way to make money. Radio advertising became big business, and sponsors like Dodge, Listerine, Wrigley, Studebaker and Gillette welcomed the opportunity to huckster their products to the invisible millions.

Meanwhile, back on the baseball beat, a radio star was being born: "The greatest announcer we ever had," Red Barber said. His name was Graham McNamee. He had been raised in the Pacific Northwest and had come to New York City with his divorced mother. There he took piano and singing lessons, and by 1923 had done well enough in recitals to have started a scrapbook of reviews. But he yearned for something else.

One day in May, on lunch recess from jury duty, the young baritone strolled up lower Broadway and into the two-room, fourth-floor studio of station WEAF, recently formed by AT&T. When he walked out a half hour or so later, he was an employee—the station's "utility infielder"—at a salary of $30 a week.

Three months later, McNamee got his first big assignment, using his rich timbre from ringside to describe Harry Greg's conquest of Johnny Wilson for the world middleweight championship. He did so well that station manager Sam Ross gave him the chance of a lifetime—to team with Grantland Rice in the 1923 World Series, the climactic third consecutive encounter between the Yankees and the Giants. Rice was to do the play-by-play, with McNamee supplying the "color."

That's how it went over the first two games. But in the fourth inning of Game 3, Rice, who felt more comfortable with a pencil in his hand, got tired of holding the microphone and turned the whole works over to McNamee. In a

Not only did radio bring fans live action in their living rooms, it delivered live interviews, like this one in 1924 with interim Giants manager Hughie Jennings (left) and Braves manager Dave Bancroft.

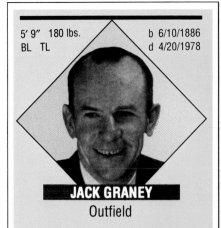

5' 9" 180 lbs.   b 6/10/1886
BL TL   d 4/20/1978

JACK GRANEY
Outfield

On the field, Jack Graney was completely unremarkable. On the air, he was a star.

In 14 years as a left fielder for Cleveland, Graney hit .250. His only claim to fame was that he was the first major leaguer to score a run off pitcher Babe Ruth.

But in 1932 Graney became the first former player to turn broadcaster. Graney had it tougher than most, since his radio career began long before broadcasters traveled with teams. Instead, Graney had to recreate away games from reports received by telegraph, using canned crowd noise and props to simulate the crack of the bat. His experience as a player, combined with his flair for drama, helped make him a master of the art form. His broadcast partner at WHK in Cleveland, Jimmy Dudley, said, "You didn't find many more accurate than Jack. You didn't find *any* more enthusiastic."

Graney disliked the broadcasting vehicle—re-creating games—that made him famous. "It was a dizzy job and more than once I'd wake up in the middle of the night in a nervous fright over what had transpired in the enclosed studio the night before."

In 1934 Graney was the first former player to broadcast a World Series. He retired 20 years later, after calling the 1954 World Series sweep by the Giants over the Indians.

box seat, surrounded by the biggest crowds in baseball history, armed with a scorecard and a saucer-shaped carbon microphone, McNamee used his "throaty, bursting" voice to draw verbal pictures of Ruth's three home runs, Bob Meusel's record-setting eight runs batted in, Frankie Frisch's spectacular fielding, and Casey Stengel's immortal bowlegged gambol around the bases. He talked himself right into the heart of America. In the week following the close of the Series, more than 1,700 complimentary letters were delivered to WEAF.

McNamee was the hottest thing in a hot new medium, and he made the most of it. He covered the big events in all the major sports, as well as some minor ones, and became known as the "father of sports broadcasting." He showed his versatility by doing political conventions, foreign coronations, and concerts. He entered the country's living rooms every week announcing "The Major Bowes Original Amateur Hour" and Ed Wynn's "The Fire Chief."

He became a celebrity himself, as much a part of the event as the event itself. When it rained during the 1923 World Series and his suit got soaked, that was news. He made the papers once more when he dropped a thermos of coffee and soaked his suit again, a gaffe that generated a flood of commiserating letters. Letters? The 1,700 he received after his baptism of fire in the 1923 Series were but a drop; there were 50,000 in the bucket after he covered the 1925 World Series.

Reporting live events, however, he often sacrificed accuracy on the altar of contrived excitement. Ring Lardner once wrote: "I don't know which game to write about—the one I saw today, or the one I heard Graham

By 1927 New York broadcaster Graham McNamee (above, right) was so popular that ballplayers clamored for his autograph. Here Waite Hoyt, who pitched in seven World Series, poses with McNamee, who broadcast 12.

McNamee announce as I sat next to him at the Polo Grounds." Not surprisingly, newspaper writers disliked and envied McNamee, and the new medium. "This was an era," wrote Robert Smith, "when the newspaper reporter was an earth-bound deity, gathering free hats, suits of clothes, meals without charge, and even more fleshly tributes, for printing, under any pretext whatever, the name of some stage or screen actor or of a store, restaurant, petty crook, big politician or professional athlete." Today we call it clout, and nobody who has it is happy seeing somebody else cutting into it.

Similar worms of jealousy and fear gnawed at the innards of the nation's newspaper moguls. The American Newspaper Publishers Association warned its members that advertising on radio would result in the splitting of advertising budgets and a corresponding dilution of revenue for the print media. Things got so bad for a while that many newspapers refused to carry radio logs in their pages, and some even decreed that the word "radio" was never to appear in their news columns.

But America was in love with its new toy, and there was no stopping the affair. Broadcasting stations were springing up all over the land, and soon there even were regular radio broadcasts at night! Wireless was still a novelty, and stunts captured listeners—interviews with flagpole sitters were good stuff, and who would want to miss the thrilling sound of a soprano trilling in the cabin of a monoplane several thousand feet above the city? Sports, with their ready-made excitement, were big, too. In 1925 WJZ began announcing baseball scores every 15 minutes, every afternoon. And by the same year, all home Cubs and White Sox games—not just scores—were being broadcast in Chicago by WMAQ, and in Los Angeles, which wasn't even in the major leagues, by KHG.

Grantland Rice was baseball's first multimedia star—adding the 1921 World Series play-by-play to his illustrious credits as a sportswriter—but his elegant prose was ill suited to the immediacy of radio. After surrendering his mike to McNamee during Game 3 of the 1923 World Series at Yankee Stadium, Rice went back to his typewriter and his job as sports editor of the New York Tribune.

Month by month, season by season, the list of stations dedicating afternoon air time to baseball grew. It didn't happen quickly or easily, for economic reasons—fear that fans would not buy tickets if they could listen for free at home. When a breakthrough did occur, there were limitations: only home games were aired, that being considered a form of advertising, and some clubs banned the wireless on Sundays and holidays, when the biggest crowds were expected. Re-creation of away games by an announcer sitting in the studio receiving brief pitch-by-pitch details from a Western Union telegrapher developed into a fantasy art form, limited only by the availability of sound effects and the announcer's imagination.

Except in New York: an agreement by the city's three clubs—Yankees, Giants and Dodgers—banned live broadcasts and even wire re-creations after 1932 right through the Depression to 1939, when the irascible Trolley Dodgers jumped the tracks and finally gave New Yorkers home-team baseball they could listen to at home. ◑

The Lively Ball
in the Lively Arts

Ballplayer gets girl . . . ballplayer gets kidnapped by evil gamblers who want him to throw the big game . . . ballplayer refuses to dishonor national pastime, escapes evil gamblers, gets to ballpark just in time to hit game-winning home run . . . ballplayer gets girl again.

In the 1920s, this was a popular variation on a familiar Hollywood theme as two national passions—baseball and movies—discovered each other. Though few were big hits and scarcely any are remembered today, 17 movies about baseball were released in the decade.

Before the twenties, films involving baseball were newsreels of actual events, and it wasn't until 1911 that first baseman Hal Chase starred in a dramatic film, "Hal Chase's Home Run." In 1916 the usually dour Ty Cobb was immortalized on celluloid in "Somewhere in Georgia," in which he escapes his kidnappers and arrives at the big game on the back of a mule. One critic called it "absolutely the worst movie I've ever seen."

In the 1920s, on the heels of the Black Sox scandal, film producers increasingly used baseball as a dramatic backdrop. The most common plot revolved around attempts to persuade, threaten or trick a player into throwing a game. The player always refused, and managed to outwit the gamblers and swindlers who threatened his life, or—in at least one case—to reveal his checkered past.

Other baseball movies were straightforward comedies or romances. Some starred actual ballplayers, most notably the biggest star of all, Babe Ruth. The Babe made his feature film debut in 1920 in "Headin' Home," a comedy-drama in which Babe plays a country bumpkin who wins the girl and saves the day as a member of the New York Yankees. In 1927 the Babe got decent reviews in "Babe Comes Home," the story of a tobacco-chewing slugger who falls in love with the team's laundress. He stops chewing in order to save the relationship, but like Samson without his hair, becomes a patsy at the plate. With the pennant on the line, the Babe's lady fair rushes to the park, hurls him a plug of tobacco, and with a chaw in his cheek, he hits the game-winning home run.

Most of the movies were silent, though late in the decade sound was added. "Warming Up," the story of the world champion Green Sox, was Paramount's first effort with sound effects and a musical score. The studio's inexperience showed, however, and one critic noted that the crack of the bat came before the pitcher had released the ball.

An exception to the decade's simplistic baseball movies was the critically acclaimed "Slide, Kelly, Slide." Former player Mike Donlin was technical adviser, and Bob Meusel, Irish Meusel and Tony Lazzeri played themselves. The story is about pitcher Jim Kelly—played by William Haines—an egotistical hero who shrinks down to size when Mickey, the team's mascot, is rushed to the hospital after being hit by a taxi. Kelly is struggling on the mound in the deciding game of the World Series when Mickey is wheeled into the ballpark, inspiring Kelly to pitch a shutout and win the game with a homer in the ninth. The film has, for its time, an unusually fresh sense of humor, built largely around Kelly's ego. When told he's been suspended for his conduct, Kelly replies, "So is the Brooklyn Bridge." And when a girls casts her dark eyes in his direction, he says, "Hold tight, boys. Eve's tossing me the apple."

In a 1917 film, The Pinch Hitter, *Glenn Hunter played a shy college student picked on by his fellow students. He's taken on as the baseball team mascot, but when the team runs out of players in a crucial game, the coach sends him in to pinch-hit. Predictably, he hits a home run and becomes the campus hero.*

Babe Ruth got a chance to relive his 1920s career *playing himself in Samuel Goldwyn's* Pride of the Yankees, *a 1942 film based on the life of Yankee first baseman Lou Gehrig. Yankees Bill Dickey, Bob Meusel and Mark Koenig also appeared in the film.* Painted People *(below) was a baseball love story filmed in black and white.*

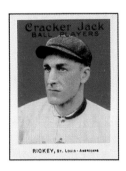

Cracker Jack
BALL PLAYERS

RICKEY, St. Louis - Americans

From Bushes to Farms

The story is told of a St. Louis Cardinals' scout driving down a country lane one day in the 1920s. A rabbit burst out of the brush, and hot behind the rabbit came a strapping, barefooted youth in tattered bib overalls. The boy caught the cottontail just as it was about to disappear into the weeds on the other side of the road. Jamming on his brakes, the astonished scout cried out, "What you doin', boy?"

"Huntin' rabbits," the youth replied.

"Is that how you *always* hunt rabbits?"

The young fellow looked surprised. "Is there any other way?" he asked.

With that, the scout whipped out a contract and said, "Boy, how'd you like to play for the Cardinals?"

It never happened, of course, but the story is a parable that explains the Cardinals' scouting theory: if a boy is swift of foot and strong of arm, sign him; you can always teach him the other stuff later. It also confirms baseball's respect for the Cardinals' vast farm system during the 1920s and 1930s. But it wasn't always that way.

When Branch Rickey began building the Cardinals' minor league empire, some baseball people were outraged at his attempts to corner the market on young talent. Others laughed, considering the idea preposterous. The second group didn't know Rickey well enough to believe he could pull it off; the first group knew him better—and was afraid he could.

Shortstop Charley Gelbert (opposite, left), a product of Branch Rickey's Cardinal farm system, beat out a bunt against Brooklyn in the heat of the 1930 pennant race. St. Louis won the September 16 game, 1–0 in ten innings, and took the NL lead for good.

Rickey ignored baseball's color line long before he brought Jackie Robinson into the majors in 1947. In 1905 Rickey (top row, far left) was coach at Ohio Wesleyan University, and his team included Charles Thomas (second row, center), one of the first black players in college baseball.

The cigar-chomping, Bible-quoting Rickey has been credited with originating baseball's farm system. But in the 1890s, John T. Brush owned not only the Cincinnati Reds but the Indianapolis club in the Western League, the high minor circuit that Ban Johnson later redesigned into the American League. Brush brought up players from Indianapolis to stock the Reds, which is the most important way traffic runs in a farm system. What Rickey did 30 years later was to pick up the concept and make it a success. If the idea was around for three decades, how come no one else grabbed it and ran? It's easier to answer why Rickey did: He was smart—maybe even a genius.

Wesley Branch Rickey was born on an Ohio farm in 1881 to Jacob Franklin Rickey—well known for his piety and his wrestling ability—and Emily Brown Rickey. The couple had five children, three of whom survived infancy: Orla Edward, Wesley Branch (named for John Wesley, founder of Methodism) and Frank. Young Wesley, nicknamed "Weck," loved sports, rooted noisily for the Cincinnati Reds, and formed a respectable baseball battery with Orla, catching the fast stuff his southpaw brother burned in.

Except on Sundays. Sundays were for big breakfasts and a day spent rejoicing in the Lord. On such a day Weck made to his mother the vow that later became famous—that he would never drink, use profanity, or defile the Lord's Day by engaging in work or sports.

After absorbing the schooling available locally, Weck got a teaching job. With $35 a month in wages, he bought a bicycle, making the 36-mile round trip to work in all kinds of weather; he gave some of his earnings to his parents, put some aside for college, and with whatever was left over bought

From the tail end of the 1913 season through 1915, Rickey managed the struggling St. Louis Browns—six days a week. He came from a devout Christian family, and promised his mother he'd never go near a ballpark on Sunday. Third baseman Jimmy Austin was the Browns' Sunday manager.

books. He taught himself Latin, rhetoric and higher mathematics. In 1900, at 18, he had saved enough to start college—$100 or so—and hopped a train for Ohio Wesleyan University. He waited tables, stoked the school furnace, and paid part of his fees by playing semipro baseball and football.

A double fracture of his leg in 1902 ended his football career, and he thereafter concentrated on baseball. Still in college, he broke into organized ball with Terre Haute of the Central League; he moved to Dallas in the Texas League, and then up to the Cincinnati Reds. Refusing to play on Sundays, he was sent back to Dallas, bought by the White Sox, and traded almost immediately to the St. Louis Browns. He played only one Browns' game in 1905, but came back the next year to bat a respectable .284 in 64 games. That year he married his childhood sweetheart, Jane Moulton, and earned a bachelor of arts degree, having been awarded a bachelor of literature in 1904. Besides playing ball and studying, he served as athletic director and football coach at Ohio Wesleyan.

The Browns traded Rickey to the New York Highlanders in 1907, his last season in the majors as a player. He missed spring training because of university commitments, and batted a puny .182 for the season. Worse, he was dead last in fielding percentage among catchers and outfielders in the American League, committing nine errors in one 11-game span. But the straw that broke the back of his modest career as a big league catcher occurred on June 28, 1907, against Washington: 13 bases were stolen on him, a record for a nine-inning game. Not surprisingly, the Highlanders released him at the end of the season.

In 1909, suffering from tuberculosis, he took a six-month rest cure at Saranac Lake in the Adirondack Mountains. On the mend, he enrolled in the

It wasn't until Rickey got out of uniform and into the front office that he became a success. He hit .239 in 343 career at-bats as a catcher for the Browns and Highlanders, and in ten years as a manager for the Browns and Cardinals, the best he could do was third place. In 1926, Rickey's first full year as an executive, the Cardinals won it all.

6' 190 lbs.   b 7/22/1893
BR TR   d 8/5/1978

POP HAINES
Pitcher

In 1919 the St. Louis Cardinals were short on cash and talent. Manager Branch Rickey wanted to buy the contract of Jesse Haines, a hard-thrower who'd gone 21–5 in the American Association, but the team didn't have the $10,000 purchase price. So Rickey persuaded the team's band of stockholders to borrow the $10,000 from a bank in order to get Haines, who immediately became a solid workhorse for the Cardinals.

As a 26-year-old rookie in 1920, Haines was one of just five NL pitchers to go over 300 innings. He also lost 20 games, despite a 2.98 ERA. When Haines developed a darting knuckleball to go with his blazing fastball, he became a consistent winner, and went on to compile a 210–158 lifetime mark. Haines sparkled in the 1926 World Series against New York, but is best remembered for the game he couldn't finish. He shut out the vaunted Yankee sluggers on just five hits in Game 3, and took a 3–2 lead into the seventh inning of Game 7. But with the bases loaded and his fingers bleeding, Haines was relieved by Grover Cleveland Alexander, who saved the game and the Series for St. Louis.

Haines' greatest thrill came in the 1930 Series, when he outdueled the great Lefty Grove 3–1 in Game 4. Haines went to the bullpen later in his career, and pitched until he was 44, thereby earning the nickname "Pop."

After spending 1920 with a semipro team, Specs Toporcer was sold to Syracuse of the International League. Syracuse became a part of Rickey's Cardinal farm system two months later, and Toporcer opened the 1921 season as the majors' only bespectacled infielder.

University of Michigan Law School and completed the three-year course in civil law in two years. He coached the baseball team at Michigan, and in 1913 became a part-time scout for the Browns. Colonel Bob Hedges, owner of the Browns, was so impressed by Rickey's reports that he hired him as assistant presidential secretary—little enough he could do for the man who brought in a young player named George Sisler from the University of Michigan team. When Rickey tried to deliver his young star to the St. Louis club, he discovered that Pittsburgh already had Sisler's signature—on a contract he had signed in high school.

Rickey, who had just won his law degree, hied himself down to Manchester, Ohio. After spending a pleasant hour or so swapping hunting and fishing stories with Sisler's parents, Rickey pointed out that the papers young George had signed were neither valid nor binding, since he was underage at the time. At that point Rickey whipped out a St. Louis Browns' contract and got Mr. Sisler's signature on the dotted line. The Pirates raised a stink, but Rickey and the Browns were upheld by the National Baseball Commission, still firmly under the thumb of AL president Ban Johnson.

Late in 1913 Hedges made his youthful assistant the manager of the Browns, then in last place, 39 games in back of Connie Mack's Athletics. Rickey led the Browns to a fifth-place finish in 1914, a modest improvement. On August 25, in a game the Browns were losing to the Athletics 7–0, Philadelphia catcher Ira Thomas, a former teammate of Rickey's on the Highlanders, started twitting him about taking a turn at the plate. Soon all the players were in on the fun, even the dignified Connie Mack. Rickey agreed when Ray Bressler, Philadelphia's 19-year-old southpaw pitcher,

Billy Southworth proved that Rickey was as good at trading for talent as he was at developing it. Southworth was 33 and had already played for four teams when Rickey traded for him in 1926. The veteran outfielder responded with a .317 average in 99 games, then hit .345 in the Cardinals' World Series win over New York.

swore he would not throw any curveballs. And so, leaning over the plate in dubious anticipation, he watched three fat fastballs go by for strikes. "My last turn at bat in the major leagues," he said later, "taught me that nothing is gained by distrusting your fellow man."

In 1915 even Sisler couldn't help the Browns; they ended in sixth place, with only 63 wins. It wasn't all the players' fault. Rickey, possessor of three university degrees, often forgot that many of his men were at best semiliterate. He sermonized endlessly about baseball theory and the game's intricacies until the bewildered players fell asleep with their eyes open. And the man they dubbed the "Ohio Wheezeleyant" cried out in frustration, "I wonder why a man trained in the law devotes his life to something so cosmically unimportant as a game!"

This frustration was an everyday burden for Rickey, especially with Jay Hanna "Dizzy" Dean. "I'm a man of some intelligence," he once complained to his family, "I've had some education, passed the bar, practiced law. I've been a teacher, and I deal with men of substance, statesmen, business leaders, the clergy. Then why, *why,* do I spend my time arguing with Dizzy Dean?" After Dean dropped by his office still one more time to prop his feet up on the desk and "talk country," Rickey exclaimed in his profanity-eschewing way, "Judas Priest! If there was one more like him, I'd get out of the game!"

Happily for baseball, he didn't get out; the game was in his blood. In 1916 Colonel Hedges sold the Browns to Phil Ball, who already owned the St Louis Federal League franchise. Loud and abrasive, with a picturesque vocabulary, Ball also owned an ice business. The consumption of ice was tied to the consumption of beer and booze, and Ball was solidly on the side of the

Catcher Pickles Dillhoefer came to the Cardinals from Philadelphia in a 1919 trade. Rickey, himself a smallish catcher in his playing days, may have had a soft spot for the 5′ 7″, 154-pound Dillhoefer.

The Birth
of the Negro Leagues

The 1920s were the golden age of baseball, but the glitter was tarnished by the fact that some of the best players in the nation weren't allowed to play in the major leagues. While black athletes were forced to play in segregated leagues, the decade was a golden one for Negro baseball as well.

From the time blacks were forced out of organized baseball in the late 1880s until the formation of the first Negro league in 1920, black professionals played on a number of independent teams that survived by barnstorming—playing against white semiprofessional, professional and off-season major league all-star teams. Teams were at the mercy of white booking agents who controlled access to stadiums, and efforts to organize black teams into stable leagues failed in 1906 and 1910.

Then along came Andrew "Rube" Foster. A great pitcher in his playing days, Foster became a player-manager in 1907, and by 1911 he was part-owner—with John Schorling, the son-in-law of Chicago White Sox owner Charlie Comiskey—of the Chicago American Giants. The Giants had the best players, the best salaries and the best stadium of any Negro teams in the 1910s, and the best manager. Foster was considered a baseball genius, and is given credit for teaching Christy Mathewson his famous fadeaway pitch, as well as for being a con-

fidante of New York Giants manager John McGraw.

Foster's vision extended far beyond mere team ownership. In February 1920, tired of dependence on booking agents and bidding wars with white-owned eastern teams for top players, he and the owners of other midwestern Negro teams organized the Negro National League. The league consisted of Foster's Chicago American Giants, the Chicago Giants, the St. Louis Giants, the Detroit Stars, the Taylor ABC's, the Cuban Stars and the Kansas City Monarchs. Foster was reluctant to admit the Monarchs, a white-owned team, but he knew they were a key to the league's success.

Inspired by Foster's creation, several southern independent teams formed the Southern Negro League in 1920. The league was denied the opportunity to play lucrative exhibitions against white teams, and lost many of its top players to the Negro National League and the Eastern Colored League, which was formed in 1923 by booking agent Nat Strong.

Despite some success, Negro leagues were far from stable in the 1920s. Since barnstorming provided many teams with a large share of their income, consistent scheduling was difficult, although the NNL drew 400,000 paying customers in 1923.

Then in 1926 Foster fell ill and was forced to

retire. He died in 1930, and in the face of the Great Depression and the loss of his leadership, the NNL folded in 1931, formed again in 1933 and lasted until the major leagues integrated in the 1940s.

Before Foster's vision of a Negro National League died, it played host to a landmark achievement in the history of the game. In 1929 J. L. Wilkinson went into debt to pay for a portable lighting system for night games, thereby enabling his Kansas City Monarchs to play under the lights six years before night baseball came to the major leagues.

Today the Hall of Fame honors the best of the Negro National League, and includes such stars as Oscar Charleston, Cool Papa Bell, Satchel Paige, John Henry Lloyd, Martin Dihigo and Judy Johnson.

The 1921 Kansas City Monarchs (top) finished second in the National Negro League, and were led by Bullet Joe Rogan (middle row, far left). Rogan invented the palmball, an off-speed pitch that is thrown like a fastball but gripped deep in the pitcher's palm. A 230-pound shortstop, John Beckwith (above) played with ten negro league teams and hit .408 lifetime.

6' 185 lbs. b 2/12/1903
BR TR d 7/2/1973

CHICK HAFEY
Outfield

Chick Hafey was cursed with bad vision, bad sinuses and bad luck, but blessed with Hall of Fame talent. Despite his maladies, Hafey was one of Branch Rickey's first and best discoveries and played a major role on Cardinal pennant-winners in 1926, 1928, 1930 and 1931.

Hafey had all the tools. He hit .317 lifetime, and almost 40 percent of his hits were for extra bases. He had good speed, a better glove, and what some called the best arm of any outfielder of his era. He was something of an enigma—a shy, soft-spoken man but a tiger at the negotiating table and one of the team's top practical jokers.

Hafey came to the Cardinals as a pitcher in 1923, but became an outfielder shortly after Rickey saw him at the plate. He hit .271 in 78 games for the Cards in 1926, but was hit in the head several times during the season, and as a result had to wear eyeglasses. In 1927 he exploded for a .329 batting average and a league-leading .590 slugging percentage. Hafey signed a three-year contract in 1928, then earned every penny by averaging .337, 27 homers and 114 RBI in those three years. In 1931 he won baseball's closest batting race, edging New York's Bill Terry .3489 to .3486.

Rickey traded him to the Reds in 1932 after a contract holdout, but recognized his talent: "If Hafey had had good eyesight and good health he might have been the finest right-handed hitter baseball has ever known."

Rickey got a bargain when he bought spitballer Allen Sothoron for a waiver price of $5,000 in 1924. Sothoron led the NL in shutouts with four and the Cardinals in wins with ten.

Wets in the bubbling temperance question. His first words to Rickey were, "So you're the goddamned Prohibitionist!" With that determined, he brought in Fielder Jones, former manager of his Federal League team, as field manager and limited Rickey to various front-office duties.

Rickey and Ball didn't take to each other, but their short-lived relationship with the Browns changed the course of the game. By merging the two clubs, Ball had more players than he could use. Rickey began placing surplus players with minor league teams, and in return obtained options on other players for much less than market value. The seeds of the farm system were planted.

Across town, a syndicate of St. Louis businessmen bought the Cardinals from Helene Hathaway Robeson Britton, "Lady Bee." They kept Miller Huggins as field manager and wanted Rickey, a popular man about town, as president. Rickey was delighted; Ball was not. He matched the Cardinals' offer, and sued when Rickey opted to leave the Browns anyhow. Attorney Rickey filed a countersuit to prove that his contract allowed him to move if a better deal came along. He won and moved on.

Tied for last place in 1916, the Cardinals leaped to third the following year, behind young Rogers Hornsby batting .327, second in the NL. Rickey finessed several key trades, and he soon developed a reputation as an extremely canny trader who usually got back more than he gave up.

He also came up with ideas to improve player performance, some of which also improved Cardinal finances, and all of which were quickly copied by other clubs: he built sliding pits for players to practice baserunning, developed new plays to catch runners off base, and deployed a five-man infield. He

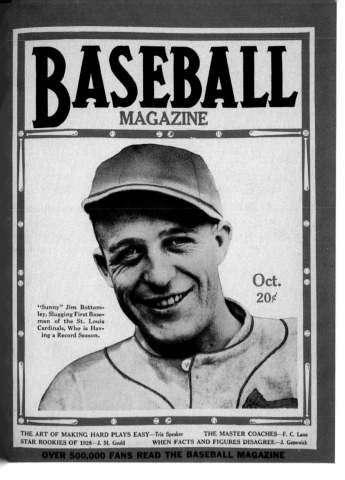

First baseman Jim Bottomley (left) was the first Hall of Famer that Rickey's farm system produced. Bottomley played for Cardinal farm teams in Houston and Syracuse before beginning an 11-year, four-pennant stint with St. Louis. First baseman Jack Fournier (above) hit .343 for the 1921 Cardinals, but was traded to Brooklyn in 1923.

brought Ladies' Day back, and formed "Knothole Gangs," distributing free tickets to poor kids, recognizing that today's youngsters are tomorrow's paying customers. And of course he inaugurated blackboard chalk-talks in which he declaimed, at length, on baseball theory to his bored players.

The Cards finished last in 1918, after the War Department's "work or fight" edict brought the season to an abrupt halt on Labor Day. Patriot Rickey entered the Army's Chemical Warfare branch, emerging as Major Rickey by the end of the war in November.

Returning to St. Louis in 1919, he found the Cardinals nearly $200,000 in debt. "We didn't even have the money to send the club south for spring training," he recalled later, "so we trained at home. We even wore the same uniforms at home and on the road. They were ragged...I had to pass up my salary to meet the payroll." He borrowed a rug from home to brighten his bare office. The bow tie that became his trademark was a necessity— "cheaper than a regular tie...it could also cover up a soiled shirt or a frayed collar."

Faced with a massive rebuilding job, Rickey appointed himself manager, and brought Burt Shotten over from the Browns to manage the team on Sundays. Players came and went as he shuffled the Cards. "We lived a precarious existence," he said. "We would trade one player for four and then sell one of them for some extra cash. We were always at a distinct disadvantage trying to get players from the minor leagues. Other clubs would outbid us; they had the money and the superior scouting machinery."

Rickey's sharp eye for talent actually worked to his disadvantage. Often, when the Cards made a bid for a good prospect in the minors, the team's owner would contact some other rich club and offer the player at a higher price, noting that Rickey was interested. Respecting Rickey's

After playing on four pennant-winners in eight years with the Giants, second baseman Frankie Frisch was dealt to the Cardinals for the legendary Rogers Hornsby. Frisch played on four Cardinal pennant-winners in the next eight years.

judgment, the other club would make a higher offer, and the Cardinals would lose another prospect. Tired of acting as a bird dog for John McGraw and other baseball fat cats, Rickey said, "That kind of thing drove me mad. I pondered long on it, and finally concluded that, if we were too poor to buy, we would have to raise our own."

Step one was to buy 18 of 100 outstanding shares of stock in the Texas League Houston Buffaloes. Quietly. That was followed—still quietly—by gaining working control of Fort Smith, Arkansas, in the Class C Western Association, and Syracuse, in the AA International League. More clubs were added, and "the Mahatma," as Rickey came to be called, even backed whole leagues. At one point the Cardinals controlled the entire player pool in the Nebraska State and Arkansas-Missouri leagues. Rickey discovered that a partial share of a minor league team led to too many conflicts. "The solution," he said, "was to own the minor league club outright."

By this time, there was no way the Cardinals' empire building could go unnoticed. At first the whole idea of a farm system feeding players to a major league club was roundly ridiculed. Muggsy McGraw, usually quick to pick up on anything that would help his Giants, called the concept a pipe dream and sneered, "It's the stupidest idea in baseball."

Muggsy was wrong. It wasn't a pipe dream—it was a pipeline. The scoffers sang a different tune as the Cardinals began to reap a rich harvest of fuzzy-cheeked young men who could run and throw and hit the ball a country mile. Rickey's method was deceptively simple: for as little as $60 a month, he signed any young fellow who showed the merest flash of talent and sent him somewhere in the Cardinals' minor league network for training. It was like

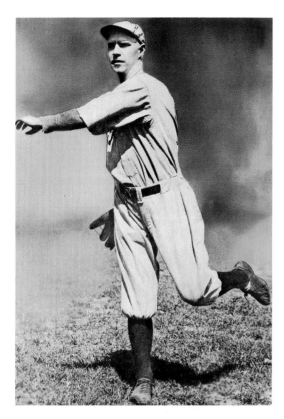

Cardinal southpaw Bill Sherdel averaged 18 wins a season from 1926 to 1928, but went 0–4 in World Series play. In 1926 he lost both of his Series starts despite a 2.12 ERA, and in 1928 he gave up two of Babe Ruth's three home runs in Game 4.

Spittin' Bill Doak was a big man in the Cardinal rotation until 1922, when his ERA ballooned from a league-leading 2.59 in 1921 to 5.54. In early 1924 Doak went to Brooklyn for pitcher Leo Dickerman in a trade that didn't help either club.

panning for gold—pick over enough pebbles, and sooner or later you come up with a nugget.

Rickey himself got involved in the search, sitting in the stands, making notes in a little black book, telling his assistants to make this boy a pitcher, this one an outfielder, this one a shortstop, regardless of the positions they wanted to play. Chick Hafey went from pitcher's mound to outfield, for example, and by the time he hung up his spikes had a career batting average of .317 and a ticket to the Hall of Fame.

Around the leagues, screams of anguish condemned "Rickey's Chain Gang" as the system began to produce a seemingly endless flow of talent. The Mahatma was able to stock the Cardinals with homegrown stars and offer *surplus* farm-bred players to other major league clubs—naturally, at handsome prices.

Then into this garden of delights glided the snake, in the person of Commissioner Kenesaw Mountain Landis. The commissioner didn't like Rickey, and he opposed the farm system from the start. A believer in local ownership and control of minor league teams, he ruled that a major league team could control only one club in each minor league. Despite arrogance and high-handed arbitrariness, Judge Landis did try to protect players from greedy club owners. One of the abuses he feared was the power of a team to keep a player, regardless of his ability, "on ice" in low-grade baseball to prevent him from getting a chance on another major league team. Landis proposed an alternative plan: cooperative support of the minor leagues by the entire body of major league baseball, with schools and tryout camps run on the same cooperative basis, and a draft at the end of each season, with the lowest club in each major league having the first choice of players.

Rickey's ability to judge and develop talent produced five Cardinal pennant-winners and three world champions in the first nine years he ran the team's front office. "Luck," he said, "is the residue of design."

With Hornsby making decisions on the field and Rickey doing the same in the front office, the Cardinals won their first pennant in 1926. The Yankees blasted a major league-high 121 homers on the way to their 1926 pennant, but Babe Ruth's four World Series homers weren't enough as St. Louis won in seven.

Sound familiar? The owners back then denounced the plan as un-American and socialist, then went their merry, patriotic way trying to do the same thing they had ridiculed, then cursed, Rickey for doing.

The 1925 season opened with the Cardinals, who had been in the league since it was created in 1876, still looking for their first pennant. The farm was beginning to bear fruit—the first graduate, Sunny Jim Bottomley, arrived in 1922 followed by Chick Hafey in 1924, both of them .300 hitters. Hornsby was doing his usual wrecking job on opposing pitchers, but the Cards were still going nowhere. The problem was Rickey. Brilliant in the front office, he just couldn't cut it as a field manager. "Too much theory and too little practice," critics said. "His players often could not understand or execute his ideas."

On Memorial Day, 1925, with the Cardinals in last place and attendance plunging, owner Sam Breadon replaced Rickey with Rogers Hornsby. It was a bitter pill for the Mahatma to swallow, for he and the Rajah, both strong-willed men, had already cemented their enmity with a no-holds-barred fistfight. Angrily, Rickey sold off his Cardinal stock, which was immediately snapped up by Hornsby, thereby adding insult to injury.

After he calmed down a notch or two—enough to admit that perhaps his cerebral approach to the game confused his players, making them "too tense, too eager"—Breadon told him, "What I'm doing for you is the greatest favor any man ever did for another. One of these days you'll see that I'm right."

They didn't have long to wait. ◑

A Minor Dynasty

Jack Dunn never managed a game in the majors, but his accomplishments in the minors were anything but bush league. From 1919 to 1925, Dunn's Baltimore Orioles not only won seven straight league championships—something no major league team has ever done—they won at least 100 games each season.

Dunn was undoubtedly one of the best baseball minds of his era. As the International League Orioles' owner-manager from 1907 to 1928, Dunn not only found and signed some of the greatest talent in the history of the game—including Babe Ruth and Lefty Grove—but he was the leading voice in support of independence for minor league teams. In 1914, faced with financial ruin because of competition from a Baltimore franchise in the newly formed Federal League—a short-lived major league—Dunn sold 19-year-old Babe Ruth to the Red Sox for $2,900. From then on he became famous for holding on to star players until he got what he considered their fair market value from major league owners. Throughout the early 1920s, Dunn steadfastly refused to sign the various agreements proposed to allow major league teams to draft minor league players. After all, his team was as good as many major league teams, and he had the gate receipts to prove it.

The Orioles opened the 1920s by winning their second International League pennant. The 1920 team, like the rest of Dunn's pennant-winners, had great pitching. Debuting on the 1920 team were Grove, who came to Baltimore halfway through the season and went 12–2 for the Orioles; Jack Ogden, who went 27–9 on his way to an International League-record 213 career wins; and Harry Frank, like Ruth a local boy, who went 25–12.

Merwin Jacobson's .404 batting average set a modern International League record, and Jack Bentley hit .371 with 20 home runs. Dunn's Orioles won 110 games that season, including their last 25 in a row, but they were just getting warm. In 1921 Baltimore got off to a slow start and was just 15–10 on May 19. The Orioles then put together a record 27 straight wins and coasted to the pennant by 20 games, winning 119 and losing 47.

While Dunn was winning pennants, major league owners were clamoring for his talented players. But Dunn was becoming a rich man and was good to his players, so most of them were in no hurry to leave Baltimore. In 1924 Grove was making $750 a month, which was more than a lot of major leaguers were paid. And in 1920, as a reward for winning the first Little World Series, the championship series between the International League and American Association champions, Dunn split up his owner's share among the players.

The ensuing pennant-winning years saw more good and great ballplayers contribute to Dunn's success, including George "Moose" Earnshaw, who went on to win 20 or more games in each of the Philadelphia Athletics' pennant years of 1929, 1930 and 1931, and Rube Parnham, who went 33–7 for Dunn's 1923 team.

In 1924 Dunn began selling off his talent, and got a record $100,600 for Grove—$600 more than Boston got for selling Ruth to the Yankees—and another $65,000 for Bentley.

Dunn won his last pennant in 1925. Though the Orioles had their eighth straight 100-win season in 1926, their string of pennants was snapped at seven. They finished second to a Toronto club that featured another fine young pitcher—Carl Hubbell.

Spirits of St. Louis

There are people who think that the seventh and deciding game of the 1926 World Series was the most dramatic baseball contest of all time, not just for the action on the field, but also because of the performance by an ancient, alcoholic, epileptic pitcher named Grover Cleveland Alexander. "I can see him yet," Cardinal third baseman Les Bell recalled, "walking in from the left-field bull pen through the gray mist. The Yankee fans recognized him right off, of course, but you didn't hear a sound from anywhere in that stadium. They just sat there and watched him walk in. And he took his time."

Grover Cleveland Alexander was never in a hurry, and especially not this day. He had pitched nine innings the day before, and he was coming into the seventh game of the World Series to face a tough young hitter with two out and the bases loaded in the bottom of the seventh inning, the score 3–2 in his favor.

The Yankee batter waiting for Alexander was rookie Tony Lazzeri, sporting a .462 season slugging average. Cardinal manager and second baseman Rogers Hornsby handed over the ball. "Okay," Alec said. "I'll tell you what I'm gonna do. I'm gonna throw the first one inside to him. Fast."

" 'No, no,' Rog said. 'You can't do that.'

"Alec nodded his head very patiently and said, 'Yes I can. Because if I do and he swings at it he'll most likely hit it on the handle, or if he doesn't hit it good it'll go foul. Then I'm going to come outside with my breaking pitch.'

"Rog looked him over for a moment, then gave Alec a slow smile and said, 'Who am I to tell you how to pitch?' "

More than a million fans welcomed the Cards home to St. Louis (opposite) after their 1926 World Series win over the Yankees. Player-manager Rogers Hornsby said, "Anybody who says he isn't nervous or excited in a World Series is either crazy or a liar."

After being dropped by the Cubs early in 1926, 39-year-old Grover Cleveland Alexander was picked up by the Cardinals and had a storybook season, ending with 2⅓ innings of shutout relief to win Game 7 of the World Series against the Yankees.

Urban Shocker's strong St. Louis connection included four straight 20-win seasons for the AL Browns from 1920 to 1923, and—after being traded to the Yankees in 1924—a loss to the Cardinals in the 1926 World Series.

There, on the mound at the same time, were two of the most famous players of the 1920s: "Old Pete" Alexander closing out a stellar career that had peaked in the preceding decade, and Rogers Hornsby riding the crest of the new power-hitting generation.

Like Ty Cobb before him and Ted Williams who followed, Hornsby was accused of "living for his next time at bat." When he stepped into the batting cage everything on the field stopped. In a literal sense, Hornsby didn't "come up to the plate" until he saw a pitch that he liked. He stood as far back in the batter's box as he could get, waited, and then strode into the ball. Few batters guarded the plate as well as he did, and nothing in the pitcher's bag of tricks mystified him. He hit everything—fastball, curve, spitter, change—and it didn't matter where it was pitched. Inside, outside, high, low, he went with the pitch, spraying hits all over the ballpark. Out of it, too. He was a line drive hitter with remarkable power. And to top it all off, he could run!

Since the American League had, in Babe Ruth, the Sultan of Swat, the National League countered with the Rajah of Swat. But there was more to the nickname that that. "Rajah" was a play on the pronunciation of his first name, but it was also a mocking reference to Hornsby's caustic personality. He was accused of being irascible, moody, petty, egotistical, too brutally frank and just downright nasty. His apologists, and he had more than a few, saw him as an honest man, up-front all the way, and outspoken, yes, but totally devoid of sham or pretense. Burleigh Grimes said, "He was a *very* good manager. Never bothered anyone. Told you exactly what he thought. I liked the guy." At the other end of the spectrum was the veteran New York sportswriter who called him "the most tactless public figure I ever met."

Even with Hornsby's great bat, the Cardinals under Branch Rickey had been going backward—from third in 1921 to sixth in 1924. In 1925, after 13 wins and 25 losses, Cardinal president Sam Breadon kicked Rickey upstairs and named Hornsby player-manager. The team responded, going 64–51 the rest of the season to finish a respectable fourth.

They continued winning in 1926. Hornsby's batting average slipped under the press of managerial duties—from .403 to .317, a poor figure for a batsman of his stature. But he got help from his teammates: Jim Bottomley hit .299 and led the league with 120 RBI; Les Bell came in at .325 with 100 RBI; Taylor Douthit and Ray Blades hit .308 and .305; veteran Billy Southworth, picked up from the Giants that summer, chipped in with .317 and 11 home runs. That summer the Cards also signed off the waiver list a grizzled, pushing-40 pitcher named Grover Cleveland Alexander, who won nine games over the rest of the season.

The combination was enough for the Cardinals to slide into first place early in September, and in a tight race they finished two games ahead of Cincinnati and four and a half in front of Pittsburgh. It was the first championship banner for the Cardinals, and St. Louis went agog. "Man, what a parade they had when we got back!" recalled Les Bell. "The train pulled in around three o'clock in the afternoon and they had a line of open touring cars waiting for us. Everybody was cheering and yelling and the ticker tape was pouring down like a blizzard. We had trouble getting out of those automobiles and into the hotel, what with everybody crowding around wanting to pat us on the back and shake our hands."

While Cardinal players and fans were preparing themselves mentally and emotionally to do battle with the redoubtable New York Yankees—hot on

In 1928—his only season with the Braves—Rogers Hornsby (right) led the NL with a .387 batting average and .632 slugging percentage. Yankee owner Jake Ruppert (above, left) tried to lure him to New York, but at the end of the season Hornsby was traded to the Cubs for five players and $200,000.

6′ 180 lbs.   b 4/23/1900
BL TL   d 12/11/1959

JIM BOTTOMLEY
First Base

Anyone who hit directly behind seven-time NL batting champ Rogers Hornsby got a lot of chances to drive in runs, and on September 16, 1924, St. Louis' Jim Bottomley went RBI crazy. With two home runs, one double and three singles, Bottomley drove in 12 runs in a 17–3 win over the Brooklyn Robins, a record that still stands.

Bottomley was a crowd-pleaser, with a constant smile that earned him the nickname "Sunny Jim." He walked with a bit of a swagger, wore his cap cocked at a jaunty angle and, before getting married late in his career, packed St. Louis' Sportsman's Park on Ladies' Day. One of the first products of Branch Rickey's farm system, Bottomley caught the Cardinals' attention with a two-homer, three-triple day for a semipro team.

In 1923, his first full season in the majors, he hit .371, second only to Hornsby. From 1924 to 1929, Bottomley averaged 126 RBI per season. He continued his remarkable string of single-day feats in 1927 with a three-triple day on June 21, and on July 15 he hit for the cycle—racking up a single, a double, a triple and a homer in a single game. In 1928 he led the NL with 31 homers, 20 triples and 136 RBI, and was named the league's MVP.

He played on four Cardinal pennant-winners, the last in 1931. In addition to his single-game RBI record, Bottomley holds the major league record of eight unassisted double plays in a season by a first baseman.

Although outfielder Ken Williams played in the shadow of Browns teammate George Sisler, he was a true slugger. In 1922 he became the second AL player to have more RBI than games played—155 in 153 games.

the comeback trail after having taken a back seat to Washington for the preceding two years—there was another group in St. Louis considerably more accustomed to the back seat. The Browns, and their diehard fans, shared the shame of being the only major league franchise, in those days of two eight-team leagues, never to have won a pennant.

Not all their seasons were totally without cheer, however. In 1922, when Rogers Hornsby was slamming the ball at a .401 pace for the Cardinals, a young fellow named George Sisler was knocking the cover off the ball for the Browns. By the time the year was over he had racked up a batting average of .420. Between them the two peerless batsmen amassed a grand total of 496 hits, and if the proud civic fathers of St. Louis had decided to hang a huge banner proclaiming their fair city the batting capital of America, no one could have disputed them.

Sisler came to the Browns in 1915, the same year that Hornsby made his debut with the Cardinals. Before that he had starred in football, baseball and basketball at the University of Michigan. Like Babe Ruth, Sisler started out as a left-handed pitcher, and was considered a pretty good one. Branch Rickey had other ideas, though. On the day Sisler, tired from traveling and rookie-nervous, joined the Browns Rickey stuck him into an out-of-reach game, saying, "Let's see what you can do in these last three innings."

As scared as he was, Sisler went out and pitched. "Did pretty good, too," he recalled later. "I gave up one hit but the Sox didn't get any runs so I figured that I was all right. Next day, though, I was out warming up and meeting more of the Browns when Rickey came over to me. He was carrying a first baseman's glove."

That wasn't the end of Sisler's career as a pitcher, for the Mahatma shuttled him between the mound, first base and the outfield. As a pitcher, he compiled a 4–4 record in 15 games with a 2.83 ERA. But he also batted .285, and Rickey figured him to be more valuable as an everyday player. The next year he settled in as a first baseman.

Sisler learned his trade at first base quickly, and so well that he has been ranked at least the equal of Hal Chase as the finest fielding first sacker in baseball history. Throw in his ability with the bat and you could make a strong case for naming him the best first baseman ever to play the game. His contemporaries called him "Gorgeous George" and "the Picture Player," and not without cause.

In 1922, the year of his .420 average—second highest ever in the American League—George Sisler led the league in four other offensive categories: 246 hits, 18 triples, 134 runs scored and 51 stolen bases. His AL record 41-game hitting streak lasted until Joe DiMaggio's great 56-game run in 1941. Not surprisingly, he was named the league's Most Valuable Player, even though the Browns didn't win the pennant—again.

But they came close! They fielded the most talented team in Brownie history that year. Besides Sisler there was Kenny Williams, a bona fide slugger, whose 39 home runs and 155 RBI led the league. Center fielder Bill "Baby Doll" Jacobson drove in 102 runs; right fielder Johnny Tobin hit .331; second baseman Marty McManus hit .312 and veteran catcher Hank Severeid batted .321. The Browns were one of the few teams ever to boast four hitters with 100 or more RBI, and overall they led the league in hitting, runs scored and stolen bases. The pitching staff was led by Urban Shocker, who posted 24 wins, and Elam Vangilder with a 19–13 record;

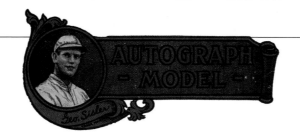

George Sisler

Branch Rickey called George Sisler "the smartest hitter that ever lived. He never stopped thinking. . . . He was a menace every time he stepped to the plate." To his teammates he was "the Picture Player." To his fans—and there were legions of them—he was simply "Gorgeous George."

George Harold Sisler could do it all. Born in Manchester, Ohio, in 1893, he was a standout pitcher in college, compiling an astonishing 50–0 mark for the University of Michigan Wolverines. He joined the St. Louis Browns in 1915 as a pitcher, one year after Babe Ruth joined the Red Sox. They both proved too valuable as hitters to be kept out of the daily lineup.

The tightly wound, 5′ 11″, 170-pounder was so talented a hitter—his lifetime average was .340—that he was quickly moved to first base, where he became a standout fielder. And he could run. Bill James claims that, at his peak, Sisler was "probably the best player in baseball with the exception of Ruth, and it was not hard to find people who felt that he was better than Ruth."

In his first four complete seasons, his batting averages were .305, .353, .341 and .352—quite a feat in the dead-ball era. In a 1917 interview with *Baseball Magazine,* which had tagged him "Ty Cobb's probable successor," Sisler said, "I cannot say that I shall ever touch the high marks that Ty has reached. A four hundred batting average is surely a big feat but . . . is not impossible to me if I get a good start and things break favorably."

A few years later, things began to "break favorably" for Sisler. In 1920 he rapped out a league-leading .407 batting average with 257 hits—still the major league record—including 49 doubles, 18 triples and 19 home runs, second in the league to Ruth. He scored 137 runs, knocked in 122, stole 42 bases and made 140 assists as a first baseman, the fourth-highest at that time.

Sisler was not a home run slugger but was more of a tactician, a spray hitter in the mold of Willie Keeler, the pint-sized batsman who used to "hit 'em where they ain't." A gentleman on and off the field, Gorgeous George was a non-smoker and a teetotaler. W. C. Fields, one of his great fans, once offered him a drink. When Sisler refused, the bulbous-nosed comedian remarked, "Even the perfect player isn't perfect in everything."

Most claim that 1922 was Sisler's best year. He had a 41-game hitting streak—only Joe DiMaggio and Pete Rose have bettered it in the modern era—and won the AL's first Most Valuable Player award with a career-high average of .420. He led the league in stolen bases with 51 and in assists for first basemen.

During the off-season Sisler developed a severe sinus infection that affected his optic nerve. Double vision caused him to sit out the 1923 season. "I never was a real good hitter again. Oh, I know I hit .345 and got 224 hits in 1925 but that never gave me much satisfaction. That isn't what I call real good hitting," said the self-effacing slugger.

When he came back, he played for seven more seasons, his batting average ranging from a low of .290 to a high of .345, with five .300-pluses in the middle. In 1930, his last year in the majors, Sisler hit .309. Not bad for a 37-year-old but a far cry from his glory years. Students of the game are tormented by the thought of what Gorgeous George would have done to the record books if he had remained healthy.

Sisler was the Browns' player-manager from 1924 to 1926. The Picture Player, undoubtedly one of the game's greatest all-rounders, was inducted into the Hall of Fame in 1939.

GEORGE SISLER

First Base
St. Louis Browns 1915–1927
Washington Senators 1928
Boston Braves 1928–1930
Hall of Fame 1939

GAMES	**2,055**
AT-BATS	**8,267**
BATTING AVERAGE	
Career	**.340**
Season High (*8th all time*)	**.420**
BATTING TITLES	**1920, 1922**
SLUGGING AVERAGE	
Career	**.468**
Season High	**.632**
HITS	
Career	**2,812**
Season High (*1st all time*)	**257**
DOUBLES	
Career	**425**
Season High	**49**
TRIPLES	
Career	**165**
Season High	**18**
HOME RUNS	
Career	**100**
Season High	**19**
TOTAL BASES	**3,868**
EXTRA-BASE HITS	**690**
RUNS BATTED IN	
Career	**1,175**
Season High	**122**
RUNS	
Career	**1,284**
Season High	**137**
MOST VALUABLE PLAYER	**1922**

Sisler was a brilliant hitter, fielder and base stealer who had his moments on the mound as well. Before being switched to first base, Sisler outpitched Walter Johnson in a 2–1 win and, in his first appearance against Ty Cobb, held him hitless in five at-bats.

Big Bats

Batting averages skyrocketed in the 1920s—the lively-ball era—giving the game's top hitters a chance to put up some astonishing numbers. The incomparable Rogers Hornsby highlighted the decade by hitting .424 in 1924.

Below are some of the top single-season averages of the decade, along with the career averages and home run totals of the players that posted them.

National League Player	Batting Average Best 1920s			Home Runs Best 1920s		
		Year	Career		Year	Career
Rogers Hornsby	.424	1924	.358	42	1922	301
Lefty O'Doul	.398	1929	.349	32	1929	113
Babe Herman	.381	1929	.324	21	1929	181
Paul Waner	.380	1927	.333	15	1929	112
Zack Wheat	.375	1924	.317	16	1922	132
Bill Terry	.372	1929	.341	20	1927	154
Freddie Lindstrom	.358	1927	.311	15	1929	103
Kiki Cuyler	.357	1925	.321	17	1925,'28	127
Ross Youngs	.356	1924	.322	10	1924	42
Lloyd Waner	.355	1927	.316	5	1928,'29	28

American League Player	Batting Average Best 1920s			Home Runs Best 1920s		
		Year	Career		Year	Career
George Sisler	.420	1922	.340	19	1920	100
Harry Heilmann	.403	1923	.342	21	1922	183
Ty Cobb	.401	1922	.367	12	1921,'25	118
Babe Ruth	.393	1923	.342	60	1927	714
Al Simmons	.392	1927	.334	34	1929	307
Tris Speaker	.389	1925	.344	17	1923	117
Joe Jackson	.382	1920	.356	12	1920	54
Goose Goslin	.379	1928	.316	18	1925,'29	248
Heinie Manush	.378	1926,'28	.330	14	1926	110
Lou Gehrig	.374	1928	.340	47	1927	493

A .247 hitter with two career home runs, Cardinal shortstop Tommy Thevenow eclipsed Babe Ruth as the hitting star of the 1926 World Series with a .417 average, one homer, five runs scored and four RBI.

the staff led the league in strikeouts, earned run average and saves.

The Browns looked good enough to win the pennant in 1922. They probably should have won it. But they lacked an inch or two of pitching depth, and when the exciting pennant race came down to the wire, the Yankees had a record of 94–60 and the Browns came in at 93–61. The burst bubble seemed to affect the fans more than the players. During the 1922 race, the Browns drew crowds that totaled 713,000—second only to the Yankees—into tiny Sportsman's Park, which at the time had a capacity of about 15,000. Nothing was the same with the Browns after that storybook year of 1922. In 1923 the fans deserted the ship and—as the fortunes of the Cardinals, stimulated by Rickey's farm system, began to rise—the Browns declined to the point where the team was playing before crowds averaging less than 1,500 per game.

But St. Louis still had the Cardinals, and in 1926 the Redbirds were NL champions. True, the Cardinals were by no stretch of the imagination a powerhouse; their 89 wins and 65 defeats gave them a pennant-winning percentage of .578, the lowest in NL history to that time. The Yankees, on the other hand, just a year away from their monstrous 1927 season, *were* a powerhouse, and nobody gave the pretenders from St. Louis much of a chance in the Series.

But it wasn't a runaway—it was a roller-coaster ride. The Yankees, behind Herb Pennock, took first blood, 2–1. The Cards took the second game, 6–2, as Alexander struck out ten men and retired the last 21 in succession. St. Louis won again, 4–0, in Game 3, with knuckleballer Jesse Haines shutting out New York and belting a two-run homer to help his own cause. Then Yankee power showed up in Sportsman's Park with the Babe blasting a

The 1926 Cardinals led the NL in runs scored, homers and slugging percentage. Their hard-hitting lineup included outfielders (from left) Billy Southworth, Taylor Douthit and Chick Hafey.

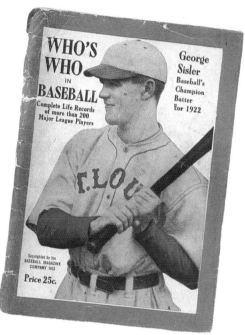

Sisler's hitting was the big story in 1922 but, over his career his speed made headlines as well. He stole home 19 times, good for a tie for sixth on the all-time list with speedsters Jackie Robinson and Frankie Frisch.

record three homers to seal up Game 4 for Waite Hoyt. Game 5 also went to the Yanks as Pennock outdueled Bill Sherdel 3–2 in a ten-inning squeaker, the winning run knocked in on a sacrifice fly from the bat of Tony "Poosh 'Em Up" Lazzeri, nicknamed for his success in advancing baserunners.

The Yankees were now ahead in games, 3–2, poised to take all the marbles and go triumphantly home. But in Game 6 Alexander ambled out to the mound for a second start, this time limiting New York to two runs while his mates, led by Les Bell's three hits and four RBI, pounded out a good imitation of a Bronx Bomber victory, 10–2.

Old Pete's best years were behind him, but there had been some grand years indeed. From 1914 to 1917 he amassed a total of 121 wins for the Philadelphia Phillies. In 1918 he went to France with the 89th Infantry Division and lost the hearing in one ear as a result of constant shelling. He also developed epilepsy, apparently from the same cause, although at the time doctors attributed the problem to his heavy drinking. Alex never denied an affection for John Barleycorn. He may not have been the far-gone alcoholic he has been painted, however. In the climate of those times, alcoholism was far more common than epilepsy, and a reputation as a heavy drinker could easily mask the physical manifestations of a much-misunderstood ailment.

Tradition, nevertheless, must be honored, and tradition says that in his 40th year, after being dumped in midseason by the Cubs as over the hill, Old Pete celebrated by winning two games in the World Series, then going out and tying on a doozy, in spite of Prohibition. Now it was Sunday, October 10, 1926, a cold, drizzly day, and Old Pete—according to tradition, at least—was huddled in a corner of the Yankee Stadium bullpen, trying to snooze his way

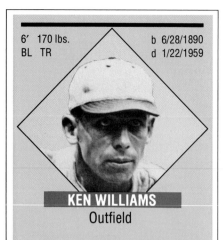

KEN WILLIAMS
Outfield

6' 170 lbs.
BL TR
b 6/28/1890
d 1/22/1959

In 1922, as St. Louis Browns first baseman George Sisler was capturing headlines with his 41-game hitting streak and .420 batting average, left fielder Ken Williams was quietly capturing the other two-thirds of the triple crown.

Williams, one of the game's first true power hitters, played in the shadow of teammate Sisler and Babe Ruth. But in 1922 he had one of finest seasons of the young lively-ball era.

As the Browns were fighting the Yankees for the pennant, Williams was on his way to breaking Ruth's stranglehold on the league's home run crown. In 1922 Williams led the league with 39 home runs—a total no one but Ruth had yet matched—and 155 RBI. And he added a few tricks the Babe hadn't performed. On April 22 he became the first AL player to hit three home runs in a single game, and on August 7 he became the first in his league to hit two home runs in the same inning. From July 28 to August 2 Williams was on fire, and set a then-major league record with at least one home run in six consecutive games.

Williams was also an excellent baserunner, and in 1922 became baseball's first 30–30 man, with 37 stolen bases to go with his 39 home runs, a feat no one else accomplished until Willie Mays in 1956.

He remained a serious home run threat for several years, finishing second to Ruth in 1923 and 1925. But in 1925 he was beaned severely, and never regained his power stroke.

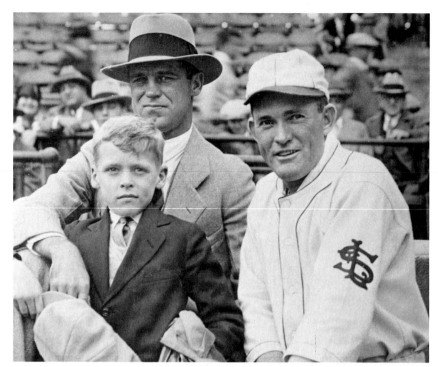

St. Louis' pair of player-managers, Sisler (top) and Hornsby (right), got together before Game 3 of the 1926 World Series. In the foreground is Sisler's son Dick, who broke into the majors in 1946. In St. Louis, where else?

through a blinding hangover during the crucial seventh game to determine the world champion of baseball.

Pitching for the Cards, Jesse Haines; for the Yanks, Waite Hoyt. In the third, Ruth unloaded his fourth home run of the Series to put New York on top, 1–0. In the fourth, St. Louis came back with three runs fashioned out of a hit by Jim Bottomley, an error by Yankee shortstop Koenig that should have been scored a hit, a dying quail pop fly that dropped in, a monstrous error by Meusel in left center, and a single by Tommy Thevenow. In the sixth, the Yankees got one back on a single by Joe Dugan and a double by Hank Severeid to make the score 3–2, Cardinals.

Haines had thrown so many knuckleballs by the bottom of the seventh that blisters were popping on his fingers—and here came the top of the Yankee batting order. Earle Combs singled, moving to second on Koenig's sacrifice bunt. Up to the plate strode Babe Ruth, with the tying run on second. Hornsby knew how to handle that threat: four intentionally wide pitches put men on first and second. Meusel followed with an infield grounder, forcing Ruth at second, Combs moving to third. Two out. Gehrig, with a .313 average in his second full season and 107 RBI, worked the count to 3–2 and drew a walk. Bases loaded. Next up, tough Tony Lazzeri, notorious for hitting with men on base. Manager Hornsby called time and waved to the bullpen. Alexander took his time getting to the mound, letting Lazzeri, the aggressive rookie, paw the earth for a while. Hornsby met Alexander at the edge of the outfield grass, stared into his eyes for a moment, and handed him the ball.

Old Pete threw eight warm-up pitches and was ready. Lazzeri stepped in. He took a ball, high and tight, then a low curve that nicked the corner for a

strike. The next pitch was up and Lazzeri took a Ruthian swing. The crowd screamed as the ball rocketed down the left field line, then groaned as it crashed into the bleachers ten feet on the wrong side of the foul pole. Old Pete passed a hand over his face, muttered to himself and stepped back on the rubber. The runners leaned away, the pitch came in, another sweeping curve that broke sharply outside. Lazzeri swung his home run swing again—and missed. *Strike three!*

Pete set the Yanks down in order in the eighth, then got Combs and Koenig in the ninth. He was one out away from winning the World Series, and the batter was Babe Ruth. Alex worked the corners—a shade too carefully, perhaps, because with the count 3–2 he walked the Bambino. The next batter was the heavy-hitting Meusel, with Gehrig bruising the air in the on-deck circle.

As Alexander reared back and delivered the first pitch, the Babe inexplicably broke for second. Bob O'Farrell, Cardinal catcher, fired the ball to Hornsby, and Ruth was out by three steps. The Cards had won the Series!

"The only dumb play I ever saw Ruth make!" screamed Ed Barrow, the Yankee business manager.

Some time later, the Babe explained the bonehead play by claiming that he was trying to get into position to score on a single by Meusel, since the way Alex was pitching it didn't look as if the Yanks were going to be able to come up with two hits back-to-back.

But right after the game his explanation was simpler. "Hell," he snorted, "I wasn't doing any friggin' good where I was!" ◖

Yankee second baseman Tony Lazzeri went about as far as he could in pursuit of a Grover Cleveland Alexander curveball, but the ball found catcher Bob O'Farrell's mitt for strike three, leaving three Yankee runners stranded in the seventh inning of Game 7 of the 1926 World Series.

Rogers Hornsby

Let's not mince words. Rogers Hornsby, perhaps the greatest right-handed hitter of all time, was a downright sonovabitch. It's 1927 and New York Giants second baseman Hornsby is having dinner with Eddie "Doc" Farrell, the team's young shortstop. A sportswriter approaches the table and asks Hornsby if he thinks the team can win the pennant. "Not," replies Hornsby, "with Mr. Farrell playing shortstop."

At the Giants' training camp that spring, Hornsby, a 12-year veteran of the majors who by now has earned the imperious nickname "the Rajah," is tongue lashing third baseman Fred Lindstrom for failing to execute a double play to Hornsby's specifications. Lindstrom explains that he's only following the instructions of John McGraw, the Giants' great manager.

"If that's the way the Old Man wants it, do it that way when he's in charge. When I'm in charge, do it my way," bellows Hornsby. "You'll do as I say. And keep your mouth shut." As if to savor the moment, Hornsby pauses, turns to the other players, and barks, "And that goes for the rest of you."

One writer noted, "He was brusque, blunt, hypercritical, dictatorial, moody and argumentative. He alienated almost everyone sooner or later." Another wrote, "Mr. Blunt thought diplomacy was a respiratory disease."

While Rogers Hornsby was definitely deficient in the charm department, he never met a letter-high fastball he didn't like, and no right-handed batter in the modern era has ever matched Hornsby's accomplishments. He won six straight NL batting titles from 1920 to 1925, plus another in 1928. From 1921 to 1925 he averaged .402. His lifetime batting average of .358 is second only to Ty Cobb's .367. His 1924 batting average of .424 has never been matched since, and barring the appearance of some miraculous superhitter, will almost certainly never be equaled.

Born on a Texas ranch in 1896, Hornsby was playing shortstop in the Texas minor leagues when he was signed by St. Louis Cardinal scout Bob Connery in 1915. "I liked him. He didn't hit very much," Connery said later, "but he could field his position and he handled himself like a ballplayer."

The Texas right-hander got off to a slow start, batting only .246 in his first year with St. Louis. His average, however, rose steadily and by 1919 he hit .318. With the arrival of the lively ball, the Rajah came into his own and unleashed one of the most spectacular hitting streaks in the history of baseball. He hit .370 in 1920 and followed with seasons of .397, .401, .384, .424, .403, .317, .361, .387 and .380. In 1922 he hit safely in 33 consecutive games; in 1931 he hit home runs in three consecutive at-bats. Hornsby played until 1937, batting .321 at the age of 41.

He was the NL home run king twice and led in doubles four times, triples once, RBI four times, and won two MVP awards. He won the Triple Crown—leading the league in batting average, home runs and RBI—in 1922 and 1925. Only 14 men have done it since 1878, and only two have done it twice—Hornsby and Ted Williams.

Hornsby hit equally well to all fields and specialized in the lightning line drive. His batting stance was unique. The 5' 11" right-hander stood

with his feet close together well back in the box, farther from the plate than other batters, and he stepped up to meet the ball. He explained, "It was impossible to hit me with a pitched ball because I was always moving with the pitch." He prided himself on judging whether a ball was a fraction of an inch inside or outside the strike zone. A teammate claimed that he "got more *fourth* strikes than any other hitter," meaning that if Hornsby let the pitch go by, the umpire was not likely to call it a strike.

Rogers Hornsby was the last man you'd want to invite to a party. But that was all right. Hornsby didn't go to parties. He didn't drink or smoke, and he didn't go to movies, either, because he was sure that sitting in a darkened theater staring at a bright light would ruin his eyesight and therefore his hitting. For similar reasons he didn't read much, except the fine print in his contracts and the racing form. His passion for baseball was rivaled only by his love of betting on horse races and playing the stock market, compulsions that got him in trouble with Commissioner Landis and gave a number of sanctimonious owners a ready excuse for getting rid of him when they could no longer abide his abrasive attitude. His compulsive gambling caused him lifelong financial woes—he was often in debt—and apparently contributed to his two divorces.

Hornsby looked on baseball as a job and approached it with a workmanlike fervor. He wasn't the type to sit around the locker room and chew over the day's events after a game. Ferdie Schupp, who played with him on the Cardinals, said, "He never talks to anybody. He just goes out and plays second base and when the game is over he comes into the clubhouse, takes off his uniform, takes a shower and gets dressed without saying a word. Then he leaves the clubhouse and nobody knows where he goes."

When he did speak, he invariably limited his conversation to baseball. "Baseball is my life. It's the only thing I know and can talk about. Some of the other fellows like to play golf in their spare time but I'm not old enough for a sport like that. I'm used to having other guys chase the balls I hit. I'll be damned if I'm going to run after a little white ball myself."

Hornsby's moody nature and bad temper led to his downfall. In 1925, his 11th year with the Cardinals, he was named player-manager. Impatient with his young players, he lost no time infuriating and alienating his teammates. He was so gifted that he couldn't understand why others didn't match up. When players complained, Hornsby shot back, "I'm running a ball club, not a popularity contest."

In four seasons, 1926 to 1929, he played for the Cards, the Giants, the Boston Braves and the Cubs, where he stayed for four years. He became Cubs' manager in 1930.

Predictably, Hornsby's managing days were also marred by his bad temper; he was unconditionally released by the Cubs two years later. Suspicious and intolerant of players and team owners alike, Hornsby continued a peripatetic existence and managed several minor league teams in the 1940s.

After his Seattle team won the Pacific Coast League pennant in 1951, he was offered a job with the St. Louis Browns working with Bill Veeck, whose father had fired Hornsby from the Cubs in 1932. True to form, Hornsby soon had the team up in arms. In the middle of the season—facing a near-rebellion—Veeck fired the hot-headed Hornsby. "It will be easier to get a new manager," explained Veeck, "than to get 25 new players."

Although Hornsby was elected to the Hall of Fame in 1942, he never garnered the public acclaim of a Ruth or a Cobb. Yet the Rajah was one of the greatest sluggers ever to play the game. As coach and trainer Clyde Sukeforth explained, "When he had a bat in his hand, he had nothing but admirers."

1926 was Hornsby's finest year as manager—he led the Cardinals to their first pennant and world championship—but it was one of his poorest years at the plate. The Rajah's batting average dropped 86 points to .317, and his homers fell from 39 in 1925 to just 11.

ROGERS HORNSBY

Second Base, Shortstop
St. Louis Cardinals 1915-1926,
  1933
New York Giants 1927
Boston Braves 1928
Chicago Cubs 1929-1932
St. Louis Browns 1933-1937
Hall of Fame 1942

GAMES	**2,259**
AT-BATS	**8,173**
BATTING AVERAGE	
Career (*2nd all time*)	**.358**
Season High (*5th all time*)	**.424**
BATTING TITLES	
	1920-1925,1928
SLUGGING AVERAGE	
Career (*7th all time*)	**.577**
Season High (*6th all time*)	**.756**
HITS	
Career	**2,930**
Season High (*5th all time*)	**250**
DOUBLES	
Career	**541**
Season High	**47**
TRIPLES	
Career	**169**
Season High	**20**
HOME RUNS	
Career	**301**
Season High	**42**
TOTAL BASES	**4,712**
EXTRA-BASE HITS	**1,011**
RUNS BATTED IN	
Career	**1,584**
Season High	**152**
RUNS	
Career	**1,579**
Season High	**156**
WORLD SERIES	**1926, 1929**
MOST VALUABLE PLAYER	
	1925, 1929

ightning

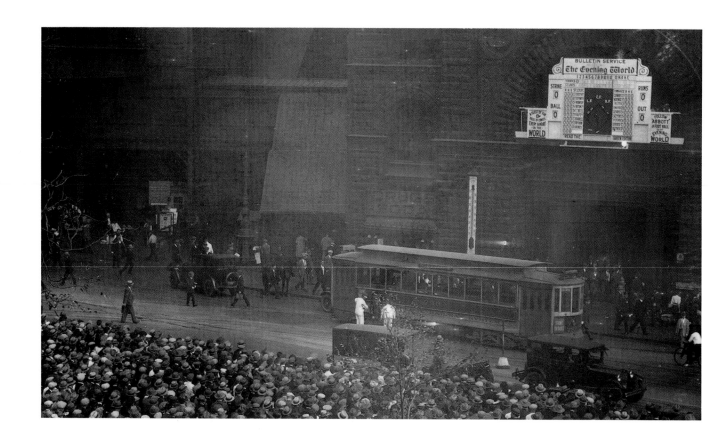

Yankee fans gather in front the New York Evening World *scoreboard for the results of Game 3 of the 1926 World Series. The crowd left unhappy, as St. Louis' Pop Haines blanked New York on five hits and the Cards won, 4–0, to take a 2–1 lead in the Series.*

The consensus among sportswriters, ballplayers and computer simulations is that the 1927 Yankees (overleaf) were indeed the greatest team ever assembled. They won 110 games, had a winning record against every other AL team, and led the league in runs scored, fewest runs allowed, triples, home runs, batting average, slugging percentage, fewest walks allowed, shutouts and earned run average.

The New York Yankees in 1918 needed a replacement for manager Wild Bill Donovan. Yankee co-owner Tillinghast L'Hommedieu Huston was all for giving the job to his buddy, Wilbert "Uncle Robbie" Robinson, fat and genial manager of the Dodgers. But Colonel Jacob Ruppert, the brewer king whose fortune fed the Yankee purse, wanted the best man available. Taking league president Ban Johnson's advice, he raided the National League and grabbed Miller Huggins, the scrawny manager of the St. Louis Cardinals.

Huggins had played 13 years for the Reds and the Cards, where he was known as "the Rabbit." He never made anybody's all-star team, and as a manager he could claim two third-place finishes, a sixth, and two lasts. When his name was announced, New York fans and sportswriters shouted *"WHO?"* and Tillinghast was aghast. The decision opened a breach between him and Ruppert that never healed, and in 1923, after trying more than once to dump Huggins, he sold his interest in the club.

But Huston wasn't the only sniper. Huggins came into town with players, fans and writers alike giving him the cold shoulder and some out actively gunning for him. He was given a sixth-place club to manage, along with some of the game's most temperamental and high-priced stars. But he took them on, even Babe Ruth, twice his size, who openly referred to him as "the Flea." Eventually he won them over. Even the Babe, who spoke for all of them, said, "He was a great guy, was Hug." But that was later. In 1921, when the Yanks won their first AL pennant, all the credit went to Ruppert's checkbook. Ditto in 1922 and 1923, although by now some perceptive souls were grudgingly admitting that the deals Hug was engineering were turning out to be pretty good. Then the first championship machine began to misfire. The

Yankees slopped to second place in 1924 and plummeted to seventh in 1925. Boom! Crash! End of era. Red Sox picked clean. End of Yankee dynasty.

Not so! In 1926 the Yankees confounded the experts, coming out of nowhere to win the pennant, then losing the World Series by a whisker to the Cardinals. Finally "the Mighty Mite" began to get some credit. "Six out of eight regulars on that team," wrote John Kieran for *The New York Times*, "were men who had never played on any other major league team. Except for Ruth in right field and Dugan at third base, the players were men who had been picked from the minors by Yankee scouts and developed into a championship array by a Yankee manager. In winning his first three pennants, Huggins had shown he knew how to buy. Now he showed that he knew how to build."

He didn't do it all by himself, of course, even though in those days field managers had a much larger say in the makeup of a team than they generally do today. Ed Barrow had also made the trip from Boston, where Ruppert installed him in the front office, and he worked with Huggins to create the team that exploded from seventh place in 1925 to the pennant in 1926, and that in 1927 became the greatest team baseball has ever seen.

It started in 1923, with Colonel Ruppert's grand new stadium—The House That Ruth Built—the likes of which no team had ever seen. In 1924 Earle Combs, "the Kentucky Colonel," was brought up from Louisville. He made 14 hits in 35 at-bats for an average of .400, then broke an ankle. In 1925, healed up, he was installed in center field, and over the next 11 seasons compiled a lifetime batting of .325. A handsome greyhound of a man, he developed into one of the league's best leadoff batters. A center of calm in the Yankees' sometimes turbulent locker room, Combs didn't drink, smoke or

Yankee manager Miller Huggins and team owner Jake Ruppert were all smiles during the 1927 World Series at Yankee Stadium. It was the Yankees' fifth trip of the decade to the Series, and brought them their second world championship.

For Huggins the player, 1911 was a pretty typical year. He hit .261, stole 37 bases, drew 96 walks, and had his own baseball card.

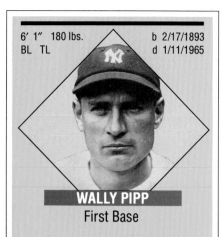

6' 1" 180 lbs.   b 2/17/1893
BL TL   d 1/11/1965

WALLY PIPP
First Base

In 1917 *Baseball Magazine* pro-claimed him "the American League's New Home Run King." In 1924 he led the league with 19 triples and drove in a career-high 113 runs. But on June 2, 1925, Wally Pipp asked to be taken out of the Yankee lineup because of a headache, and turned his last name into a verb.

When Pipp, who had been the Yankees' regular first baseman for ten years, sat out that day, he didn't know he'd never get back into the Yankee starting lineup. For the next 14 years, Lou Gehrig manned first base for the Yankees. As a result, Paul Dickson's *Baseball Dictionary* defines "Pipp" as "To be replaced due to an injury or illness and never regain one's position."

Pipp's role in launching Gehrig's record streak of 2,130 consecutive games played has consistently obscured what was an excellent career. Pipp was an outstanding dead-ball slugger, and in 1916—just his second full season in the majors—his 12 home runs earned him the American League home run title. Pipp led the league again in 1917, giving him two home run crowns.

Pipp averaged 98 RBI in the Yankee pennant years of 1921, 1922 and 1923, but he was slumping in 1925 when he took himself out of the lineup. The Reds claimed Pipp for $7,500 in February of 1926, and he had three solid seasons with Cincinnati before retiring with a .281 batting average and 996 career RBI.

Wally Pipp was more than just a good hitter made famous for losing his job to Lou Gehrig. In 1915, his first season with the Yankees, he led AL first basemen in putouts, assists and fielding percentage.

swear; he read his Bible with the daily dedication other players gave to the racing forms, and was known affectionately to his mates as "the Choir Boy."

By 1925 Babe Ruth seemed back on track after his problems, mostly behavioral, of the previous few seasons. Bob Meusel was as steady as ever in left, and with backup Benny Paschal, who had done such a fine job filling in for the Babe, the outfield was set.

But the infield was falling apart. Baseball wisdom says that to win, a team must be solid up the middle. Aaron Ward, dependable at second for so many years, could no longer make the plays. Everett "Deacon" Scott, a fixture at shortstop since coming from the Red Sox in 1922, had racked up 1,307 consecutive games, a major league record, and now was paying the price with exhaustion. So in 1925 Huggins experimented with a shortstop named Pee Wee Wanninger, whose main claim to fame is the fact that Lou Gehrig pinch-hit for him on June 1 to start his consecutive game string. When Wanninger came up short at short, Hug replaced him with Mark Koenig, a strapping 180-pound six-footer who was a solid hitter and an outstanding fielder. The following year he picked up Tony Lazzeri, who had hit 60 homers and knocked in 222 runs in a 200-game season for Salt Lake City in the Pacific Coast League. Installed at second base, Lazzeri matched up with Koenig as one of the best keystone combinations in the league.

Jumping Joe Dugan at third, imported from Philadelphia by way of the Red Sox, was nearing the end of the line, his playing time reduced by injuries. But he was still a fine fielder and dependable batter. And Wally Pipp at first base—well everybody knows what happened to Wally Pipp . . .

Lou Gehrig—"Larrupin' Lou," "Buster," "the Crown Prince of Swat," "Old Biscuit Pants," "the Pride of the Yankees"—wasn't a surprise package

to the baseball world. At the High School of Commerce in New York, he was considered one of the best young players in the nation. He won a scholarship to Columbia University, where his German-born parents worked in a fraternity house, but in the summer of 1921 the Giants' John McGraw signed him—under the name Lou Lewis—to play with Hartford in the Eastern League. Columbia officials got wind of the move before 18-year-old Lou had played more than a dozen games, rescued him, and somehow got his amateur status restored.

As a penalty for his foolishness, Gehrig had to sit out his freshman year, but in 1923 he starred as a pitcher and outfielder for Columbia in his only year of college baseball. Major league scouts were baying at his door, and the Yankees, offering a $1,500 signing bonus and $3,000 for the balance of the season, won the bidding war. To Lou's frugal parents, $3,000 for four months' work seemed like a fortune.

The Yankees sent the young prospect back to Hartford for seasoning, and the results were definitely spicy. In 59 games, Gehrig batted .304 with 69 hits, 45 of them for extra bases, and 24 home runs. Huggins brought him up for a closer look at the end of the 1923 season. In 13 games he batted .423 and hit his first major league home run. When regular first baseman Pipp injured himself in the last week of the season, the Yankees asked Judge Landis to waive World Series eligibility requirements so that Gehrig could take his place. Landis approved, pending an okay by the NL champion Giants. But McGraw, long on memory and unforgiving, flatly refused. So Gehrig sat while Pipp, trussed up, played.

Pipp was still doing the job in 1924, and Gehrig, now 21, spent another summer in Hartford, where he batted .369, banging out 40 doubles, 13 trip-

Although they weren't called Murderers' Row in 1921, the heart of the Yankee lineup could still do some damage. From left to right, the killers were first baseman Wally Pipp (8 HRs), left fielder Babe Ruth (59 HRs), shortstop Roger Peckinpaugh (8 HRs), right fielder Bob Meusel (24 HRs) and, in the twilight of his career, third baseman Frank "Home Run" Baker (9 HRs).

les and 37 home runs. He was recalled again at season's end and belted six hits and five RBI in 12 at-bats. He started 1925 with the Yankees, but only as a pinch hitter and occasional outfielder. Then, on June 2, Wally Pipp complained of a bad headache and asked Huggins for the day off. Gehrig took over first base and stayed, not missing a game for the next 14 years.

Wally Schang went to the Browns after the 1925 season, so Pat Collins and Benny Bengough split time behind the plate with Johnny Grabowski, another good journeyman catcher brought over from the White Sox in 1927. Yankee catching was only average until Bill Dickey took over in 1929, but the pitching staff was strong and well balanced: Waite Hoyt and Herb Pennock, Urban Shocker from the Browns, and young George Pipgras. Behind them were Dutch Ruether, Myles Thomas, Bob Shawkey and Joe Giard. But the real surprise was Wilcy Moore, a balding rookie who came out of nowhere to enjoy the kind of season that could have been scripted into baseball fiction.

A big, slow-talking, easygoing dirt farmer from Oklahoma, Moore admitted to being 28, but everybody knew he was at least 30. He had knocked around the minors for years, and kept playing partly out of habit and partly to pick up extra money for his farm. Still, 1926 had been a pretty good year; pitching for Greenville in the South Atlantic League, he had won 30 games and lost only four. When big Ed Barrow read that in *The Sporting News* his nostrils quivered. "Anybody who can win 30 games in any league is worth taking a look at," he said, and bought Moore's contract sight unseen.

Moore brought with him to the major leagues a fast, sharp-breaking sinker, almost flawless control, and unflappable nerves. He thought he also had a curve, but Huggins wouldn't let him use it. "Your curve ball," he said, "wouldn't go around a button on my vest."

The good-natured rookie was a favorite with other Yankee players, who had great fun teasing him about his hitting. Ruth took one look at him in batting practice during spring training and bet him $300 to $100 that he wouldn't get three hits all season. Moore collected six hits in 75 at-bats. From back home in Oklahoma he wrote the Babe a letter: "The $300 came in handy. I used it to buy a fine pair of mules. I named one Babe and the other one Ruth."

T he 1927 season wasn't very old before the rest of the AL got the message that there wasn't going to be much of a pennant race. The Yankees opened at home before a capacity-plus crowd of over 70,000 and beat the Athletics, 8–3. They ended the day in first place, and never relinquished it. From Combs in the leadoff spot down to the pitcher, there wasn't a man in the batting order—Ruth, Meusel, Gehrig, Lazzeri, Dugan, Koenig, even the three-headed catcher—who couldn't bust a game wide open. The lineup terrorized opposing pitchers, and many a hurler who had to face that "Murderers' Row" must have felt he was walking the last mile.

Yankee pitchers, on the other hand, performed superbly. Waite Hoyt, who had suffered from a sore arm in 1926, rebounded to win 22 games. Pennock won 19; Shocker took 18; Ruether added 13, Pipgras 10 and Thomas 7. And when a Yankee pitcher did falter, out from the bullpen came Wilcy Moore, and more often than not the fire withered and died. It was a magical year for the old rookie, who appeared in 50 games, both as a starter and as a reliever. He won 19 and lost only seven, with a league-leading 13 saves and an impressive 2.28 ERA.

Did the Yanks appreciate Moore? One night in Detroit the players were watching firemen fight a raging blaze near their hotel. When only wisps of

Boisterous Babe Ruth and introverted Lou Gehrig were a study in contrasts, except when it came to slugging. In 1927 they hit 107 home runs, more than any entire AL team.

In 1923, Joe Dugan's first full season with the Yankees, he led the AL with 644 at-bats, then drove in five runs in the World Series against the Giants, including a three-run inside-the-park home run.

Yankee Stadium

Ten stadiums' worth of drama has unfolded within its walls. It welcomed baseball's greatest players to the majors, hosted their greatest feats, and bade them tearful farewells. Sportswriters liked to refer to it as The House That Ruth Built, but ever since it opened in 1923, it's been known simply as Yankee Stadium.

Yankee Stadium has hosted 31 World Series, more than any other ballpark. For entire decades it was the home park and namesake of the most dominant team in baseball, yet it took just 185 working days to build. And while Ruth himself didn't build it, his skill with a bat set in motion the chain of events that led to its construction.

After sharing the Polo Grounds with the Giants for seven years, Yankee owners Jake Ruppert and Til Huston settled on a 10-acre plot on the north side of the Harlem River, across from the Polo Grounds. The Yankees' first year in their new stadium, 1923, was their best yet, even if their enthusiasm caused them to announce an Opening Day crowd of more than 74,000 when the stadium had just 62,000 seats. Babe Ruth homered on Opening Day, the Yankees won their third straight pennant, and went on to beat the Giants for their first World Series triumph. And it just kept getting better.

On September 30, 1927, Ruth smacked his 60th homer of the season into the right field seats, near the spot where, 34 years and one day later, Roger Maris broke the unbreakable record with his 61st. Before the 1928 season began, second and third decks were added in left center field, increasing the stadium's capacity to more than 80,000. The Yankees celebrated with their second straight World Series win.

The 1930s brought five more world championship flags to Yankee Stadium, but the decade ended on a tragic note. On July 4, 1939, Lou Gehrig said goodbye to 61,808 fans in one of baseball's most indelible moments. The Iron Horse, stricken with amyotrophic lateral sclerosis, a degenerative muscular disease, died two years later. Shortly before Gehrig's death, Yankee Stadium was the scene of a magical beginning: on May 15, 1941, Yankee center fielder Joe DiMaggio got a single against Chicago, starting a hitting streak that ran a record 56 games and ended in Cleveland.

The stadium hosted eight World Series in the 1950s—six were won by the Yanks—and some of the fall classic's most dramatic moments. The Yankees beat the Giants in 1951 despite losing Mickey Mantle, who injured his knee in a bout with a drainage outlet in right center field. The Yankees lost the 1955 Series when Brooklyn's Sandy Amoros made a lunging catch on a Yogi Berra fly ball to preserve a 2–0 win in Game 7. In 1956 Don Larsen made Yankee Stadium his own private showcase as he pitched the only perfect game in World Series history.

There's a debate about whether a ball has ever been hit out of Yankee Stadium in fair territory, but Mantle came close in 1963 when he hit the facade of the third deck in right field with a home run that was on its way to a 600-foot flight. After the 1973 season, the stadium got a $100 million renovation that forced the Yankees to share Shea Stadium with the Mets for two years, and reduced the stadium's capacity to 57,545. And in 1976 the team opened Yankee Stadium II in the same manner as the original—with an AL pennant.

In 1976 Yankee Stadium reopened after a two-year, $100 million renovation (above), and Chris Chambliss' ninth-inning home run in Game 5 of the AL Championship Series gave the Yankees their first pennant since 1964. In 1926, the heyday of Babe Ruth, the stadium's right field foul pole (left) was a cozy 295 feet from home plate.

Yankee Stadium

161st Street and
 River Avenue
Bronx, New York

Built 1923
Renovated 1976

New York Yankees, AL
 1923–present

Seating Capacity
57,545

Style
Grass Surface,
Major League Classic,
permanent baseball

Height of Outfield Fence
Left Field: 3′ 11″ (1923)
            8′   (1976)
Left Center: 13′ 10″ (1923)
             7′   (1976)
Right Center: 14′ 6″ (1923)
              8′   (1976)

Right Field: 3′ 9″ (1923)
            10′   (1976)

Dugouts
Home: 1st base side
Visitor: 3rd base side

Bullpens
Home: Right field
Visitor: Left field

YANKEE STADIUM

411 410 353 312 310 84

As a sophomore at Columbia University in
1923, Lou Gehrig played his only year of
college baseball. He set all sorts of hitting
records, but his only surviving record is in
the pitching column. Gehrig struck out 17
batters in a game on his way to a 5–1 record.

Consistency was Gehrig's trademark. From
1926 to 1938, he drove in at least 107 runs
each season. "Gehrig never learned that a
ballplayer couldn't be good every day," said
Braves catcher Hank Gowdy.

smoke curled up from the stricken walls, utility infielder Mike Gazella said,
"We can go home now. They got Wilcy Moore in."

The Yanks sparkled in the field, but their bats made them famous—and
feared. Harry Heilmann of Detroit won the AL batting title that year with
.398, and George Sisler of the Browns stole 27 bases. But in every other offensive category the Yankees excelled. Babe Ruth unloaded his record 60
home runs, driving in 164 and batting .356. Gehrig exploded with 47 home
runs, 175 RBI and a .373 average. Meusel drove home 103 and batted .337.
Combs batted .356 with 231 hits. Lazzeri batted .309 and drove in 102.

The stats are overwhelming: Ruth, Gehrig and Lazzeri paced the
league in homers; Ruth and Gehrig ranked one-two in slugging average;
Gehrig, Ruth and Combs swept the top three spots in total bases; Gehrig and
Ruth had the most RBI; Combs and Gehrig had the most hits; Ruth, Gehrig
and Combs scored the most runs; Gehrig hit the most doubles; Combs and
Gehrig hit the most triples. It was murder.

As a team, the Yankees batted .307, and people began calling them "the
Window Breakers." But Earle Combs came up with an even better name for
the Yank attack. Baseball was played in the daylight, of course, most games
starting at three-thirty in the afternoon. Opposing pitchers might hold the
Window Breakers in check for a while, but the mighty bats usually spoke up
in the late innings—so often that Combs called the delayed explosions "five
o'clock lightning." The phrase spread through the league, and few were the
men who stood on the mound, ball in hand, facing the Yankees of 1927 who
didn't dread the approach of five o'clock and the eighth inning.

Any doubts about the outcome of the 1927 season were gone by the
Fourth of July. The Senators, riding a hot June spurt, had moved up on

the front-running Yanks. A holiday doubleheader between the rivals packed the stadium, but the expected Donnybrook never materialized. The Yankees won the opener, 12–1, then nearly giggled themselves through the nightcap, 21–1.

With the pennant race a foregone conclusion, fans shifted their attention to the home run battle between Ruth and Gehrig. It was the first time anybody had ever challenged the Babe directly. The only years since 1920 that he hadn't won the title, 1922 and 1925, he hadn't played a full schedule. In 1927 Gehrig made a horse race out of it, and by mid-August was ahead of the Bambino, 38 to 36. Then Larrupin' Lou slowed down, hitting only nine more, just as Ruth got hot—and Ruth hot was something incredible.

Nobody really expected him to challenge his 1921 record of 59 round-trippers, especially since he was far behind his previous pace as he entered September. Then the homers started coming in bunches, until he had 53, and everybody got excited. With only nine games left in the season, no one gave him a chance to match 1921, but the Babe hit a homer in each of the next three games for 56, skipped two days, then got number 57, a grand slam off Lefty Grove. Numbers 58 and 59 came the next day, and on September 30, in the next-to-last game of the year, he sliced one down the right field line to establish one of baseball's most cherished records—still.

The Yankees waltzed to the pennant, winning by a league-record 19 games. Their 110 wins and .714 percentage were league high-water marks. And while all *that* was going on, the Pirates, Cardinals and Giants were showing the National League what a pennant race was all about. The Pirates surged ahead at the wire with a winning record of 94–60, the Cards following at 92–61 and the Giants at 92–62. The Pirates, under Donie Bush, were a

When it came to putting his case before the umpires in his 12-year tenure as Yankee manager, Miller Huggins (above, second from right) was a pro. He received his law degree from the University of Cincinnati, and passed the Ohio bar exam in 1902.

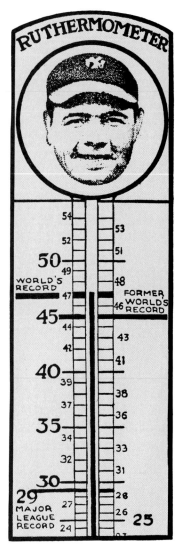

Brothers Irish (above, left) and Bob Meusel played in ten World Series. Irish's career batting average was one point higher than Bob's, .310 to .309, but Bob played in six Yankee Series to his brother's four for the Giants.

By September 10, 1920, Babe Ruth had long since smashed all existing home run records, but readers of the New York American *were still treated to a homer-by-homer check of the Babe's progress. He reached 54 by season's end.*

good team. In the outfield they had Clyde Barnhart and the Waner brothers, Paul and Lloyd—"Big Poison" and "Little Poison"—Joe Harris at first, George Grantham at second, Glenn Wright at short, and Pie Traynor, about the best hot corner man in the business. Earl Smith and Johnny Gooch divided the catching. The pitching staff was solid, with Ray Kremer, Vic Aldridge, Lee Meadows, Carmen Hill and Johnny Miljus. A good team—but no match for the Yankees.

The story of how the Pirates lost the 1927 World Series before it began is cemented in baseball lore. The Series opened in Pittsburgh, and in the morning the Pirates took batting practice. Most of the Pirates were showered, dressed and in the stands as the Yankees took their turn. With Hoyt throwing fastballs over the center of the plate, Murderers' Row walked up one after the other and slammed balls against the fences, into the stands, over the roof, out of the ballpark. At one point, so the story goes, Lloyd Waner turned to brother Paul and said in a hushed voice, "Jesus! They're big guys!"

Little Poison denies that anything like that ever happened, but there was no denying the result of the Series. The Yankees won the first game, 5–4, behind Hoyt, with Moore mopping up. They romped to victory in the second game behind Pipgras, 6–2. In New York for Game 3, Pennock didn't allow a hit for seven innings, cooling off on the bench while his mates played five o'clock lightning with Lee Meadows. Pennock didn't get his perfect game, but came away with a three-hit victory, 8–1, that still stands as a classic. Huggins let Wilcy Moore start the fourth game as a reward for his great work during the year; the farm boy hung on to win, although the victory was hardly in the window-breaking tradition. The score was tied 3–3 in the ninth

Pittsburgh's Lloyd (far left) and Paul Waner are the only pair of brothers in the Hall of Fame, but they lost their only chance at a World Series win in 1927 to the Yankees. As a rookie that season, Lloyd hit .355, including a major league record 198 singles, while Paul led the NL with a .380 average and 131 RBI. They combined for 11 hits in the four-game Series.

110 Wins, 44 Losses

The 1927 New York Yankees—with the strongest combination of batting and pitching ever assembled by a single team—set an AL record for most wins that stood unchallenged until the 1954 Cleveland Indians bested it by one.

Yankees	VS	Opponent
21–1		St. Louis
18–4		Boston
12–10		Cleveland
14–8		Detroit
17–5		Chicago
14–8		Washington
14–8		Philadelphia

Record at Home: 57–19
Record Away: 53–25

when the Yankees loaded the bases. Miljus pitched heroically, fanning both Gehrig and Meusel, but then wild-pitched to Lazzeri over the catcher's head and watched Combs scamper home from third with the winning run.

It was the shortest Series on record, but the Pirates got a little something to take back home: Ruth and Gehrig got ten hits and a combined .354 average, but the Waner boys got 11 hits and a .366 average.

It had been some year: Lindy soloed across the Atlantic, the Bambino hit 60 big ones, and the Yankees were without doubt the greatest team of all time. The 1927 season also ended the run of Ban Johnson. In poor health and at loggerheads with Landis and the team owners, the tyrannical, tempestuous founder and president of the American League submitted a pencil-written resignation that the owners quickly accepted.

The Yankees picked up in 1928 where they had left off, and by July 1 their lead was up to 13½ games. Ruth and Gehrig were superlative again, but everybody else was hurting, one way or the other. Lazzeri banged his shoulder and missed 40 games. Dugan missed 60 games with a bad knee in what was to be his last year with the Yankees. Koenig missed 30 games at short, Meusel was hurt, and both showed signs of slipping. Combs sprained his wrist late in the year. Pennock developed arm trouble and was never again a topflight pitcher. Wilcy Moore lost the stardust sprinkled on him by his fairy godmother and assumed his normal shape, more like a pumpkin than Prince Charming. The worst shock of all: Urban Shocker, out all season with a serious heart condition, died in September at 38.

Hobbled with injuries, the team had lost much of its unbeatable mystique, and a hungry young team from Philadelphia mounted a serious chal-

Pitchers in Pinstripes

Waite Hoyt said it best: "The secret of success as a pitcher lies in getting a job with the Yankees." For much of the 20th century, Yankee pitchers had the easiest jobs in baseball, and at no time was this more true than in the 1920s.

Yankee teams averaged 5.5 runs per game from 1920 through 1929, and led the AL in runs scored four times in the decade. Understandably, the great Yankee teams are remembered more for the bats of Ruth, Gehrig, Combs and Meusel than for the arms of Hoyt, Herb Pennock, Bob Shawkey and George Pipgras. But the Yankee pitching staffs in the 1920s were among the best in baseball, and when October rolled around, it was often Yankee arms, not bats, that made the difference.

Hoyt was arguably the best of the lot, and pitched in all six Yankee World Series in the 1920s. He earned the nickname "Schoolboy" after being signed by the Giants at age 15, but pitched just one inning for John McGraw. After two mediocre seasons with the Red Sox, Hoyt was traded to the Yanks, where he made an immediate impression, winning 19 games. In the World Series against the Giants, Hoyt allowed no earned runs in 27 innings, but was a 1–0 loser in Game 8 because of an error by shortstop Roger Peckinpaugh. Hoyt was a classic stylist who worked quickly and stayed ahead of the hitters, but often didn't receive as much offensive support as did his fellow Yankee starters, and once it almost cost him money. During salary negotiations, Yankee owner Jake Ruppert screamed, "Hoyt, you make me so nervous with those 2–1 and 3–2 games. Why can't you be like Pennock? He

wins 7–1 and 8–2." A two-time 20-game winner, Hoyt was toughest to hit in October, and compiled a 1.83 ERA in 83⅔ World Series innings.

Like Hoyt, most of the other great Yankee pitchers of the 1920s—Pennock, Sad Sam Jones, Bullet Joe Bush and Carl Mays—were acquired from the Red Sox. Shawkey was the lone acquisition from elsewhere—Ruppert had paid a generous $18,000 to get him from the Philadelphia A's in 1915. These Yankee pitching staffs received little fanfare, but were dominant throughout the decade. Four times the Yankee staff had the lowest team ERA in the American League, and three times it finished second. Take the pennant years, for example. In 1921 Mays paced the staff with 27 wins, and he and Hoyt were among the top five in ERA. In 1922 Bush won 26, Shawkey 20 and Hoyt 19, as the Yankees led the AL in complete games and missed the team ERA title by 0.01. Balance was the key in 1923 as five starters won 16 or more games and the staff led the league in ERA, strikeouts and complete games. Pennock and Urban Shocker, who'd been traded by the Browns, led the way in 1926 with 42 wins between them. In 1927 rookie Wilcy Moore's 19 wins and 13 saves led a dazzling staff whose 3.20 ERA was more than half a run lower than that of any other team in the league. Pipgras had his finest year in 1928, winning 24 games to go with Hoyt's 23 and Pennock's 2.56 ERA.

The Yankees went three for six in World Series in the 1920s. Surprisingly, the three losses were more the result of anemic hitting than poor pitching. In the three Series they lost—1921, 1922 and 1926—Yankee pitching staffs posted ERAs of

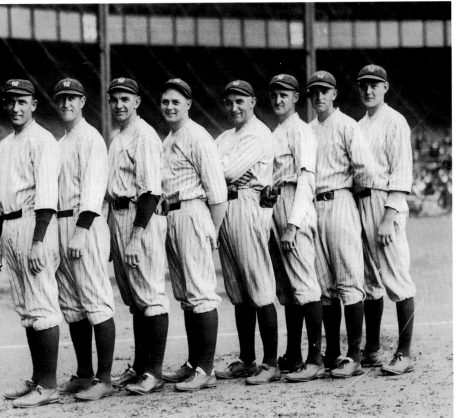

The 1923 Yankee pitching staff (left) led the AL with a 3.66 ERA, 102 complete games and 506 strikeouts. From far left: Sad Sam Jones, Bullet Joe Bush, Bob Shawkey, Waite Hoyt, Carl Mays, Herb Pennock, Oscar Roettger and George Pipgras. In 1927 Wilcy Moore (below) was the Yankees' bullpen ace, with 13 relief wins and 13 saves in 38 relief appearances.

3.09, 3.35 and 3.14, while the Yankee offense averaged only 2.75, 2.75 and 3.00 runs a game.

By 1931 the Philadelphia A's were baseball's new dynasty, and the great Yankee pitching staff had broken up, with only Pipgras and Pennock still in pinstripes. Bush, Shawkey, and Mays had retired, Moore was with the Red Sox, and Jones was with the Senators. In the nine years after leaving New York in 1930, Hoyt pitched for five teams, including two stints with Brooklyn. But at heart he remained a Yankee. In 1933, while pitching for Pittsburgh, Hoyt was taking a beating from Cub hitters and a lot of verbal abuse from the Cub bench. He left the mound and headed for the Chicago dugout. "If you guys don't shut up," he said, "I'll put on my old Yankee uniform and scare you to death."

The 1927 Yankees were supposed to blast opponents away with their power, but in Game 2 of the World Series against Pittsburgh they pecked their way to a 6–2 win. Bob Meusel scored on an eighth-inning wild pitch by Pittsburgh pitcher Vic Aldridge (right, above) as batter Joe Dugan bails out and catcher Johnny Gooch looks on.

lenge. On September 8, nibbling away at New York's advantage, the Athletics moved ahead by half a game to take over the league lead. In the strange way that baseball schedules sometimes seem fated, the Athletics came into Yankee Stadium the next day for a Sunday doubleheader that opened a four-game series. It was what sports fans live for, and thousands of them were turned away from the jam-packed stadium. Those who were there saw the Yankees win twice, 5–0 and 7–3, to push the challengers back. They completed the job the next day, as Ruth broke a 3–3 tie in the eighth with a two-run homer, courtesy of the five o'clock lightning crew. That was it for the Athletics—that year.

For a while during the season Ruth appeared to be on track to break the home run record again. He entered August with 42, an incredible 26 games ahead of his 1927 pace. But Gehrig, who had an excellent year otherwise, knocked out only 27 four-baggers, and the lack of competition may have taken something off the Bambino's swing. He tailed off during the last two months of the season and finished with "only" 54.

But Babe made up for it in the Series. So did Gehrig. It was St. Louis again in 1928, and the Yanks quickly exacted revenge for what the Cardinals had done to them in 1926. Four games and out—the first time a team had ever swept two consecutive Series. The Yankees took the lead in the first inning of the first game and went on to win the Series 4–1, 9–3, 7–3 and 7–3. The big story was the mayhem wreaked on Cardinal pitching by New York's twin terrors. Ruth batted .625 on ten hits, swatted three home runs, scored nine; Gehrig batted .545, hit four homers, and brought in nine runs. Together they outscored the Cardinals in the Series, 14–10.

For the second time that decade, the New Yorkers had won three pennants in a row, and the cry went up throughout the land: *Break Up the Yankees!* But any dreams the Yanks had of adding a fourth pennant in 1929 went glimmering. The cracks that started to show in 1928 widened, and the once magnificent pitching staff disintegrated. They were well out of the race in September when Huggins, who hadn't been himself for weeks, turned the team over to coach Art Fletcher and went home. Five days later the Yanks were playing the Red Sox in Fenway. In the third inning, the flag in center field fluttered slowly down to half-mast. An inning later the Yankees learned why—Huggins had died in a hospital of blood poisoning. The dugout was deathly quiet until sweet-tempered Earle Combs broke down and cried. A reporter punched in, asking questions, but a scowl from the Babe cut him off in midsentence. The teams gathered at home plate for a minute of silence, then the Yanks filed slowly back to their dugout. From far back in the shadows Fletcher finally cleared his throat and growled, "Well, let's get it over with."

The Yankees won the game 11–10, in ten innings, but everyone knew that an era had ended.

The Philadelphia Athletics, stepping into the spotlight, took up the challenge the rest of the league longed for. Connie Mack had put together a remarkable team on the solid foundation of four of baseball's grandest names: Lefty Grove threw baseballs so fast that they looked, said one batter, "like a piece of white thread coming to the plate." First baseman Jimmie Foxx, only 21 years old, was already touted as "the right-handed Babe Ruth." Mickey Cochrane, a strong candidate for baseball's best all-time catcher, had a fierce determination to win and was light-footed enough to

Hat tricks are usually reserved for ice hockey, but after Ruth punctuated the Yankees' sweep of the Cardinals with his third home run in Game 4 of the 1928 World Series, the St. Louis crowd sent its toppers flying onto the field in appreciation of the Babe's power.

After 15 years without a pennant, Philadelphia A's owner-manager Connie Mack was back atop baseball as his A's played .781 ball at home and dethroned the Yankees.

serve occasionally as leadoff batter. Left fielder Al Simmons—baptized Aloys Szymanski—was a brute with a bat.

Philadelphia won 104 games in 1929 and cruised to the pennant, 18 games in front of the pitching-poor Yanks. In the opposing dugout at the World Series they found the Chicago Cubs, who had won the NL pennant with a flourish under Joe McCarthy, 10½ lengths ahead of Pittsburgh. The Cubs had excellent pitching with Pat Malone, 22–10; Charlie Root, 19–6; and Guy Bush, 18–7. But their strength was their hitting: Rogers Hornsby, .380 and 39 home runs; Kiki Cuyler, .360; Riggs Stephenson, .362; and Hack Wilson, .345 and another 39 home runs—all right-handed hitters— plus southpaw first baseman Charlie Grimm. And therein lies the tale of the 1929 World Series.

Connie Mack, a great player of percentages, made note of the starboard-leaning batting order of the Cubs. He surprised no one by not starting Grove, his left-handed ace, but he passed over his premier right-hander, George Earnshaw, who was almost as fast as Grove and who had won 24 games during the season, in favor of 35-year-old Howard Ehmke, seldom used and on his way out. Canny Connie figured that Ehmke's slow, sidearm stuff would throw the Cubs' fastball bashers off balance. The strategy worked. Old man Ehmke struck out 13 Chicago batters and won, 3–1.

In the seventh inning of Game 4—with ace Charlie Root working an 8–0 lead—the Cubs looked to be well on their way to evening the Series. Then the roof fell in. Simmons started the inning with a home run to left, and before the dust had time to settle the Athletics had scored ten runs for one of the most remarkable comebacks in Series history. Goat of the game was Cubs center fielder Hack Wilson, who lost two balls in the sun, one of which fell for a single

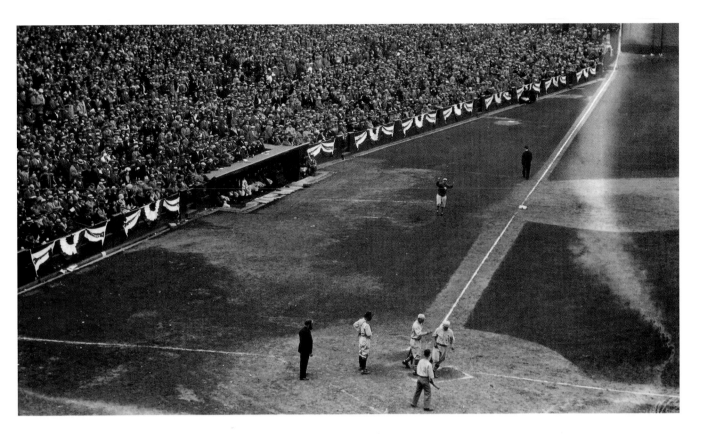

and the other for a three-run homer, giving the Athletics the game and ultimately the Series, four games to one.

Wilson, destined to establish in 1930 new NL home run and RBI records, had to take some terrible ragging. A cheerful fireplug of a man, he knew how to do better than simply turn the other cheek. With the ribbing at its peak, he entered a hotel dining room, pulled the window shades, and loudly asked the maitre d' to dim the lights so he wouldn't misjudge his soup. Considering what happened to the stock market a few weeks after the 1929 World Series went into the history books, the country needed a good laugh.

And so ended a decade. Baseball still mirrored the wackiness, the excitement, the gaudy prosperity and the inevitable changeability of the times. It was a decade that started in baseball's darkest hour, with the stain of the Black Sox disgrace tainting everything it touched, and ended in the cheerless gray light of America's bleakest dawn. But in between—oh, what a glorious, golden time it was for the old ballgame! ◑

Philadelphia first baseman Jimmie Foxx broke a scoreless tie in Game 1 of the 1929 World Series with a seventh-inning homer off Chicago's Charlie Root. Foxx hit 33 regular-season homers, and added two more in the Series, as the A's won in five.

The A's galloped off with three straight AL pennants from 1929 to 1931, winning by margins of 18, 8 and 13½ games.

1920s Statistics

1920

American League

	W	L	PCT	GB
Cleveland	98	56	.636	—
Chicago	96	58	.623	2
New York	95	59	.617	3
St. Louis	76	77	.497	21½
Boston	72	81	.471	25½
Washington	68	84	.447	29
Detroit	61	93	.396	37
Philadelphia	48	106	.312	50

League Leaders

Batting	G. Sisler, StL	.407
Runs	B. Ruth, NY	158
Home Runs	B. Ruth, NY	54
RBI	B. Ruth, NY	137
Steals	S. Rice, WAS	63
Wins	J. Bagby, CLE	31
Saves	D. Kerr, CHI	5
	U. Shocker, StL	5
ERA	B. Shawkey, NY	2.45
Strikeouts	S. Coveleski, CLE	133

World Series

Best-of-9-Games Series
Cleveland (AL) def. Brooklyn (NL) 5-2

Record Setters

Highest slugging percentage, season—.847, Babe Ruth, NY (AL)

Most hits, season—257, George Sisler, StL (AL)

Most consecutive hits by a team, single game —12, St. Louis (NL), September 17 vs. Boston (tied in 1930 by Brooklyn)

Most walks, team, single game—20, Boston (AL), September 17 vs. Detroit, 12 innings

Most innings pitched, single game—26, Leon Cadore, BKN, and Joe Oeschger, BOS, May 1

Most consecutive scoreless innings, single game —21, Joe Oeschger, BOS (NL), 6th through 26th inning, May 1

Longest game—26 innings, May 1, Brooklyn vs. Boston, 1-1

National League

	W	L	PCT	GB
Brooklyn	93	61	.604	—
New York	86	68	.558	7
Cincinnati	82	71	.536	10½
Pittsburgh	79	75	.513	14
Chicago	75	79	.487	18
St. Louis	75	79	.487	18
Boston	62	90	.408	30
Philadelphia	62	91	.405	30½

League Leaders

Batting	R. Hornsby, StL	.370
Runs	G. Burns, NY	115
Home Runs	C. Williams, PHI	15
RBI	G. Kelly, NY	94
	R. Hornsby, StL	94
Steals	M. Carey, PIT	52
Wins	G. Alexander, CHI	27
Saves	B. Sherdel, StL	6
ERA	G. Alexander, CHI	1.91
Strikeouts	G. Alexander, CHI	173

1921

American League

	W	L	PCT	GB
New York	98	55	.641	—
Cleveland	94	60	.610	4½
St. Louis	81	73	.526	17½
Washington	80	73	.523	18
Boston	75	79	.487	23½
Detroit	71	82	.464	27
Chicago	62	92	.403	36½
Philadelphia	53	100	.346	45

League Leaders

Batting	H. Heilmann, DET	.394
Runs	B. Ruth, NY	177
Home Runs	B. Ruth, NY	59
RBI	B. Ruth, NY	171
Steals	G. Sisler, StL	35
Wins	C. Mays, NY	27
	U. Shocker, StL	27
Saves	J. Middleton, DET	7
	C. Mays, NY	7
ERA	R. Faber, CHI	2.48
Strikeouts	W. Johnson, WAS	143

World Series

New York (NL) def. New York (AL) 5-3

Record Setters

Most runs scored, AL, season—177, Babe Ruth, NY

Most total bases, season—457, Babe Ruth, NY (AL)

Most extra-base hits, season—119 (44 doubles, 16 triples, 59 home runs), Babe Ruth, NY (AL)

Highest team batting average, AL—.316, Detroit

Most hits by a team, season—1,724, Detroit

Fewest errors by a first baseman, season (150 games or more), AL—1, Stuffy McInnis, BOS, 152 games

National League

	W	L	PCT	GB
New York	94	59	.614	—
Pittsburgh	90	63	.588	4
St. Louis	87	66	.569	7
Boston	79	74	.516	15
Brooklyn	77	75	.507	16½
Cincinnati	70	83	.458	24
Chicago	64	89	.418	30
Philadelphia	51	103	.331	43½

League Leaders

Batting	R. Hornsby, StL	.397
Runs	R. Hornsby, StL	131
Home Runs	G. Kelly, NY	23
RBI	R. Hornsby, StL	126
Steals	F. Frisch, NY	49
Wins	B. Grimes, BKN	22
	W. Cooper, PIT	22
Saves	L. North, StL	7
ERA	B. Doak, StL	2.59
Strikeouts	B. Grimes, BKN	136

Records listed in **Record Setters** still stand as of publication date.

1922

American League	W	L	PCT	GB
New York	94	60	.610	—
St. Louis	93	61	.604	1
Detroit	79	75	.513	15
Cleveland	78	76	.506	16
Chicago	77	77	.500	17
Washington	69	85	.448	25
Philadelphia	65	89	.422	29
Boston	61	93	.396	33

Most Valuable Player   G. Sisler, StL
(first year awarded AL)

League Leaders

Batting	G. Sisler, StL	.420
Runs	G. Sisler, StL	134
Home Runs	K. Williams, StL	39
RBI	K. Williams, StL	155
Steals	G. Sisler, StL	51
Wins	E. Rommel, PHI	27
Saves	S. Jones, NY	8
ERA	R. Faber, CHI	2.80
Strikeouts	U. Shocker, StL	149

World Series

Best-of-7-Games Series
New York (NL) def. New York (AL) 4-0

Record Setters

Highest batting average, season, AL left-hander
—.420, George Sisler, StL
Most total bases, NL, season—450, Rogers
Hornsby, StL
Most at-bats, NL, 154-game season—672, Rabbit
Maranville, PIT
Most at-bats without a home run, season—672,
Rabbit Maranville, PIT
Most consecutive games with at least one RBI
—17, Ray Grimes, CHI (NL)
Most runs in a game, both clubs—49: Chicago
(NL) 26, Philadelphia (NL) 23, August 25

National League	W	L	PCT	GB
New York	93	61	.604	—
Cincinnati	86	68	.558	7
Pittsburgh	85	69	.552	8
St. Louis	85	69	.552	8
Chicago	80	74	.519	13
Brooklyn	76	78	.494	17
Philadelphia	57	96	.373	35½
Boston	53	100	.346	39½

League Leaders

Batting	R. Hornsby, StL	.401
Runs	R. Hornsby, StL	141
Home Runs	R. Hornsby, StL	42
RBI	R. Hornsby, StL	152
Steals	M. Carey, PIT	51
Wins	E. Rixey, CIN	25
Saves	C. Jonnard, NY	5
ERA	R. Ryan, NY	3.01
Strikeouts	D. Vance, BKN	134

1923

American League	W	L	PCT	GB
New York	98	54	.645	—
Detroit	83	71	.539	16
Cleveland	82	71	.536	16½
Washington	75	78	.490	23½
St. Louis	74	78	.487	24
Philadelphia	69	83	.454	29
Chicago	69	85	.448	30
Boston	61	91	.401	37

Most Valuable Player   B. Ruth, NY

League Leaders

Batting	H. Heilmann, DET	.403
Runs	B. Ruth, NY	151
Home Runs	B. Ruth, NY	41
RBI	B. Ruth, NY	130
	T. Speaker, CLE	130
Steals	E. Collins, CHI	47
Wins	G. Uhle, CLE	26
Saves	A. Russell, WAS	9
ERA	S. Coveleski, CLE	2.76
Strikeouts	W. Johnson, WAS	130

World Series

New York (AL) def. New York (NL) 4-2

Record Setters

Most walks, season—170, Babe Ruth, NY (AL)
Most runs scored in an inning after two outs—13,
Cleveland, sixth inning, July 7 vs. Boston (tied by
Kansas City in 1956)
Most hits by a team, AL, single game—30,
New York vs. Boston, September 28
Most runs allowed, inning, AL—13, Lefty O'Doul,
BOS, July 7
Most home games lost, 154-game season, NL
—55, Philadelphia and Boston (tied by
Philadelphia in 1945)
Most days in first place, 154-game season—174,
New York (NL), entire season (tied in 1927 by
New York [AL])

National League	W	L	PCT	GB
New York	95	58	.621	—
Cincinnati	91	63	.591	4½
Pittsburgh	87	67	.565	8½
Chicago	83	71	.539	12½
St. Louis	79	74	.516	16
Brooklyn	76	78	.494	19½
Boston	54	100	.351	41½
Philadelphia	50	104	.325	45½

League Leaders

Batting	R. Hornsby, StL	.384
Runs	R. Youngs, NY	121
Home Runs	C. Williams, PHI	41
RBI	I. Meusel, NY	125
Steals	M. Carey, PIT	51
Wins	D. Luque, CIN	27
Saves	C. Jonnard, NY	5
ERA	D. Luque, CIN	1.93
Strikeouts	D. Vance, BKN	197

Records listed in **Record Setters** still stand as of publication date.

1920s STATISTICS
1924

American League	W	L	PCT	GB
Washington	92	62	.597	—
New York	89	63	.586	2
Detroit	86	68	.558	6
St. Louis	74	78	.487	17
Philadelphia	71	81	.467	20
Cleveland	67	86	.438	24½
Boston	67	87	.435	25
Chicago	66	87	.431	25½

Most Valuable Player   W. Johnson, WAS

League Leaders

Batting	B. Ruth, NY	.378
Runs	B. Ruth, NY	143
Home Runs	B. Ruth, NY	46
RBI	G. Goslin, WAS	129
Steals	E. Collins, CHI	42
Wins	W. Johnson, WAS	23
Saves	F. Marberry, WAS	15
ERA	W. Johnson, WAS	2.72
Strikeouts	W. Johnson, WAS	158

World Series
Washington (AL) def. New York (NL) 4-3

Record Setters
Highest batting average, season (since 1900)
—.424, Rogers Hornsby, StL (NL)

Most RBI, single game—12, Jim Bottomley, StL
(NL), September 16

Most innings pitched without a wild pitch or hit
batter, season, NL—268, Jesse Barnes, BOS

Most unassisted double plays by a third baseman,
season—4, Joe Dugan, NY (AL)

Most assists by a shortstop, 154-game season
—601, Glenn Wright, PIT

Most at-bats, 7-game World Series—33, Bucky
Harris, WAS (tied in 1925 by Sam Rice, WAS,
and in 1979 by Omar Moreno, PIT)

Youngest manager, World Series winner—27
years, 11 months, 2 days, Bucky Harris, WAS

National League	W	L	PCT	GB
New York	93	60	.608	—
Brooklyn	92	62	.597	1½
Pittsburgh	90	63	.588	3
Cincinnati	83	70	.542	10
Chicago	81	72	.529	12
St. Louis	65	89	.422	28½
Philadelphia	55	96	.364	37
Boston	53	100	.346	40

Most Valuable Player   D. Vance, BKN
(first year awarded NL)

League Leaders

Batting	R. Hornsby, StL	.424
Runs	F. Frisch, NY	121
	R. Hornsby, StL	121
Home Runs	J. Fournier, BKN	27
RBI	G. Kelly, NY	136
Steals	M. Carey, PIT	49
Wins	D. Vance, BKN	28
Saves	J. May, CIN	6
ERA	D. Vance, BKN	2.16
Strikeouts	D. Vance, BKN	262

1925

American League	W	L	PCT	GB
Washington	96	55	.636	—
Philadelphia	88	64	.579	8½
St. Louis	82	71	.536	15
Detroit	81	73	.526	16½
Chicago	79	75	.513	18½
Cleveland	70	84	.455	27½
New York	69	85	.448	28½
Boston	47	105	.309	49½

Most Valuable Player   R. Peckinpaugh, WAS

League Leaders

Batting	H. Heilmann, DET	.393
Runs	J. Mostil, CHI	135
Home Runs	B. Meusel, NY	33
RBI	B. Meusel, NY	138
Steals	J. Mostil, CHI	43
Wins	E. Rommel, PHI	21
	T. Lyons, CHI	21
Saves	F. Marberry, WAS	15
ERA	S. Coveleski, WAS	2.84
Strikeouts	L. Grove, PHI	116

World Series
Pittsburgh (NL) def. Washington (AL) 4-3

Record Setters
Highest slugging percentage, season, NL—.756,
Rogers Hornsby, StL

Highest batting average, season, pitcher—.433,
Walter Johnson, WAS

Most consecutive years leading the league in
batting average, NL—6, 1920 through 1925,
Rogers Hornsby, StL

Longest hitting streak, start of season, AL—34
games, George Sisler, StL, April 14 through
May 19

Fewest strikeouts, season, at least 150 games—4,
Joe Sewell, CLE, 155 games (tied his own record
in 1929 playing in 152 games)

National League	W	L	PCT	GB
Pittsburgh	95	58	.621	—
New York	86	66	.566	8½
Cincinnati	80	73	.523	15
St. Louis	77	76	.503	18
Boston	70	83	.458	25
Brooklyn	68	85	.444	27
Philadelphia	68	85	.444	27
Chicago	68	86	.442	27½

Most Valuable Player   R. Hornsby, StL

League Leaders

Batting	R. Hornsby, StL	.403
Runs	K. Cuyler, PIT	144
Home Runs	R. Hornsby, StL	39
RBI	R. Hornsby, StL	143
Steals	M. Carey, PIT	46
Wins	D. Vance, BKN	22
Saves	J. Morrison, PIT	4
	G. Bush, CHI	4
ERA	D. Luque, CIN	2.63
Strikeouts	D. Vance, BKN	221

Records listed in **Record Setters** still stand as of publication date.

American League | 1926 | National League

World Series
St. Louis (NL) def. New York (AL) 4-3

	W	L	PCT	GB
New York	91	63	.591	—
Cleveland	88	66	.571	3
Philadelphia	83	67	.553	6
Washington	81	69	.540	8
Chicago	81	72	.529	9½
Detroit	79	75	.513	12
St. Louis	62	92	.403	29
Boston	46	107	.301	44½

Most Valuable Player — G. Burns, CLE

League Leaders

Batting	H. Manush, DET	.378
Runs	B. Ruth, NY	139
Home Runs	B. Ruth, NY	47
RBI	B. Ruth, NY	145
Steals	J. Mostil, CHI	35
Wins	G. Uhle, CLE	27
Saves	F. Marberry, WAS	22
ERA	L. Grove, PHI	2.51
Strikeouts	L. Grove, PHI	194

Record Setters
Most consecutive games played, from the start of a career—394, Al Simmons, PHI (AL), April 15, 1924, through July 20, 1926

First player ever to get nine hits in a doubleheader, AL—Ray Morehart, CHI, August 31

Longest Opening Day game—15 innings, April 13, Washington vs. Philadelphia, 1-0 (tied in 1960 by Detroit and Cleveland)

Shortest game, AL—55 minutes, September 26, St. Louis vs. New York, 6-2

Most total bases, World Series game—12, Babe Ruth, NY (AL) (tied in 1928 by Ruth and in 1977 by Reggie Jackson, NY [AL])

Most walks, 7-game World Series—11, Babe Ruth, NY (AL) (tied in 1973 by Gene Tenace, OAK)

	W	L	PCT	GB
St. Louis	89	65	.578	—
Cincinnati	87	67	.565	2
Pittsburgh	84	69	.549	4½
Chicago	82	72	.532	7
New York	74	77	.490	13½
Brooklyn	71	82	.464	17½
Boston	66	86	.434	22
Philadelphia	58	93	.384	29½

Most Valuable Player — B. O'Farrell, StL

League Leaders

Batting	B. Hargrave, CIN	.353
Runs	K. Cuyler, PIT	113
Home Runs	H. Wilson, CHI	21
RBI	J. Bottomley, StL	120
Steals	K. Cuyler, PIT	35
Wins	L. Meadows, PIT	20
	P. Donahue, CIN	20
	R. Kremer, PIT	20
	F. Rhem, StL	20
Saves	C. Davies, NY	6
ERA	R. Kremer, PIT	2.61
Strikeouts	D. Vance, BKN	140

American League | 1927 | National League

World Series
New York (AL) def. Pittsburgh (NL) 4-0

	W	L	PCT	GB
New York	110	44	.714	—
Philadelphia	91	63	.591	19
Washington	85	69	.552	25
Detroit	82	71	.536	27½
Chicago	70	83	.458	39½
Cleveland	66	87	.431	43½
St. Louis	59	94	.386	50½
Boston	51	103	.331	59

Most Valuable Player — L. Gehrig, NY

League Leaders

Batting	H. Heilmann, DET	.398
Runs	B. Ruth, NY	158
Home Runs	B. Ruth, NY	60
RBI	L. Gehrig, NY	175
Steals	G. Sisler, StL	27
Wins	W. Hoyt, NY	22
	T. Lyons, CHI	22
Saves	G. Braxton, WAS	13
	W. Moore, NY	13
ERA	W. Hoyt, NY	2.63
Strikeouts	L. Grove, PHI	174

Record Setters
Most runs scored, rookie season (since 1900) —133, Lloyd Waner, PIT

Most hits, rookie season—223, Lloyd Waner, PIT

Most home runs, 154-game season—60, Babe Ruth, NY (AL)

Most home runs on the road, season—32, Babe Ruth, NY (AL)

Most home runs, month of September—17, Babe Ruth, NY (AL)

Fewest strikeouts, switch-hitter, season, NL—10, Frankie Frisch, StL, 153 games

	W	L	PCT	GB
Pittsburgh	94	60	.610	—
St. Louis	92	61	.601	1½
New York	92	62	.597	2
Chicago	85	68	.556	8½
Cincinnati	75	78	.490	18½
Brooklyn	65	88	.425	28½
Boston	60	94	.390	34
Philadelphia	51	103	.331	43

Most Valuable Player — P. Waner, PIT

League Leaders

Batting	P. Waner, PIT	.380
Runs	L. Waner, PIT	133
Home Runs	H. Wilson, CHI	30
	C. Williams, PHI	30
RBI	P. Waner, PIT	131
Steals	F. Frisch, StL	48
Wins	C. Root, CHI	26
Saves	B. Sherdel, StL	6
ERA	R. Kremer, PIT	2.47
Strikeouts	D. Vance, BKN	184

BASEBALL MAGAZINE

Harry Heilmann

March 20c.

OVER 500,000 FANS READ THE BASEBALL MAGAZINE

Records listed in **Record Setters** still stand as of publication date.

1920s STATISTICS

1928

American League

	W	L	PCT	GB
New York	101	53	.656	—
Philadelphia	98	55	.641	2½
St. Louis	82	72	.532	19
Washington	75	79	.487	26
Chicago	72	82	.468	29
Detroit	68	86	.442	33
Cleveland	62	92	.403	39
Boston	57	96	.373	43½

Most Valuable Player   M. Cochrane, PHI

League Leaders

Batting	G. Goslin, WAS	.379
Runs	B. Ruth, NY	163
Home Runs	B. Ruth, NY	54
RBI	L. Gehrig, NY	142
	B. Ruth, NY	142
Steals	B. Myer, BOS	30
Wins	L. Grove, PHI	24
	G. Pipgras, NY	24
Saves	W. Hoyt, NY	8
ERA	G. Braxton, WAS	2.51
Strikeouts	L. Grove, PHI	183

World Series
New York (AL) def. St. Louis (NL) 4-0

Record Setters

Most hits allowed, shutout game, AL—14, Milt Gaston, WAS, July 10 vs. CLE

Fewest shutout games won by a team, season, NL (since 1900)—1, Boston

Most putouts by an outfielder, season—547, Taylor Douthit, StL (NL)

Most consecutive doubleheaders lost on consecutive days—5, Boston (NL), September 8-14

Highest batting average, 4-game World Series—.625 (10 hits in 16 at-bats), Babe Ruth, NY (AL)

Highest slugging percentage, 4-game World Series—1.727 (4 home runs, 1 double and 1 single in 11 at-bats), Lou Gehrig, NY (AL)

National League

	W	L	PCT	GB
St. Louis	95	59	.617	—
New York	93	61	.604	2
Chicago	91	63	.591	4
Pittsburgh	85	67	.559	9
Cincinnati	78	74	.513	16
Brooklyn	77	76	.503	17½
Boston	50	103	.327	44½
Philadelphia	43	109	.283	51

Most Valuable Player   J. Bottomley, StL

League Leaders

Batting	R. Hornsby, BOS	.387
Runs	P. Waner, PIT	142
Home Runs	H. Wilson, CHI	31
	J. Bottomley, StL	31
RBI	J. Bottomley, StL	136
Steals	K. Cuyler, CHI	37
Wins	L. Benton, NY	25
	B. Grimes, PIT	25
Saves	B. Sherdel, StL	5
	H. Haid, StL	5
ERA	D. Vance, BKN	2.09
Strikeouts	D. Vance, BKN	200

1929

American League

	W	L	PCT	GB
Philadelphia	104	46	.693	—
New York	88	66	.571	18
Cleveland	81	71	.533	24
St. Louis	79	73	.520	26
Washington	71	81	.467	34
Detroit	70	84	.455	36
Chicago	59	93	.388	46
Boston	58	96	.377	48

Most Valuable Player   No Selection

League Leaders

Batting	L. Fonseca, CLE	.369
Runs	C. Gehringer, DET	131
Home Runs	B. Ruth, NY	46
RBI	A. Simmons, PHI	157
Steals	C. Gehringer, DET	28
Wins	G. Earnshaw, PHI	24
Saves	F. Marberry, WAS	11
ERA	L. Grove, PHI	2.81
Strikeouts	L. Grove, PHI	170

World Series
Philadelphia (AL) def. Chicago (NL) 4-1

Record Setters

Most hits, NL, season—254, Lefty O'Doul, PHI (tied with Bill Terry, NY, 1930)

Most doubles, rookie season—52, Johnny Frederick, BKN

Most triples, rookie season, AL—17, Russ Scarritt, BOS

Most consecutive games without a strikeout, season—115, Joe Sewell, CLE, May 17 through September 19, 437 at-bats

Most players on one team, 200 or more hits—4, PHI (NL): Lefty O'Doul (254), Chuck Klein (219), Fresco Thompson (202), Pinky Whitney (200)

Most grand slams by a team, NL, season—9, Chicago

National League

	W	L	PCT	GB
Chicago	98	54	.645	—
Pittsburgh	88	65	.575	10½
New York	84	67	.556	13½
St. Louis	78	74	.513	20
Philadelphia	71	82	.464	27½
Brooklyn	70	83	.458	28½
Cincinnati	66	88	.429	33
Boston	56	98	.364	43

Most Valuable Player   R. Hornsby, CHI

League Leaders

Batting	L. O'Doul, PHI	.398
Runs	R. Hornsby, CHI	156
Home Runs	C. Klein, PHI	43
RBI	H. Wilson, CHI	159
Steals	K. Cuyler, CHI	43
Wins	P. Malone, CHI	22
Saves	J. Morrison, BKN	8
	G. Bush, CHI	8
ERA	B. Walker, NY	3.09
Strikeouts	P. Malone, CHI	166

Records listed in **Record Setters** still stand as of publication date.

Boldface indicates picture.

FOR FURTHER READING

Robert W. Creamer, *Babe.* Simon &
 Schuster, 1974.

Harvey Frommer, *Rickey & Robinson.*
 MacMillan, 1982.

Robert Smith, *Baseball.* Simon &
 Schuster, 1947.

Damon Rice, *Seasons Past.* Praeger
 Publishers, 1976.

Robert W. Creamer, *Stengel.* Simon &
 Schuster, 1984.

Glenn Dickey, *History of American League
 Baseball.* Stein & Day, 1982.

Glenn Dickey, *History of National League
 Baseball.* Stein & Day, 1982.

Curt Smith, *Voices of the Game.* Diamond
 Communications, Inc., South Bend, IN,
 1987.

Robert Obojski, *Bush League.* MacMillan,
 1975.

Fred Lieb, *Baseball As I Have Known It.*
 Coward, McCann & Geoghegan, 1977.

Bill James, *The Bill James Baseball
 Historical Abstract.* Villard Books, 1988.

Eliot Asinof, *Eight Men Out.* Henry Holt
 and Company, 1963.

Harold Seymour, *Baseball: The Golden
 Age.* Oxford University Press, 1971.

PICTURE CREDITS

National Baseball Library, Cooperstown, NY; 32 (right) The Bettmann Archive; 33 The Bettmann Archive; 34 *The Sporting News*; 35 (left) National Baseball Library, Cooperstown, NY; 35 (right) National Baseball Library, Cooperstown, NY; 37 (top) National Baseball Library, Cooperstown, NY; 37 (bottom) National Baseball Library, Cooperstown, NY; 38 National Baseball Library, Cooperstown, NY; 39 (left) UPI/Bettmann Newsphotos; 39 (right) National Baseball Library, Cooperstown, NY; 40 National Baseball Library, Cooperstown, NY; 41 UPI/Bettmann Newsphotos; 42 National Baseball Library, Cooperstown, NY; 43 (top) National Baseball Library, Cooperstown, NY; 43 (bottom left) AP/Wide World Photos; 43 (bottom right) Brown Brothers

Dunnie's Babe
44 The Babe Ruth Museum; 45 National Baseball Library, Cooperstown, NY; 46 (left) Ron Menchine Collection/Renée Comet Photography; 46 (right) National Baseball Library, Cooperstown, NY; 47 (left) National Baseball Library, Cooperstown, NY; 47 (right) National Baseball Library, Cooperstown, NY; 48 Library of Congress; 49 The Babe Ruth Museum; 50 The Babe Ruth Museum; 51 National Baseball Library, Cooperstown, NY; 52 Ron Menchine Collection/Renée Comet Photography; 53 (left) The Bettmann Archive; 53 (right) National Baseball Library, Cooperstown, NY; 54 Brown Brothers; 56 The Babe Ruth Museum; 57 (left) Barry Halper Collection/Henry Groskinsky Photography; 57 (right) National Baseball Library, Cooperstown, NY; 58 (left) Thomas Carwile Collection/Renée Comet Photography; 58 (right) Brown Brothers; 59 Culver Pictures, Inc.; 60 National Baseball Library, Cooperstown, NY; 61 National Baseball Library, Cooperstown, NY

Thunder At The Plate
62 Culver Pictures, Inc.; 63 Ron Menchine Collection/Renée Comet Photography; 64 (left) National Baseball Library, Cooperstown, NY; 64 (right) National Baseball Library, Cooperstown, NY; 65 (left) National Baseball Library, Cooperstown, NY; 65 (right) Ron Menchine Collection/Renée Comet Photography; 66 (left) National Baseball Library, Cooperstown, NY; 66 (right) National Baseball Library, Cooperstown, NY; 67 (left) National Baseball Library, Cooperstown, NY; 67 (right) National Baseball Library, Cooperstown, NY; 68 National Baseball Library, Cooperstown, NY; 69 (top left) UPI/Bettmann Newsphotos; 69 (top right) UPI/Bettmann Newsphotos; 69 (bottom) Cleveland Public Library; 70 (left) National Baseball Library, Cooperstown, NY; 70 (right) National Baseball Library, Cooperstown, NY; 71 National Baseball Library, Cooperstown, NY; 72 Courtesy of Detroit Tigers; 73 (left) National Baseball Library, Cooperstown, NY; 73 (right) Cleveland Public Library; 74 UPI/Bettmann Newsphotos; 75 Brown Brothers; 76 (left) Ron Menchine Collection/Renée Comet Photography; 76 (right) The Historial Society of Pennsylvania; 77 Brown Brothers; 78 National Baseball Library, Cooperstown, NY; 79 National Baseball Library, Cooperstown, NY;

Mr. New York
80 UPI/Bettmann Newsphotos; 81 National Baseball Library, Cooperstown, NY; 82 (left) National Baseball Library, Cooperstown, NY; 82 (right) National Baseball Library, Cooperstown, NY; 83 (left) National Baseball Library, Cooperstown, NY; 83 (right) National Baseball Library, Cooperstown, NY; 84 National Baseball Library, Cooperstown, NY; 85 (top) FPG International; 85 (bottom) The Bettmann Archive; 86 National Baseball Library, Cooperstown, NY; 87 National Baseball Library, Cooperstown, NY; 88 National Baseball Library, Cooperstown, NY; 89 National Baseball Library, Cooperstown, NY; 90 (left) Ron Menchine Collection/Renée Comet Photography; 90 (right) National Baseball Library, Cooperstown, NY; 91 (left) Mike Mumby Collection; 91 (right) National Baseball Library, Cooperstown, NY; 92 (left) UPI/Bettmann Newsphotos; 92 (right) Dennis Goldstein Collection; 93 (top) UPI/Bettmann Newsphotos; 93 (bottom) The Bettmann Archive; 94 (left) National Baseball Library, Cooperstown, NY; 94 (right) National Baseball Library, Cooperstown, NY; 95 UPI/Bettmann Newsphotos; 96 Ron Menchine Collection/Renée Comet Photography; 97 (top) Ron Menchine Collection/Renée Comet Photography; 97 (middle) National Baseball Library, Cooperstown, NY; 97 (bottom) National Baseball Library, Cooperstown, NY

The Big Train
98 Library of Congress; 99 Ron Menchine Collection/Renée Comet Photography; 100 (left) National Baseball Library, Cooperstown, NY; 100 (right) Library of Congress; 101 (left) Library of Congress; 101 (right) Ron Menchine Collection/Renée Comet Photography; 102 (left) Library of Congress; 102 (right) Library of Congress; 103 (left) Culver Pictures Inc.; 103 (right) National Baseball Library, Cooperstown, NY; 104 National Baseball Library, Cooperstown, NY; 105 (top) National Baseball Library, Cooperstown, NY; 105 (bottom) UPI/Bettmann Newsphotos; 106 (left) National Baseball Library, Cooperstown, NY; 106 (right) National Baseball Library, Cooperstown, NY; 107 (left) Ron Menchine Collection/Renée Comet Photography; 107 (right) National Baseball Library, Cooperstown, NY; 108 The Bettmann Archive; 109 National Baseball Library, Cooperstown, NY; 110 (left) Ron Menchine Collection/Renée Comet Photography; 110 (right) National Baseball Library, Cooperstown, NY; 111 Mike Mumby Collection; 112 The Bettmann Archive; 113 (left) National Baseball Library, Cooperstown, NY; 113 (right) Ron Menchine Collection/Renée Comet Photography; 114 Ron Menchine Collection/Renée Comet Photography; 115 (left) UPI/Bettmann Newsphotos; 115 (right) National Baseball Library, Cooperstown, NY

Radio Waves
116 Thomas Carwile Collection/Renée Comet Photography; 117 National Baseball Library, Cooperstown, NY; 118 (left) UPI/Bettmann Newsphotos; 118 (right) Courtesy of KDKA Radio, Pittsburgh, PA; 119 National Baseball Library, Cooperstown, NY; 120 The Western Reserve Historical Society;

121 The Bettmann Archive; 122 National Baseball Library, Cooperstown, NY; 124 National Baseball Library, Cooperstown, NY; 125 (top) AP/Wide World Photos; 125 (bottom) *The Sporting News*; 127 (left) National Baseball Library, Cooperstown, NY; 127 (right) *The Sporting News*; 128 National Baseball Library, Cooperstown, NY; 129 The Bettmann Archive; 130 Dennis Goldstein Collection; 131 (top) Dennis Goldstein Collection; 131 (lower Left) Culver Pictures, Inc.; 131 (lower right) Dennis Goldstein Collection

From Bushes to Farms
132 FPG International; 133 National Baseball Library, Cooperstown, NY; 134 Courtesy of Ohio Wesleyan University; 135 (left) Library of Congress; 135 (right) National Baseball Library, Cooperstown, NY; 136 (left) National Baseball Library, Cooperstown, NY; 136 (right) Dennis Goldstein Collection; 137 (left) UPI/Bettmann Newsphotos; 137 (right) Ron Menchine Collection/Renée Comet Photography; 138 Dennis Goldstein Collection; 139 (top) Larry Lester Collection; 139 (bottom) Dennis Goldstein Collection; 140 (left) National Baseball Library, Cooperstown, NY; 140 (right) The Bettmann Archive; 141 (left) National Baseball Library, Cooperstown, NY; 141 (right) Ron Menchine Collection/Renée Comet Photography; 142 National Baseball Library, Cooperstown, NY; 143 (left) The Bettmann Archive; 143 (right) National Baseball Library, Cooperstown, NY; 144 (left) Ron Menchine Collection/ Renée Comet Photography; 144 (right) AP/Wide World Photos; 145 Ron Menchine Collection/Renée Comet Photography

Spirits of St. Louis
146 National Baseball Library, Cooperstown, NY; 147 Ron Menchine Collection/Renée Comet Photography; 148 (left) National Baseball Library, Cooperstown, NY; 148 (right) National Baseball Library, Cooperstown, NY; 149 UPI/Bettmann Newsphotos; 150 (left) National Baseball Library, Cooperstown, NY; 150 (right) National Baseball Library, Cooperstown, NY; 151 The Bettmann Archive; 152 Hillerich and Bradsby Company

Records; University of Louisville Archives, Louisville, KY ; 153 (left) National Baseball Library, Cooperstown, NY; 153 (right) National Baseball Library, Cooperstown, NY; 154 National Baseball Library, Cooperstown, NY; 155 (left) UPI/ Bettmann Newsphotos; 155 (right) Ron Menchine Collection/Renée Comet Photography; 156 (left) National Baseball Library, Cooperstown, NY; 156 (right) Dennis Goldstein Collection; 157 UPI/Bettmann Newsphotos; 158 Ron Menchine Collection/Renée Comet Photography; 159 UPI/Bettmann Newsphotos; 161 National Baseball Library, Cooperstown, NY

Five O'Clock Lightning
162-3 UPI/Bettmann Newsphotos; 164 (top) UPI/Bettmann Newsphotos; 164 (bottom) Library of Congress; 165 UPI/Bettmann Newsphotos; 166 (left) National Baseball Library, Cooperstown, NY; 166 (right) National Baseball Library, Cooperstown, NY; 167 Library of Congress; 168 The Bettmann Archive; 169 (top) UPI/ Bettmann Newsphotos; 169 (bottom) Ron Menchine Collection/Renée Comet Photography; 170 Ron Menchine Collection/Renée Comet Photography; 171 (top) Comstock; 171 (bottom) National Baseball Library, Cooperstown, NY; 172 (left) UPI/ Bettmann Newsphotos; 172 (right) UPI/Bettmann Newsphotos; 173 Library of Congress; 174 Library of Congress; 175 AP/Wide World Photos; 176 Dennis Goldstein Collection; 177 (left) Mike Mumby Collection; 177 (right) AP/Wide World Photos; 178 National Baseball Library, Cooperstown, NY; 179 (top) National Baseball Library, Cooperstown, NY; 179 (bottom) National Baseball Library, Cooperstown, NY; 180 (top) UPI/Bettmann Newsphotos; 180 (bottom) Smithsonian Institution; 181 The Bettman Archive

182-186 Ron Menchine Collection/ Renée Comet Photography except 183 (top) Smithsonian Institution; 184 (top) Thomas Carwile Collection/Renée Comet Photography; 185 (bottom) National Baseball Library, Cooperstown, NY.

The author and editors wish to thank:

Peter P. Clark, Tom Heitz, Bill Deane, Patricia Kelly, Dan Bennett and the staffs of the National Baseball Hall of Fame and the National Baseball Library, Cooperstown, New York; George Hobart and Mary Ison, Prints and Photographs Division, Library of Congress, Washington, D.C.; David Gibson, Photo Equipment Museum, Eastman Kodak Company, Rochester, New York; Candice Cochrane, Boston, Massachusetts; Clarence "Lefty" Blasco, Van Nuys, California; Dennis Goldstein, Atlanta, Georgia; Morris Eckhouse, Cleveland, Ohio; Adrienne Auricchio, New York, New York; Lloyd Johnson, New England Sports Museum, Boston, Massachusetts; Stanley Arnold, Afro-American Historical and Cultural Museum, Philadelphia, Pennsylvania; Mrs. Meredith Collins, Brown Brothers, Sterling, Pennsylvania; Tom Logan, Culver Pictures, Inc, New York, New York; Helen Bowie Campbell and Gregory J. Schwalenberg, Babe Ruth Museum, Baltimore, Maryland; Stephen P. Gietschier, The Sporting News, St. Louis, Missouri; Ellen Hughes, National Museum of American History, Smithsonian Institution, Washington, D.C.; Nat Andriani, Wide World Photos, New York, New York; Renee Comet Photography, Washington, D.C.; Thomas Carwile, Petersburg, Virginia; Marcy Silver and Carolyn Park, Historical Society of Pennsylvania; Lillian Clark and Mary Perencevic, Cleveland Public Library, Cleveland, Ohio; Pam Nicholson, Bettmann; Ed Dixon, Dixon and Turner Research Associates, Bethesda, MD; Victoria Salin, Washington D.C.; Julie Harris, Arlington, Virginia; Joe Borras, Accokeek, Maryland; Kenneth E. Hancock, Annandale, Virginia; Dorothy A. Gergel, Springfield, Virginia; Ronald G. Liebman, Flushing, New York; Dave Kelly, Library of Congress, Washington, D.C.; Robert F. Bluthardt, San Angelo, Texas.

World of Baseball is produced and
published by Redefinition, Inc.

WORLD OF BASEBALL

Editor	Glen B. Ruh
Design Director	Robert Barkin
Production Director	Irv Garfield
Senior Writer	Jonathan Kronstadt
Text Editor	Sharon Cygan
Picture Research	Rebecca Hirsh
	Louis P. Plummer
	Catherine M. Chase
Design	Edwina Smith
	Sue Pratt
	Collette Conconi
	Sharon M. Greenspan
	Monique Strawderman
Copy Editing	Anthony K. Pordes
	Ginette Gauldfeldt
Production Assistant	Kimberly Fornshill Holmlund
Editorial Research	Janet Pooley
Illustrations	Dale Glasgow
Copy Preparation	Gail Cerra
Index	Lee McKee

REDEFINITION

Administration	Margaret M. Higgins
	June M. Nolan
Marketing Director	Harry Sailer
Finance Director	Vaughn A. Meglan
PRESIDENT	Edward Brash

CONTRIBUTORS

James A. Cox, author of *The Lively Ball,* is a frequent contributor to leading magazines, and specializes in American sports figures. A former writer and editor for *Life* and *National Geographic,* he is the author of six books, among them *Slashing Blades,* a hockey novel for young readers. On the school baseball diamond, he was never much of a hitter, but he walked a lot and stole bases like crazy.

Henry Staat is Series Consultant for World of Baseball. A member of the Society for American Baseball Research since 1982, he helped initiate the concept for the series. He is an editor with Wadsworth, Inc., a publisher of college textbooks.

Ron Menchine, an advisor and special sports collector, shared baseball materials he has been collecting for 40 years. A sportscaster and sports director for numerous radio stations, he announced the last three seasons played by the Senators in Washington, D.C. He currently freelances on radio and television and has had roles in two motion pictures.

The editors also wish to thank the following writers for their contributions: Leonard Hochberg, Falls Church, Virginia; David Hoff, Washington, D.C.; Robert Kiener, Washington, D.C.

Library of Congress Cataloging-in-Publication Data
The lively ball/James A. Cox
    (World of Baseball)
    Includes index.
    1. Baseball—United States—History.
    2. Baseball players—
United States—Biography. I.Title II.Series
GV863.A1C67   1989   89-10276
796.357 0973—dc20
ISBN 0-924588-03-9

Printed in U.S.A.
10 9 8 7 6 5 4 3 2 1

This book is one of a series that celebrates America's national pastime.

Redefinition also offers a World of Baseball Top Ten Stat Finder.

For subscription information and prices please write:
    Customer Service, Redefinition, Inc., P.O. Box 25336,
    Alexandria, Virginia 22313

The text of this book is set in Century Old Style; display type is Helvetica and Gill Sans. The paper is 70 pound Warrenflo Gloss supplied by Stanford Paper Company. Typesetting by Darby Graphics, Alexandria, Virginia and Intergraphics, Inc., Alexandria, Virginia. Color separation by Colotone, Inc., North Branford, Connecticut. Printed and bound by W.A. Krueger Company, New Berlin, Wisconsin.